Amiga

Hardware Reference Manual

Commodore-Amiga, Incorporated

Amiga Technical Reference Series

Addison-Wesley Publishing Company, Inc.

Reading, Massachusetts   Menlo Park, California   New York
Don Mills, Ontario   Wokingham, England   Amsterdam   Bonn
Sydney   Singapore   Tokyo   Madrid   San Juan

This manual covers the A1000, A500, and A2000 release machines.

This edition of the manual was edited and typeset on an Amiga 2500 running AMIX.

The text of the original version of this manual was written by Robert Peck, Susan Deyl, Jay Miner, and Chris Raymond; other contributors included Bill Kolb, Dave Needle, Lee Ho, and Dale Luck.

This manual was revised by Joe Augenbraun, Dan Baker, Greg Berlin, Ken Farinsky, Glenn Keller, Bryce Nesbitt, Nancy Rains, and Carolyn Scheppner.

Special thanks to Thomas Rokicki of Radical Eye Software and Jez San of Argonaut Software Ltd. for their contributions.

This book is for all the "busy guys" who made Amiga and are Amiga.

CBM Product Number 327272-04

ISBN 0-201-18157-6

ABCDEFGHIJ-BA-89
First Printing, September 1989

WARNING:

The information described in this manual may contain errors or bugs and may not function as described. All information is subject to enhancement or upgrade for any reason including to fix bugs, add features or change performance. As with all upgrades, full compatibility, although a goal, cannot be guaranteed and is in fact unlikely.

DISCLAIMER:

THIS INFORMATION IS PROVIDED TO YOU "AS IS" WITH OUT WARRANTY OF ANY KIND, EITHER EXPRESS OR IMPLIED. THE ENTIRE RISK AS TO THE USE OF THE INFORMATION IS ASSUMED BY YOU. COMMODORE-AMIGA, INC., ("COMMODORE") SPECIFICALLY DOES NOT MAKE ANY REPRESENTATIONS OR ENDORSEMENTS, REGARDING THE USE OF, THE RESULTS OF, OR PERFORMANCE OF THE INFORMATION (INCLUDING BUT NOT LIMITED TO ITS APPROPRIATENESS, ACCURACY, RELIABILITY, CURRENTNESS, OR OTHERWISE.) IN NO EVENT WILL COMMODORE BE LIABLE FOR DIRECT, INDIRECT, INCIDENTAL, OR CONSEQUENTIAL DAMAGES RESULTING FROM ANY DEFECT IN THIS INFORMATION EVEN IF IT HAS BEEN ADVISED OF THE POSSIBILITY OF SUCH DAMAGES. SOME LAWS DO NOT ALLOW THE EXCLUSION OR LIMITATION OF IMPLIED WARRANTIES OR LIABILITIES FOR INCIDENTAL OR CONSEQUENTIAL DAMAGES, SO THE ABOVE LIMITATION OR EXCLUSION MAY NOT APPLY.

PREFACE

The Amiga® Technical Reference Series is the official guide to programming the Commodore Amiga computers. This revised edition of the *Amiga Hardware Reference Manual* has been updated for version 1.3 of the Amiga operating system and the new Amiga computer systems. This manual provides information about the Amiga graphics, audio hardware, and how the Amiga talks to the outside world through peripheral devices. A portion of this manual is a tutorial on writing assembly language programs to directly control the Amiga's graphics and hardware.

This book is intended for the following audiences:

- Assembly language programmers who need a more direct way of interacting with the system than the routines described in the *Amiga ROM Kernel Reference Manual: Includes and Autodocs* and *Amiga ROM Kernel Reference Manual: Libraries and Devices*.

- Designers who want to interface with new peripherals to the Amiga.

- Anyone who wants to know how the Amiga hardware works.

Here is a brief overview of the contents:

Chapter 1, *Introduction*. An overview of the hardware and survey of the Amiga's graphics and audio features.

Chapter 2, *Coprocessor Hardware*. Using the Copper coprocessor to control the entire graphics and audio system; directing mid-screen modifications in graphics displays and directing register changes during the time between displays.

Chapter 3, *Playfield Hardware*. Creating, displaying and scrolling the playfields, one of the basic display elements of the Amiga; how the Amiga produces multi-color, multi-graphical bit-mapped displays.

Chapter 4, *Sprite Hardware*. Using the eight sprite direct-memory access (DMA) channels to make sprite movable objects; creating their data structures, displaying and moving them, reusing the DMA channels.

Chapter 5, *Audio Hardware*. Overview of sampled sound; how to produce quality sound, simple and complex sounds, and modulated sounds.

Chapter 6, *Blitter Hardware*. Using the blitter DMA channel to create animation effects and draw lines into playfields.

Chapter 7, *System Control Hardware*. Using the control registers to define depth arrangement of graphics objects, detect collisions between graphics objects, control direct memory access, and control interrupts.

Chapter 8, *Interface Hardware*. How the Amiga talks to the outside world through controller ports, keyboard, audio jacks and video connectors, serial and parallel interfaces; information about the disk controller and RAM expansion slot.

Appendixes. Alphabetical and address-order listings of all the graphics and audio system registers and the functions of their bits, system memory map, descriptions of internal and external connectors, specifications for the peripheral interface ports, and specifications for the keyboard.

Glossary. After the appendixes, there is a glossary of important terms.

We suggest that you use this book according to your level of familiarity with the Amiga system. Here are some suggestions:

• If this is your initial exposure to the Amiga, read chapter 1, which gives a survey of all the hardware features and a brief rundown of graphics and audio effects created by hardware interaction.

• If you are already familiar with the system and want to acquaint yourself with how the various bits in the hardware registers govern the way the system functions, browse through chapters 2 through 8. Examples are included in these chapters.

• For advanced users, the appendixes give a concise summary of the entire register set and the uses of the individual bits. Once you are familiar with the effects of changes in the various bits, you may wish to refer more often to the appendixes than to the explanatory chapters.

The other manuals in this series are the *Amiga ROM Kernel Reference Manual: Libraries and Devices*, with tutorial-style chapters on the use of each Amiga system library and device, and the *Amiga ROM Kernel Reference Manual: Includes and Autodocs*, an alphabetically organized reference of autodoc function summaries, Amiga system include files, and the IFF file format specifications.

Hardware designers should contact Commodore Amiga Technical Support for appropriate documents.

Commodore Amiga Technical Support (CATS)

Commodore maintains a technical support group dedicated to helping developers achieve their goals with the Amiga. Available technical support programs are tailored both to the needs of smaller independent developers and larger corporations. Subscription to the support publication *AmigaMail*™ is available to anyone with an interest in the latest news, Commodore software and hardware changes, and tips for developers.

To request an application for the Commodore Amiga Developer Programs, lists of CATS technical publications, or information regarding electronic developer support, send a self-addressed, stamped, 9'' x 12'' envelope to:

> CATS-Information
> 1200 West Wilson Drive
> West Chester, PA 19380-4231

Error Reports

In a complex technical manual, errors are often found after publication. When errors in this manual are found, they will be corrected in the following printing. Updates will be published in the AmigaMail technical support publication.

Bug reports can be sent to Commodore electronically or by mail. Submitted reports must be clear, complete, and concise. Reports must include a telephone number and enough information so that the bug can be quickly verified from your report. (I.e. please describe the bug *and* all the steps needed to reproduce it.)

> Amiga Software Engineering Group
> ATTN: BUG REPORTS
> Commodore Business Machines
> 1200 Wilson Drive
> West Chester, PA 19380-4231
> USA
>
> BIX: afinkel
> USENET: bugs@commodore.COM or uunet!cbmvax!bugs
>   or suggestions@commodore.COM

Table of Contents

List of Figures

List of Tables

Chapter 1

INTRODUCTION

The Amiga family of computers consists of several models, each of which has been designed on the same premise — to provide the user with a low cost computer that features high cost performance. The Amiga does this through the use of custom silicon hardware that yields advanced graphics and sound features.

There are three distinct models that make up the Amiga computer family: the A500, A1000, and A2000. Though the models differ in price and features, they have a common hardware nucleus that makes them software compatible with one another. This chapter describes the Amiga's hardware components and gives a brief overview of its graphics and sound features.

Components of the Amiga

These are the hardware components of the Amiga:

- Motorola MC68000 16/32 bit main processor. The Amiga also supports the 68010, 68020, and 68030 processors as an option.

- 512K bytes of internal RAM, expandable to 1 MB on the A500 and A2000.

- 256K bytes of ROM containing a real time, multitasking operating system with sound, graphics, and animation support routines.

- Built-in 3.5 inch double sided disk drive.

- Expansion disk port for connecting up to three additional disk drives, which may be either 3.5 inch or 5.25 inch, double sided.

- Fully programmable RS-232-C serial port.

- Fully programmable parallel port.

- Two button opto-mechanical mouse.

- Two reconfigurable controller ports (for mice, joysticks, light pens, paddles, or custom controllers).

- A professional keyboard with numeric keypad, 10 function keys, and cursor keys. A variety of international keyboards are also supported.

- Ports for simultaneous composite video, and analog or digital RGB output.

- Ports for left and right stereo audio from four special purpose audio channels.

- Expansion options that allow you to add RAM, additional disk drives (floppy or hard), peripherals, or coprocessors.

THE MC68000 AND THE AMIGA CUSTOM CHIPS

The Motorola 68000 is a 16/32 bit microprocessor. The system clock speed for NTSC Amigas is 7.15909 megahertz (PAL 7.09379 MHz). These speeds may vary when using an external system clock, such as from a genlock. The 68000 has an address space of 16 megabytes. In the Amiga, the 68000 can address over 8 megabytes of contiguous random access memory (RAM).

In addition to the 68000, the Amiga contains special purpose hardware known as the "custom chips" that greatly enhance system performance. The term "custom chips" refers to the 3 integrated circuits which were designed specifically for the Amiga computer. These three custom chips (called Agnus, Paula, and Denise) each contain the logic to handle a specific set of tasks, such as video, sound, direct memory access (DMA), or graphics.

Among other functions, the custom chips provide the following:

• Bitplane generated, high resolution graphics capable of supporting both PAL and NTSC video standards.

  - On NTSC systems the Amiga typically produces a 320 by 200 non-interlaced or 320 by 400 interlaced display in 32 colors and a 640 by 200 non-interlaced or 640 by 400 interlaced display in 16 colors.

  - On PAL systems, the Amiga typically produces a 320 by 256 non-interlaced or 320 by 512 interlaced display in 32 colors, and a 640 by 256 non-interlaced or 640 by 512 interlaced display in 16 colors.

  Additional video modes allow for the display of up to 4,096 colors on screen simultaneously (hold-and-modify) or provide for larger, higher resolution displays (overscan).

• A custom display coprocessor that allows changes to most of the special purpose registers in synchronization with the position of the video beam. This allows such special effects as mid-screen changes to the color palette, splitting the screen into multiple horizontal slices each having different video resolutions and color depths, beam synchronized interrupt generation for the 68000 and more. The coprocessor can trigger many times per screen, in the middle of lines, and at the beginning or during the blanking interval. The coprocessor itself can directly affect most of the registers in the other custom chips, freeing the 68000 for general computing tasks.

• 32 system color registers, each of which contains a twelve bit number as four bits of RED, four bits of GREEN, and four bits of BLUE intensity information. This allows a system color palette of 4,096 different choices of color for each register.

• Eight reusable 16 bit wide sprites with up to 15 color choices per sprite pixel (when sprites are paired). A sprite is an easily movable graphics object whose display is entirely independent of the background (called a playfield); sprites can be displayed over or under this background. A sprite is 16 low resolution pixels wide and an arbitrary number of lines tall. After producing the last line of a sprite on the screen, a sprite DMA channel may be used to produce yet another sprite image elsewhere on screen (with at least one horizontal line between each reuse of a sprite processor). Thus, many small sprites can be produced by simply reusing the sprite processors appropriately.

• Dynamically controllable inter-object priority, with collision detection. This means that the system can dynamically control the video priority between the sprite objects and the bitplane backgrounds (playfields). You can control which object or objects appear over or under the background at any time.

Additionally, you can use system hardware to detect collisions between objects and have your program react to such collisions.

- Custom bit blitter used for high speed data movement, adaptable to bitplane animation. The blitter has been designed to efficiently retrieve data from up to three sources, combine the data in one of 256 different possible ways, and optionally store the combined data in a destination area. This is one of the situations where the 68000 gives up memory cycles to a DMA channel that can do the job more efficiently (see below). The bit blitter, in a special mode, draws patterned lines into rectangularly organized memory regions at a speed of about 1 million dots per second; and it can efficiently handle area fill.

- Audio consisting of four digital channels with independently programmable volume and sampling rate. The audio channels retrieve their control and data via direct memory access. Once started, each channel can automatically play a specified waveform without further processor interaction. Two channels are directed into each of the two stereo audio outputs. The audio channels may be linked together to provide amplitude or frequency modulation or both forms of modulation simultaneously.

- DMA controlled floppy disk read and write on a full track basis. This means that the built-in disk can read over 5600 bytes of data in a single disk revolution (11 sectors of 512 bytes each).

The internal memory shared by the custom chips and the 68000 CPU is also called "chip memory". The original custom chips in the Amiga were designed to be able to physically access up to 512K bytes of shared memory. The new version of the Agnus custom chip was created which allows the graphics and audio hardware to access up to a full megabyte of memory.

The Amiga 500 and 2000 models were designed to be able to accept the new Agnus custom chip, called "Fat Agnus," due to its square shape. Hence, the A500 and A2000 have allocated a chip memory space of 1 MB. This entire 1 MB space is subject to the arbitration logic that controls the CPU and custom chip accesses. On the A1000, only the first 512K bytes of memory space is shared, chip memory.

These custom chips and the 68000 share memory on a fully interleaved basis. Since the 68000 only needs to access the memory bus during each alternate clock cycle in order to run full speed, the rest of the time the memory bus is free for other activities. The custom chips use the memory bus during these free cycles, effectively allowing the 68000 to run at full rated speed most of the time. We say "most of the time" because there are some occasions when the special purpose hardware steals memory cycles from the 68000, but with good reason. Specifically, the coprocessor and the data moving DMA channel called the blitter can each steal time from the 68000 for jobs they can do better than the 68000. Thus, the system DMA channels are designed with maximum performance in mind. The job to be done is performed by the most efficient hardware element available. Even when such cycle stealing occurs, it only blocks the 68000's access to the internal, shared memory. When using ROM or external memory, the 68000 always runs at full speed.

Another primary feature of the Amiga hardware is the ability to dynamically control which part of the chip memory is used for the background display, audio, and sprites. The Amiga is not limited to a small, specific area of RAM for a frame buffer. Instead, the system allows display bitplanes, sprite processor control lists, coprocessor instruction lists, or audio channel control lists to be located anywhere within chip memory.

This same region of memory can be accessed by the bit blitter. This means, for example, that the user can store partial images at scattered areas of chip memory and use these images for animation effects by rapidly replacing on screen material while saving and restoring background images. In fact, the Amiga includes firmware support for display definition and control as well as support for animated objects embedded within playfields.

VCR AND DIRECT CAMERA INTERFACE

In addition to the connectors for monochrome composite, and analog or digital RGB monitors, the Amiga can be expanded to include a VCR or camera interface. This system is capable of synchronizing with an external video source and replacing the system background color with the external image. This allows development of fully integrated video images with computer generated graphics. Laser disk input is accepted in the same manner.

PERIPHERALS

Floppy disk storage is provided by a built in, 3.5 inch floppy disk drive. Disks are 80 track, double sided, and formatted as 11 sectors per track, 512 bytes per sector (over 900,000 bytes per disk). The disk controller can read and write 320/360K IBM PC™ (MS-DOS™) formatted 3.5 or 5.25 inch disks, and 640/720K IBM PC (MS-DOS) formatted 3.5 inch disks. External 3.5 inch or 5.25 inch disk drives can be added to the system through the expansion connector.

Circuitry for some of the peripherals resides on Paula. Other chips handle various signals not specifically assigned to any of the custom chips, including modem controls, disk status sensing, disk motor and stepping controls, ROM enable, parallel input/output interface, and keyboard interface.

The Amiga includes a standard RS-232-C serial port for external serial input/output devices.

A keyboard with numeric keypad, cursor controls and 10 function keys is included in the base system. For maximum flexibility, both key-down and key-up signals are sent. The Amiga also supports a variety of international keyboards. Many other types of controllers can be attached through the two controller ports on the base unit. You can use a mouse, joystick, keypad, trackball, light pen, or steering wheel controller in either of the controller ports.

SYSTEM EXPANDABILITY AND ADAPTABILITY

New peripheral devices may be easily added to all Amiga models. These devices are automatically recognized and used by system software through a well defined, well documented linking procedure called AUTOCONFIG™.

On the A500 and A1000 models, peripheral devices can be added to the Amiga's 86 pin expansion connector, including additional external RAM. Extra disk units may be added from a connector at the rear of the unit.

The A2000 model provides the user with the same features as the A500 or A1000, but with the added convenience of simple and extensive expandability. The 86 pin, external connector of the A1000 and A500 is not externally accessible on the A2000. Instead, the A2000 contains 7 internal slots that allow many types of expansion boards to be quickly and easily added inside the machine. These expansion boards may contain coprocessors, RAM expansion, hard disk controllers, video or I/O ports. There is also room to mount both floppy and hard disks internally. The A2000 also supports the special Bridgeboard™ coprocessor card. This provides a complete IBM PC™ on a card and allows the Amiga to run MS-DOS™ compatible software, while simultaneously running native Amiga software.

About the Examples

The examples in this book all demonstrate direct manipulation of the Amiga hardware. However, as a general rule, it is not permissible to directly access the hardware in the Amiga unless your software either has full control of the system, or has arbitrated via the OS for exclusive access to the particular parts of the hardware you wish to control.

Almost all of the hardware discussed in this manual, most notably the Blitter, Copper, playfield, sprite, CIA, trackdisk, and system control hardware, are in either exclusive or arbitrated use by portions of the Amiga OS in any running Amiga system. Additional hardware, such as the audio, parallel, and serial hardware, may be in use by applications which have allocated their use through the system software.

Before attempting to directly manipulate any part of the hardware in the Amiga's multitasking environment, your application must first be granted exclusive access to that hardware by the operating system library, device, or resource which arbitrates its ownership. The operating system functions for requesting and receiving control of parts of the Amiga hardware are varied and are not within the scope of this manual. Generally such functions, when available, will be found in the library, device, or resource which manages that portion of the Amiga hardware in the multitasking environment. The following list will help you to find the appropriate operating system functions or mechanisms which may exist for arbitrated access to the hardware discussed in this manual.

> Copper, Playfield, Sprite, Blitter - graphics.library
> Audio - audio.device
> Trackdisk - trackdisk.device, disk.resource
> Serial - serial.device, misc.resource
> Parallel - parallel.device, cia.resource, misc.resource
> Gameport - input.device, gameport.device, potgo.resource
> Keyboard - input.device, keyboard.device
> System Control - graphics.library, exec.library (interrupts)

Most of the examples in this book use the hw_examples.i file (see Appendix J) to define the chip register names. Hw_examples.i uses the system include file hardware/custom.i to define the chip structures and relative addresses. The values defined in hardware/custom.i and hw_examples.i are offsets from the base chip register address space. In general, this base value is defined as _custom and is resolved during linking from amiga.lib. (_ciaa and _ciab are also resolved in this way.)

Normally, the base address is loaded into an address register and the offsets given by hardware/custom.i and hw_examples.i are then used to address the correct register.

The offset values of the registers are the addresses that the Copper must use to talk to the registers.

For example, in assembler:

```
        INCLUDE "exec/types.i"
        INCLUDE "hardware/custom.i"

        XREF    _custom                 ; External reference...

Start:  lea     _custom,a0              ; Use a0 as base register
        move.w  #$7FFF,intena(a0)       ; Disable all interupts
```

In C, you would use the structure definitions in hardware/custom.h For example:

```
#include         "exec/types.h"
#include         "hardware/custom.h"

extern  struct  Custom  custom;

/* You may need to define the above external as
**   extern struct Custom far custom;
**   Check you compiler manual.
*/

main()
{
custom.intena = 0x7FFF;          /* Disable all interupts */
}
```

The Amiga hardware include files are generally supplied with your compiler or assembler. Listings of the hardware include files may also be found in the Addison-Wesley Amiga ROM Kernel Manual "Includes and Autodocs". Generally, the include file label names are very similar to the equivalent hardware register list names with the following typical differences.

- Address registers which have low word and high word components are generally listed as two word sized registers in the hardware register list, with each register name containing either a suffix or embedded "L" or "H" for low and high. The include file label for the same register will generally treat the whole register as a longword (32 bit) register, and therefore will not contain the "L" or "H" distinction.

- Related sequential registers which are given individual names with number suffixes in the hardware register list, are generally referenced from a single base register definition in the include files. For example, the color registers in the hardware list (COLOR00, COLOR01, etc.) would be referenced from the "color" label defined in "hardware/custom.i" (color+0, color+2, etc.).

- Examples of how to define the correct register offset can be found in the hw_examples.i file listed in Appendix J.

Some Caveats to Hardware Level Programmers

The Amiga is available in a variety of models and configurations, and is further diversified by a wealth of add-on expansion peripherals and processor replacements. In addition, even standard Amiga hardware such as the keyboard and floppy disks, are supplied by a number of different manufacturers and may vary subtly in both their timing and in their ability to perform outside of their specified capabilities.

The Amiga operating system is designed to operate the Amiga hardware within spec, adapt to different hardware and RAM configurations, and generally provide upward compatibility with any future hardware upgrades or "add ons" envisioned by the designers. For maximum upward compatibility, it is strongly suggested that programmers deal with the hardware through the commands and functions provided by the Amiga operating system.

If you find it necessary to program the hardware directly, then it is your responsibility to write code which will work properly on various models and configurations. Be sure to properly request and gain control of the hardware you are manipulating, and be especially careful in the following areas:

Do not jump into ROM. Beware of any example code that calls routines in the $F80000 to $FFFFFF range. These are ROM addresses and the ROM routines WILL move with every OS revision. The only supported interface to system ROM code is through the provided library, device, and resource calls.

Do not modify or depend on the format of any private system structures. This includes the poking of copper lists, memory lists, and library bases.

Do not depend on any address containing any particular system structure or type of memory. The system modules dynamically allocate their memory space when they are initialized. The addresses of system structures and buffers differ with every OS, every model, and every configuration, as does the amount of free memory and system stack usage. Remember that all data for direct custom chip access must be in CHIP RAM. This includes bit images (bitplanes, sprites, etc), sound samples, trackdisk buffers, and copper lists.

Do not write spurious data to, or interpret undefined data from currently unused bits or addresses in the custom chip space. All undefined bits must be set to zero for writes, and ignored on reads.

Do not write data past the current end of custom chip space. Custom chips may be extended or enhanced to provide additional registers, or to use currently undefined bits in existing registers.

All custom chip registers are read only OR write only. Do not read write only registers, and do not write to read only registers.

Do not read, write, or use any currently undefined address ranges. The current and future usage of such areas is reserved by Commodore and is definitely subject to change.

If you are using the system libraries, devices, and resources, you must follow the defined interface. Assembler programmers (and compiler writers) must enter functions through the library base jump tables, with arguments passed as longs and library base address in A6. Results returned in D0 must be tested, and the contents of D0-D1/A0-A1 must be assumed gone after a system call.

NOTE

The assembler TAS instruction should not be used in any Amiga program. The TAS instruction assumes an indivisible read-modify-write but this can be defeated by system DMA. Instead use BSET and BCLR. These instructions perform a test and set operation which cannot be interrupted.

TAS is only needed for a multiple CPU system. On a single CPU system, the BSET and BCLR instructions are identical to TAS, as the 68000 does not interrupt instructions in the middle. BSET and BCLR first test, then set bits.

Do not use assembler instructions which are privileged on any 68000 family processor, most notably MOVE SR,<ea> which is privileged on the 68010/20/30. Use the Exec function GetCC() instead of MOVE SR, or use the appropriate non-privileged instruction as shown below:

CPU	User Mode	Super Mode
68000	MOVE SR,<ea>	MOVE SR,<ea>
68010/20/30	MOVE CCR,<ea>	MOVE SR,<ea>

All addresses must be 32 bits. Do not use the upper 8 bits for other data, and do not use signed variables or signed math for addresses. Do not execute code on your stack or use self-modifying code since such code can be defeated by the caching capabilities of some 68xxx processors. And never use processor or clock speed dependent software loops for timing delays. See Appendix F for information on using an 8520 timer for delays.

NOTE

When strobing any register which responds to either a read or a write, (for example copjmp2) be sure to use a MOVE.W #$00, not CLR.W. The CLR instruction causes a read and a clear (two accesses) on a 68000, but only a single access on 68020 and above. This will give different results on different processors.

If you are programming at the hardware level, you must follow hardware interfacing specifications. All hardware is NOT the same. Do not assume that low level hacks for speed or copy protection will work on all drives, or all keyboards, or all systems, or future systems. Test your software on many different systems, with different processors, OS, hardware, and RAM configurations.

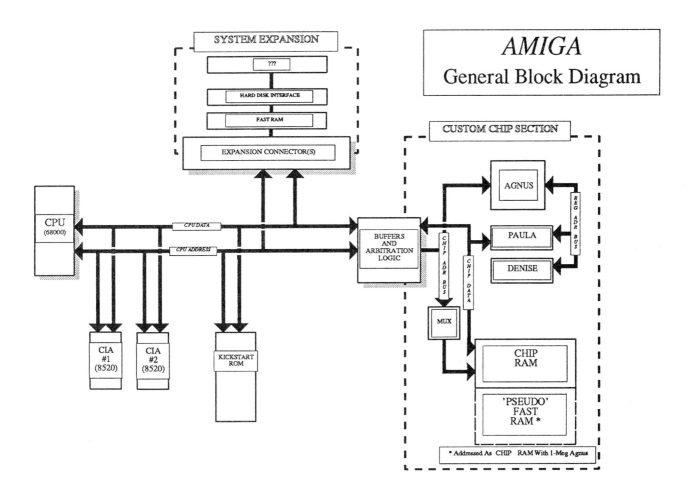

Figure 1-1: Block Diagram for the Amiga Computer Family

Chapter 2

COPROCESSOR HARDWARE

Introduction

The Copper is a general purpose coprocessor that resides in one of the Amiga's custom chips. It retrieves its instructions via direct memory access (DMA). The Copper can control nearly the entire graphics system, freeing the 68000 to execute program logic; it can also directly affect the contents of most of the chip control registers. It is a very powerful tool for directing mid-screen modifications in graphics displays and for directing the register changes that must occur during the vertical blanking periods. Among other things, it can control register updates, reposition sprites, change the color palette, update the audio channels, and control the blitter.

One of the features of the Copper is its ability to WAIT for a specific video beam position, then MOVE data into a system register. During the WAIT period, the Copper examines the contents of the video beam position counter directly. This means that while the Copper is waiting for the beam to reach a specific position, it does not use the memory bus at all. Therefore, the bus is freed for use by the other DMA channels or by the 68000.

When the WAIT condition has been satisfied, the Copper steals memory cycles from either the blitter or the 68000 to move the specified data into the selected special-purpose register.

The Copper is a two-cycle processor that requests the bus only during odd-numbered memory cycles. This prevents collision with audio, disk, refresh, sprites, and most low-resolution display DMA access, all of which use only the even-numbered memory cycles. The Copper, therefore, needs priority over only the 68000 and the blitter (the DMA channel that handles animation, line drawing, and polygon filling).

As with all the other DMA channels in the Amiga system, the Copper can retrieve its instructions only from the chip RAM area of system memory.

ABOUT THIS CHAPTER

In this chapter, you will learn how to use the special Copper instruction set to organize mid-screen register value modifications and pointer register set-up during the vertical blanking interval. The chapter shows how to organize Copper instructions into Copper lists, how to use Copper lists in interlaced mode, and how to use the Copper with the blitter. The Copper is discussed in this chapter in a general fashion. The chapters that deal with playfields, sprites, audio, and the blitter contain more specific suggestions for using the Copper.

What is a Copper Instruction?

As a coprocessor, the Copper adds its own instruction set to the instructions already provided by the 68000. The Copper has only three instructions, but you can do a lot with them:

- WAIT for a specific screen position specified as x and y coordinates.

- MOVE an immediate data value into one of the special-purpose registers.

- SKIP the next instruction if the video beam has already reached a specified screen position.

All Copper instructions consist of two 16-bit words in sequential memory locations. Each time the Copper fetches an instruction, it fetches both words. The MOVE and SKIP instructions require two memory cycles and two instruction words. Because only the odd memory cycles are requested by the Copper, four memory cycle times are required per instruction. The WAIT instruction requires three memory cycles and six memory cycle times; it takes one extra memory cycle to wake up.

Although the Copper can directly affect only machine registers, it can affect the memory by setting up a blitter operation. More information about how to use the Copper in controlling the blitter can be found in the sections called "Control Register" and "Using the Copper with the Blitter."

The WAIT and MOVE instructions are described below. The SKIP instruction is described in the "Advanced Topics" section.

The MOVE Instruction

The MOVE instruction transfers data from RAM to a register destination. The transferred data is contained in the second word of the MOVE instruction; the first word contains the address of the destination register. This procedure is shown in detail in the section called "Summary of Copper Instructions."

FIRST INSTRUCTION WORD (IR1)

Bit 0   Always set to 0.

Bits 8 - 1   Register destination address (DA8-1).

Bits 15 - 9   Not used, but should be set to 0.

SECOND INSTRUCTION WORD (IR2)

Bits 15 - 0   16 bits of data to be transferred (moved)
                 to the register destination.

The Copper can store data into the following registers:

- Any register whose address is $20 or above.[1]

- Any register whose address is between $10 and $20 if the Copper danger bit is a 1. The Copper danger bit is in the Copper's control register, COPCON, which is described in the "Control Register" section.

- The Copper cannot write into any register whose address is lower than $10.

Appendix B contains all of the machine register addresses.

The following example MOVE instructions point bit-plane pointer 1 at $21000 and bit-plane pointer 2 at $25000.[2]

```
DC.W    $00E0,$0002    ;Move $0002 to register $0E0 (BPL1PTH)
DC.W    $00E2,$1000    ;Move $1000 to regsiter $0E2 (BPL1PTL)
DC.W    $00E4,$0002    ;Move $0002 to register $0E4 (BPL2PTH)
DC.W    $00E6,$5000    ;Move $5000 to register $0E6 (BPL2PTL)
```

Normally, the appropriate assembler ".i" files are included so that names, rather than addresses, may be used for referencing hardware registers. It is strongly recommended that you reference all hardware addresses via their defined names in the system include files. This will allow you to more easily adapt your software to take advantage of future hardware or enhancements. For example:

```
INCLUDE "hardware/custom.i"

DC.W    bplpt+$00,$0002 ;Move $0002 into register $0E0 (BPL1PTH)
DC.W    bplpt+$02,$1000 ;Move $1000 into register $0E2 (BPL1PTL)
DC.W    bplpt+$04,$0002 ;Move $0002 into register $0E4 (BPL2PTH)
DC.W    bplpt+$06,$5000 ;Move $5000 into register $0E6 (BPL2PTL)
```

For use in the hardware manual examples, we have made a special include file (see Appendix J) that defines all of the hardware register names based off of the "hardware/custom.i" file. This was done to make the examples easier to read from a hardware point of view. Most of the examples in this manual are here to help explain the hardware and are, in most cases, not useful without modification and a good deal of additional code.

---

[1] Hexadecimal numbers are distinguished from decimal numbers by the $ prefix.

[2] All sample code segments are in assembly language.

The WAIT Instruction

The WAIT instruction causes the Copper to wait until the video beam counters are equal to (or greater than) the coordinates specified in the instruction. While waiting, the Copper is off the bus and not using memory cycles.

The first instruction word contains the vertical and horizontal coordinates of the beam position. The second word contains enable bits that are used to form a "mask" that tells the system which bits of the beam position to use in making the comparison.

FIRST INSTRUCTION WORD (IR1)

Bit 0	Always set to 1.
Bits 15 - 8	Vertical beam position (called VP).
Bits 7 - 1	Horizontal beam position (called HP).

SECOND INSTRUCTION WORD (IR2)

Bit 0	Always set to 0.
Bit 15	The blitter-finished-disable bit. Normally, this bit is a 1. (See the "Advanced Topics" section below.)
Bits 14 - 8	Vertical position compare enable bits (called VE).
Bits 7 - 1	Horizontal position compare enable bits (called HE).

The following example WAIT instruction waits for scan line 150 ($96) with the horizontal position masked off.

```
DC.W    $9601,$FF00     ;Wait for line 150,
                        ;   ignore horizontal counters.
```

The following example WAIT instruction waits for scan line 255 and horizontal position 254. This event will never occur, so the Copper stops until the next vertical blanking interval begins.

```
DC.W    $FFFF,$FFFE     ;Wait for line 255,
                        ;   H = 254 (ends Copper list).
```

To understand why position VP=$FF HP=$FE will never occur, you must look at the comparison operation of the Copper and the size restrictions of the position information. Line number 255 is a valid line to wait for, in fact it is the maximum value that will fit into this field. Since 255 is the maximum number, the next line will wrap to zero (line 256 will appear as a zero in the comparison.) The line number will never be greater than $FF. The horizontal position has a maximum value of $E2. This means that the largest number that will ever appear in the comparison is $FFE2. When waiting for $FFFE, the line $FF will be reached, but the horizontal position $FE will never happen. Thus, the position will never reach $FFFE.

You may be tempted to wait for horizontal position $FE (since it will never happen), and put a smaller number into the vertical position field. This will not lead to the desired result. The comparison operation is waiting for the beam position to become greater than or equal to the entered position. If the vertical position is not $FF, then as soon as the line number becomes higher than the entered number, the comparison will evaluate to true and the wait will end.

The following notes on horizontal and vertical beam position apply to both the WAIT instruction and to the SKIP instruction. The SKIP instruction is described below in the ''Advanced Topics'' section.

HORIZONTAL BEAM POSITION

The horizontal beam position has a value of $0 to $E2. The least significant bit is not used in the comparison, so there are 113 positions available for Copper operations. This corresponds to 4 pixels in low resolution and 8 pixels in high resolution. Horizontal blanking falls in the range of $0F to $35. The standard screen (320 pixels wide) has an unused horizontal portion of $04 to $47 (during which only the background color is displayed).

All lines are not the same length in NTSC. Every other line is a long line (228 color clocks, 0-$E3), with the others being 227 color clocks long. In PAL, they are all 227 long. The display sees all these lines as 227 1/2 color clocks long, while the copper sees alternating long & short lines.

VERTICAL BEAM POSITION

The vertical beam position can be resolved to one line, with a maximum value of 255. There are actually 262 NTSC (312 PAL) possible vertical positions. Some minor complications can occur if you want something to happen within these last six or seven scan lines. Because there are only eight bits of resolution for vertical beam position (allowing 256 different positions), one of the simplest ways to handle this is shown below.

Instruction	Explanation
[... other instructions ...]	
WAIT for position (0,255)	*At this point, the vertical counter appears to wrap to 0 because the comparison works on the least significant bits of the vertical count.*
WAIT for any horizontal position with vertical position 0 through 5, covering the last 6 lines of the scan before vertical blanking occurs.	*Thus the total of 256 + 6 = 262 lines of video beam travel during which Copper instructions can be executed.*

NOTE

The vertical is like the horizontal—as there are alternating long and short lines, there are also long and short fields (interlace only). In NTSC, the fields are 262, then 263 lines and in PAL, 312,313.

This alternation of lines & fields produces the standard NTSC 4 field repeating pattern:

    short field ending on short line
    long field ending on long line
    short field ending on long line
    long field ending on short line
    & back to the beginning...

1 horiz count takes 1 cycle of the system clock. (Processor is twice this)

    NTSC- 3,579,545 Hz
    PAL- 3,546,895 Hz
    genlocked- basic clock frequency plus or minus about 2%.

THE COMPARISON ENABLE BITS

Bits 14-1 are normally set to all 1s. The use of the comparison enable bits is described later in the "Advanced Topics" section.

Using the Copper Registers

There are several machine registers and strobe addresses dedicated to the Copper:

- Location registers

- Jump address strobes

- Control register

LOCATION REGISTERS

The Copper has two sets of location registers:

COP1LCH	High 3 bits of first Copper list address.
COP1LCL	Low 16 bits of first Copper list address.
COP2LCH	High 3 bits of second Copper list address.
COP2LCL	Low 16 bits of second Copper list address.

In accessing the hardware directly, you often have to write to a pair of registers that contains the address of some data. The register with the lower address always has a name ending in "H" and contains the most significant data, or high 3 bits of the address. The register with the higher address has a name ending in "L" and contains the least significant data, or low 15 bits of the address. Therefore, you write the 18-bit address by moving one long word to the register whose name ends in "H." This is because when you write long words with the 68000, the most significant word goes in the lower addressed word.

In the case of the Copper location registers, you write the address to COP1LCH. In the following text, for simplicity, these addresses are referred to as COP1LC or COP2LC.

The Copper location registers contain the two indirect jump addresses used by the Copper. The Copper fetches its instructions by using its program counter and increments the program counter after each fetch. When a jump address strobe is written, the corresponding location register is loaded into the Copper program counter. This causes the Copper to jump to a new location, from which its next instruction will be fetched. Instruction fetch continues sequentially until the Copper is interrupted by another jump address strobe.

At the start of each vertical blanking interval, COP1LC is automatically used to start the program counter. That is, no matter what the Copper is doing, when the end of vertical blanking occurs, the Copper is automatically forced to restart its operations at the address contained in COP1LC.

JUMP STROBE ADDRESS

When you write to a Copper strobe address, the Copper reloads its program counter from the corresponding location register. The Copper can write its own location registers and strobe addresses to perform programmed jumps. For instance, you might MOVE an indirect address into the COP2LC location register. Then, any MOVE instruction that addresses COPJMP2 strobes this indirect address into the program counter.

There are two jump strobe addresses:

COPJMP1   Restart Copper from address contained in COP1LC.

COPJMP2   Restart Copper from address contained in COP2LC.

CONTROL REGISTER

The Copper can access some special-purpose registers all of the time, some registers only when a special control bit is set to a 1, some registers not at all. The registers that the Copper can always affect are numbered $20 through $FF inclusive. Those it cannot affect at all are numbered $00 to $0F inclusive. (See Appendix B for a list of registers in address order.) The Copper control register is within this group ($00 to $0F). Thus it takes deliberate action on the part of the 68000 to allow the Copper to write into a specific range of the special-purpose registers.

The Copper control register, called COPCON, contains only one bit, bit #1. This bit, called CDANG (for Copper Danger Bit) protects all registers numbered between $10 and $1F inclusive. This range includes the blitter control registers. When CDANG is 0, these registers cannot be written by the Copper. When CDANG is 1, these registers can be written by the Copper. Preventing the Copper from accessing the blitter control registers prevents a "runaway" Copper (caused by a poorly formed instruction list) from accidentally affecting system memory.

The CDANG bit is cleared after a reset.

Putting Together a Copper Instruction List

The Copper instruction list contains all the register resetting done during the vertical blanking interval and the register modifications necessary for making mid-screen alterations. As you are planning what will happen during each display field, you may find it easier to think of each aspect of the display as a separate subsystem, such as playfields, sprites, audio, interrupts, and so on. Then you can build a separate list of things that must be done for each subsystem individually at each video beam position.

When you have created all these intermediate lists of things to be done, you must merge them together into a single instruction list to be executed by the Copper once for each display frame. The alternative is to create this all-inclusive list directly, without the intermediate steps.

For example, the bit-plane pointers used in playfield displays and the sprite pointers must be rewritten during the vertical blanking interval so the data will be properly retrieved when the screen display starts again. This can be done with a Copper instruction list that does the following:

       WAIT until first line of the display
       MOVE data to bit-plane pointer 1
       MOVE data to bit-plane pointer 2
       MOVE data to sprite pointer 1
       and so on

As another example, the sprite DMA channels that create movable objects can be reused multiple times during the same display field. You can change the size and shape of the reuses of a sprite; however, every multiple reuse normally uses the same set of colors during a full display frame. You can change sprite colors mid-screen with a Copper instruction list that waits until the last line of the first use of the sprite processor and changes the colors before the first line of the next use of the same sprite processor:

       WAIT for first line of display
       MOVE firstcolor1 to COLOR17
       MOVE firstcolor2 to COLOR18
       MOVE firstcolor3 to COLOR19
       WAIT for last line +1 of sprite's first use
       MOVE secondcolor1 to COLOR17
       MOVE secondcolor2 to COLOR18
       MOVE secondcolor3 to COLOR19
       and so on

As you create Copper instruction lists, note that the final list must be in the same order as that in which the video beam creates the display. The video beam traverses the screen from position (0,0) in the upper left hand corner of the screen to the end of the display (226,262) NTSC (or (226,312) PAL) in the lower right hand corner. The first 0 in (0,0) represents the x position. The second 0 represents the y position. For example, an instruction that does something at position (0,100) should come after an instruction that affects the display at position (0,60).

NOTE

Given the form of the WAIT instruction, you can sometimes get away with not sorting the list in strict video beam order. The WAIT instruction causes the Copper to wait until the value in the beam counter is equal to *or greater than* the value in the instruction.

This means, for example, if you have instructions following each other like this:

    WAIT for position (64,64)
    MOVE data

    WAIT for position (60,60)
    MOVE data

the Copper will perform *both* moves, even though the instructions are out of sequence. The "greater than" specification prevents the Copper from locking up if the beam has already passed the specified position. A side effect is that the second MOVE below will be performed:

    WAIT for position (60,60)
    MOVE data

    WAIT for position (60,60)
    MOVE data

At the time of the second WAIT in this sequence, the beam counters will be greater than the position shown in the instructions. Therefore, the second MOVE will also be performed.

Note also that the above sequence of instructions could just as easily be

    WAIT for position (60,60)
    MOVE data
    MOVE data

because multiple MOVEs can follow a single WAIT.

COMPLETE SAMPLE COPPER LIST

The following example shows a complete Copper list. This list is for two bit-planes—one at $21000 and one at $25000. At the top of the screen, the color registers are loaded with the following values:

Register	Color
COLOR00	white
COLOR01	red
COLOR02	green
COLOR03	blue

At line 150 on the screen, the color registers are reloaded:

Register	Color
COLOR00	black
COLOR01	yellow
COLOR02	cyan
COLOR03	magenta

The complete Copper list follows.

```
;
; Notes:
;       1. Copper lists must be in CHIP ram.
;       2. Bitplane addresses used in the example are arbitrary.
;       3. Destination register addresses in copper move instructions
;          are offsets from the base address of the custom chips.
;       4. As always, hardware manual examples assume that your
;          application has taken full control of the hardware,
;          and is not conflicting with operating system use of
;          the same hardware.
;       5. Many of the examples just pick memory addresses to
;          be used.  Normally you would need to allocate the
;          required type of memory from the system with AllocMem()
;       6. As stated earlier, the code examples are mainly to help
;          clarify the way the hardware works.
;       7. The following INCLUDEs are required by all example code
;          in this chapter.
;

        INCLUDE "exec/types.i"
        INCLUDE "hardware/custom.i"
        INCLUDE "hardware/dmabits.i"
        INCLUDE "hardware/hw_examples.i"
```

```
COPPERLIST:
;
;  Set up pointers to two bit planes
;
        DC.W    BPL1PTH,$0002    ;Move $0002 into register $0E0 (BPL1PTH)
        DC.W    BPL1PTL,$1000    ;Move $1000 into register $0E2 (BPL1PTL)
        DC.W    BPL2PTH,$0002    ;Move $0002 into register $0E4 (BPL2PTH)
        DC.W    BPL2PTL,$5000    ;Move $5000 into register $0E6 (BPL2PTL)
;
;  Load color registers
;
        DC.W    COLOR00,$0FFF    ;Move white into register $180 (COLOR00)
        DC.W    COLOR01,$0F00    ;Move red into register   $182 (COLOR01)
        DC.W    COLOR02,$00F0    ;Move green into register $184 (COLOR02)
        DC.W    COLOR03,$000F    ;Move blue into register  $186 (COLOR03)
;
;   Specify 2 lo-res bitplanes
;
        DC.W    BPLCON0,$2200    ;2 lores planes, coloron
;
;  Wait for line 150
;
        DC.W    $9601,$FF00      ;Wait for line 150, ignore horiz. position
;
;  Change color registers mid-display
;
        DC.W    COLOR00,$0000    ;Move black into register $0180 (COLOR00)
        DC.W    COLOR01,$0FF0    ;Move yellow into register $0182 (COLOR01)
        DC.W    COLOR02,$00FF    ;Move cyan into register $0184 (COLOR02)
        DC.W    COLOR03,$0F0F    ;Move magenta into register $0186 (COLOR03)
;
; End Copper list by waiting for the impossible
;
        DC.W    $FFFF,$FFFE      ;Wait for line 255, H = 254 (never happens)
```

For more information about color registers, see Chapter 3, ''Playfield Hardware.''

LOOPS AND BRANCHES

Loops and branches in Copper lists are covered in the ''Advanced Topics'' section below.

Starting and Stopping the Copper

STARTING THE COPPER AFTER RESET

At power-on or reset time, you must initialize one of the Copper location registers (COP1LC or COP2LC) and write to its strobe address before Copper DMA is turned on. This ensures a known start address and known state. Usually, COP1LC is used because this particular register is reused during each vertical blanking time. The following sequence of instructions shows how to initialize a location register. It is assumed that the user has already created the correct Copper instruction list at location "mycoplist."

```
;
; Install the copper list
;
        LEA     CUSTOM,a1               ; a1 = address of custom chips
        LEA     MYCOPLIST(pc),a0        ; Address of our copper list
        MOVE.L  a0,COP1LC(a1)           ; Write whole longword address
        MOVE.W  COPJMP1(a1),d0          ; Causes copper to load PC from COP1LC
;
; Then enable copper and raster dma
;
        MOVE.W  #(DMAF_SETCLR!DMAF_COPPER!DMAF_RASTER!DMAF_MASTER),DMACON(a1)
;
```

Now, if the contents of COP1LC are not changed, every time vertical blanking occurs the Copper will restart at the same location for each subsequent video screen. This forms a repeatable loop which, if the list is correctly formulated, will cause the displayed screen to be stable.

STOPPING THE COPPER

No stop instruction is provided for the Copper. To ensure that it will stop and do nothing until the screen display ends and the program counter starts again at the top of the instruction list, the last instruction should be to WAIT for an event that cannot occur. A typical instruction is to WAIT for VP = $FF and HP = $FE. An HP of greater than $E2 is not possible. When the screen display ends and vertical blanking starts, the Copper will automatically be pointed to the top of its instruction list, and this final WAIT instruction never finishes.

You can also stop the Copper by disabling its ability to use DMA for retrieving instructions or placing data. The register called DMACON controls all of the DMA channels. Bit 7, COPEN, enables Copper DMA when set to 1.

For information about controlling the DMA, see Chapter 7, "System Control Hardware."

Advanced Topics

THE SKIP INSTRUCTION

The SKIP instruction causes the Copper to skip the next instruction if the video beam counters are equal to or greater than the value given in the instruction.

The contents of the SKIP instruction's words are shown below. They are identical to the WAIT instruction, except that bit 0 of the second instruction word is a 1 to identify this as a SKIP instruction.

FIRST INSTRUCTION WORD (IR1)

Bit 0	Always set to 1.
Bits 15 - 8	Vertical position (called VP).
Bits 7 - 1	Horizontal position (called HP).
	Skip if the beam counter is equal to or greater than these combined bits (bits 15 through 1).

SECOND INSTRUCTION WORD (IR2)

Bit 0	Always set to 1.
Bit 15	The blitter-finished-disable bit. (See ''Using the Copper with the Blitter'' below.)
Bits 14 - 8	Vertical position compare enable bits (called VE).
Bits 7 - 1	Horizontal position compare enable bits (called HE).

The notes about horizontal and vertical beam position found in the discussion of the WAIT instruction apply also to the SKIP instruction.

The following example SKIP instruction skips the instruction following it if VP (vertical beam position) is greater than or equal to 100 ($64).

```
DC.W    $6401,$FF01     ;If VP >= 100,
                        ;  skip next instruction (ignore HP)
```

COPPER LOOPS AND BRANCHES AND COMPARISON ENABLE

You can change the value in the location registers at any time and use this value to construct loops in the instruction list. Before the next vertical blanking time, however, the COP1LC registers *must* be repointed to the beginning of the appropriate Copper list. The value in the COP1LC location registers will be restored to the Copper's program counter at the start of the vertical blanking period.

Bits 14-1 of instruction word 2 in the WAIT and SKIP instructions specify which bits of the horizontal and vertical position are to be used for the beam counter comparison. The position in instruction word 1 and the compare enable bits in instruction word 2 are tested against the actual beam counters before any further action is taken. A position bit in instruction word 1 is used in comparing the positions with the actual beam counters *if and only if* the corresponding enable bit in instruction word 2 is set to 1. If the corresponding enable bit is 0, the comparison is always true. For instance, if you care only about the value in the last four bits of the vertical position, you set only the last four compare enable bits, bits (11-8) in instruction word 2.

Not all of the bits in the beam counter may be masked. If you look at the description of the IR2 (second instruction word) you will notice that bit 15 is the blitter-finished-disable bit. This bit is not part of the beam counter comparison mask, it has its own meaning in the Copper WAIT instruction. Thus, you can not mask the most significant bit in WAIT or SKIP instructions. In most situations this limitation does not come into play, however, the following example shows how to deal with it.

This example will instruct the Copper to issue an interrupt every 16 scan lines. It might seem that the way to do this would be to use a mask of $0F and then compare the result with $0F. This should compare "true" for $1F, $2F, $3F, etc. Since the test is for greater than or equal to, this would *seem to allow* checking for every 16th scan line. However, the highest order bit cannot be masked, so it will always appear in the comparisons. When the Copper is waiting for $0F and the vertical position is past 128 (hex $80), this test will always be true. In this case, the minimum value in the comparison will be $80, which is always greater than $0F, and the interrupt will happen on every scan line. Remember, the Copper only checks for greater than or equal to.

In the following example, the Copper lists have been made to loop. The COP1LC and COP2LC values are either set via the CPU or in the Copper list before this section of Copper code. Also, it is assumed that you have correctly installed an interrupt server for the Copper interrupt that will be generated every 16 lines. Note that these are non-interlaced scan lines.

How it works:

Both loops are, for the most part, exactly the same. In each, the Copper waits until the vertical position register has $?F (? is any hex digit) in it, at which point we issue a Copper interrupt to the Amiga hardware. To make sure that the Copper does not loop back before the vertical position has changed and cause another interrupt on the same scan line, wait for the horizontal position to be $E2 after each interrupt. Position $E2 is horizontal position 113 for the Copper and the last real horizontal position available. This will force the Copper to the next line before the next WAIT. The loop is executed by writing to the COPJMP1 register. This causes the Copper to jump to the address that was initialized in COP1LC.

The masking problem described above makes this code fail after vertical position 127. A separate loop must be executed when vertical position is greater than or equal 127. When the vertical position becomes greater than or equal to 127, the the first loop instruction is skipped, dropping the Copper into the second loop. The second loop is much the same as the first, except that it waits for $?F with the high bit set (binary 1xxx1111). This is true for both the vertical and the horizontal WAIT instructions. To cause the second loop, write to the COPJMP2 register. The list is put into an infinite wait when VP >= 255 so that it will end before the vertical blank. At the end of the vertical blanking period COP1LC is written to by the operating system, causing the first loop to start up again.

NOTE

The COP1LC register is written at the end of the vertical blanking period by a graphics interrupt handler which is in the vertical blank interrupt server chain. As long as this server is intact, COP1LC will be correctly strobed at the end of each vertical blank.

```
;
;  This is the data for the Copper list.
;
;  It is assumed that COPPERL1 is loaded into COP1LC and
;  that COPPERL2 is loaded into COP2LC by some other code.
;
COPPERL1:
        DC.W    $0F01,$8F00     ; Wait for VP=0xxx1111
        DC.W    INTREQ,$8010    ; Set the copper interrupt bit...

        DC.W    $00E3,$80FE     ; Wait for Horizontal $E2
                                ; This is so the line gets finished before
                                ; we check if we are there  (The wait above)

        DC.W    $7F01,$7F01     ; Skip if VP>=127
        DC.W    COPJMP1,$0      ; Force a jump to COP1LC

COPPERL2:
        DC.W    $8F01,$8F00     ; Wait for VP=1xxx1111
        DC.W    INTREQ,$8010    ; Set the copper interrupt bit...

        DC.W    $80E3,$80FE     ; Wait for Horizontal $E2
                                ; This is so the line gets finished before
                                ; we check if we are there  (The wait above)

        DC.W    $FF01,$FE01     ; Skip if VP>=255
```

```
        DC.W    COPJMP2,$0      ; Force a jump to COP2LC

; Whatever cleanup copper code that might be needed here...
; Since there are 262 lines in NTSC, and we stopped at 255, there is a
; bit of time available

        DC.W    $FFFF,$FFFE     ; End of Copper list
;
```

USING THE COPPER IN INTERLACED MODE

An interlaced bit-plane display has twice the normal number of vertical lines on the screen. Whereas a normal NTSC display has 262 lines, an interlaced NTSC display has 524 lines. PAL has 312 lines normally and 625 in interlaced mode. In interlaced mode, the video beam scans the screen twice from top to bottom, displaying, in the case of NTSC, 262 lines at a time. During the first scan, the odd-numbered lines are displayed. During the second scan, the even-numbered lines are displayed and interlaced with the odd-numbered ones. The scanning circuitry thus treats an interlaced display as two display fields, one containing the even-numbered lines and one containing the odd-numbered lines. Figure 2-1 shows how an interlaced display is stored in memory.

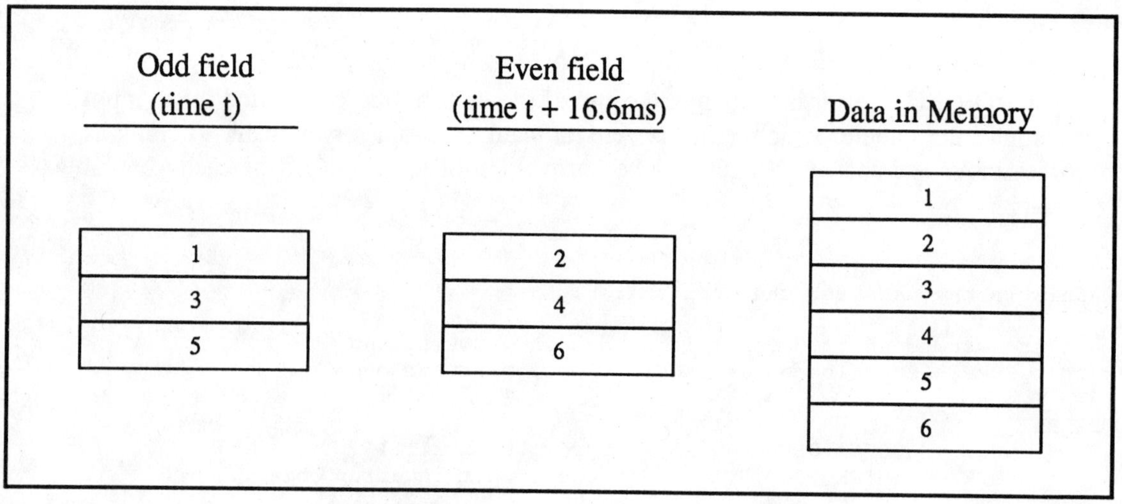

Figure 2-1: Interlaced Bit-Plane in RAM

The system retrieves data for bit-plane displays by using pointers to the starting address of the data in memory. As you can see, the starting address for the even-numbered fields is one line greater than the starting address for the odd-numbered fields. Therefore, the bit-plane pointer must contain a different value for alternate fields of the interlaced display.

Simply, the organization of the data in memory matches the apparent organization on the screen (i.e., odd and even lines are interlaced together). This is accomplished by having a separate Copper instruction list for each field to manage displaying the data.

To get the Copper to execute the correct list, you set an interrupt to the 68000 just after the first line of the display. When the interrupt is executed, you change the contents of the COP1LC location register to point to the second list. Then, during the vertical blanking interval, COP1LC will be automatically reset to point to the original list.

For more information about interlaced displays, see Chapter 3, "Playfield Hardware."

USING THE COPPER WITH THE BLITTER

If the Copper is used to start up a sequence of blitter operations, it must wait for the blitter-finished interrupt before starting another blitter operation. Changing blitter registers while the blitter is operating causes unpredictable results. For just this purpose, the WAIT instruction includes an additional control bit, called BFD (for blitter finished disable). Normally, this bit is a 1 and only the beam counter comparisons control the WAIT.

When the BFD bit is a 0, the logic of the Copper WAIT instruction is modified. The Copper will WAIT until the beam counter comparison is true *and* the blitter has finished. The blitter has finished when the blitter-finished flag is set. This bit should be unset with caution. It could possibly prevent some screen displays or prevent objects from being displayed correctly.

For more information about using the blitter, see Chapter 6, "Blitter Hardware."

THE COPPER AND THE 68000

On those occasions when the Copper's instructions do not suffice, you can interrupt the 68000 and use its instruction set instead. The 68000 can poll for interrupt flags set in the INTREQ register by various devices. To interrupt the 68000, use the Copper MOVE instruction to store a 1 into the following bits of INTREQ:

Table 2-1: Interrupting the 68000

Bit Number	Name	Function
15	SET/CLR	Set/Clear control bit. Determines if bits written with a 1 get set or cleared.
4	COPEN	Coprocessor interrupting 68000.

See Chapter 7, "System Control Hardware," for more information about interrupts.

Summary of Copper Instructions

The table below shows a summary of the bit positions for each of the Copper instructions. See Appendix A for a summary of all registers.

Table 2-2: Copper Instruction Summary

Bit#	Move		Wait		Skip	
	IR1	IR2	IR1	IR2	IR1	IR2
15	X	RD15	VP7	BFD	VP7	BFD
14	X	RD14	VP6	VE6	VP6	VE6
13	X	RD13	VP5	VE5	VP5	VE5
12	X	RD12	VP4	VE4	VP4	VE4
11	X	RD11	VP3	VE3	VP3	VE3
10	X	RD10	VP2	VE2	VP2	VE2
09	X	RD09	VP1	VE1	VP1	VE1
08	DA8	RD08	VP0	VE0	VP0	VE0
07	DA7	RD07	HP8	HE8	HP8	HE8
06	DA6	RD06	HP7	HE7	HP7	HE7
05	DA5	RD05	HP6	HE6	HP6	HE6
04	DA4	RD04	HP5	HE5	HP5	HE5
03	DA3	RD03	HP4	HE4	HP4	HE4
02	DA2	RD02	HP3	HE3	HP3	HE3
01	DA1	RD01	HP2	HE2	HP2	HE2
00	0	RD00	1	0	1	1

X = don't care, but should be a 0 for upward compatibility
IR1 = first instruction word
IR2 = second instruction word
DA = destination address
RD = RAM data to be moved to destination register
VP = vertical beam position bit
HP = horizontal beam position bit
VE = enable comparison (mask bit)
HE = enable comparison (mask bit)
BFD = blitter-finished disable

Chapter 3

PLAYFIELD HARDWARE

Introduction

The screen display of the Amiga consists of two basic parts—playfields, which are sometimes called backgrounds, and sprites, which are easily movable graphics objects. This chapter describes how to directly access hardware registers to form playfields.

ABOUT THIS CHAPTER

This chapter begins with a brief overview of playfield features, including definitions of some fundamental terms, and continues with the following major topics:

- Forming a single "basic" playfield, which is a playfield the same size as the display screen. This section includes concepts that are fundamental to forming any playfield.

- Forming a dual-playfield display in which one playfield is superimposed upon another. This procedure differs from that of forming a basic playfield in some details.

- Forming playfields of various sizes and displaying only part of a larger playfield.

- Moving playfields by scrolling them vertically and horizontally.

- Advanced topics to help you use playfields in special situations.

For information about movable sprite objects, see Chapter 4, "Sprite Hardware." There are also movable playfield objects, which are subsections of a playfield. To move portions of a playfield, you use a technique called playfield animation, which is described in Chapter 6, "Blitter Hardware."

PLAYFIELD FEATURES

The Amiga produces its video displays with raster display techniques. The picture you see on the screen is made up of a series of horizontal video lines displayed one after the other. Each horizontal video line is made up of a series of pixels. You create a graphic display by defining one or more bit-planes in memory and filling them with "1"s and "0"s The combination of the "1"s and "0"s will determine the colors in your display.

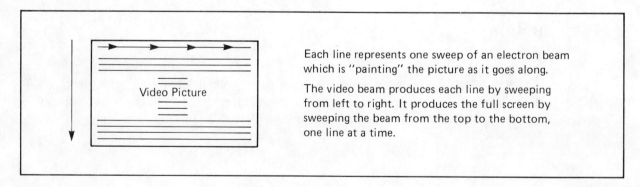

Video Picture

Each line represents one sweep of an electron beam which is "painting" the picture as it goes along.

The video beam produces each line by sweeping from left to right. It produces the full screen by sweeping the beam from the top to the bottom, one line at a time.

Figure 3-1: How the Video Display Picture Is Produced

The video beam produces about 262 video lines from top to bottom, of which 200 normally are visible on the screen with an NTSC system. With a PAL system, the beam produces 312 lines, of which 256 are normally visible. Each complete set of lines (262/NTSC or 312/PAL) is called a display field. The field time, i.e. the time required for a complete display field to be produced, is approximately 1/60th of a second for an NTSC system and approximately 1/50th of a second for PAL. Between display fields, the video beam traverses the lines that are not visible on the screen and returns to the top of the screen to produce another display field.

The display area is defined as a grid of pixels. A pixel is a single picture element, the smallest addressable part of a screen display. The drawings below show what a pixel is and how pixels form displays.

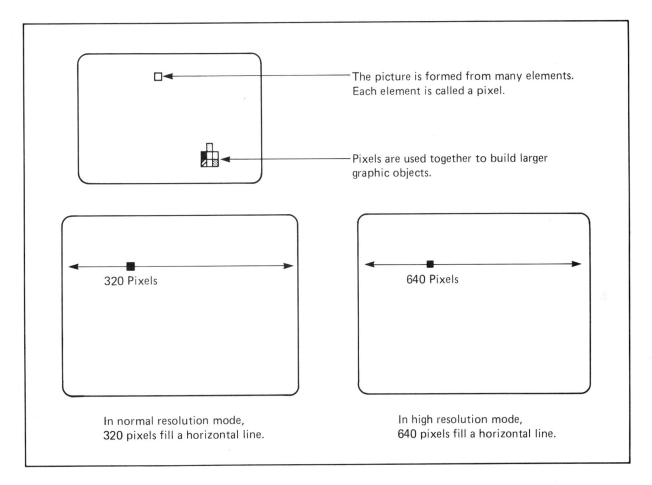

The picture is formed from many elements. Each element is called a pixel.

Pixels are used together to build larger graphic objects.

320 Pixels

640 Pixels

In normal resolution mode, 320 pixels fill a horizontal line.

In high resolution mode, 640 pixels fill a horizontal line.

Figure 3-2: What Is a Pixel?

The Amiga offers a choice in both horizontal and vertical resolutions. Horizontal resolution can be adjusted to operate in low resolution or high resolution mode. Vertical resolution can be adjusted to operate in interlaced or non-interlaced mode.

- In low-resolution mode, the normal playfield has a width of 320 pixels.

- High-resolution mode gives finer horizontal resolution — 640 pixels in the same physical display area.

- In non-interlaced mode, the normal NTSC playfield has a height of 200 video lines. The normal PAL screen has a height of 256 video lines.

- Interlaced mode gives finer vertical resolution — 400 lines in the same physical display area in NTSC and 512 for PAL.

These modes can be combined, so you can have, for instance, an interlaced, high-resolution display.

Note that the dimensions referred to as "normal" in the previous paragraph are *nominal* dimensions and represent the normal values you should expect to use. Actually, you can display larger playfields; the maximum dimensions are given in the section called "Bit-Planes and Playfields of All Sizes." Also, the dimensions of the playfield in memory are often larger than the playfield displayed on the screen. You choose which part of this larger memory picture to display by specifying a different size for the display window.

A playfield taller than the screen can be scrolled, or moved smoothly, up or down. A playfield wider than the screen can be scrolled horizontally, from left to right or right to left. Scrolling is described in the section called "Moving (Scrolling) Playfields."

In the Amiga graphics system, you can have up to thirty-two different colors in a single playfield, using normal display methods. You can control the color of each individual pixel in the playfield display by setting the bit or bits that control each pixel. A display formed in this way is called a bit-mapped display.

For instance, in a two-color display, the color of each pixel is determined by whether a single bit is on or off. If the bit is 0, the pixel is one user-defined color; if the bit is 1, the pixel is another color. For a four-color display, you build two bit-planes in memory. When the playfield is displayed, the two bit-planes are overlapped, which means that each pixel is now two bits deep. You can combine up to five bit-planes in this way. Displays made up of three, four, or five bit-planes allow a choice of eight, sixteen, or thirty-two colors, respectively.

The color of a pixel is always determined by the binary combination of the bits that define it. When the system combines bit-planes for display, the combination of bits formed for each pixel corresponds to the number of a color register. This method of coloring pixels is called *color indirection*. The Amiga has thirty-two color registers, each containing bits defining a user-selected color (from a total of 4,096 possible colors).

Figure 3-3 shows how the combination of up to five bit-planes forms a code that selects which one of the thirty-two registers to use to display the color of a playfield pixel.

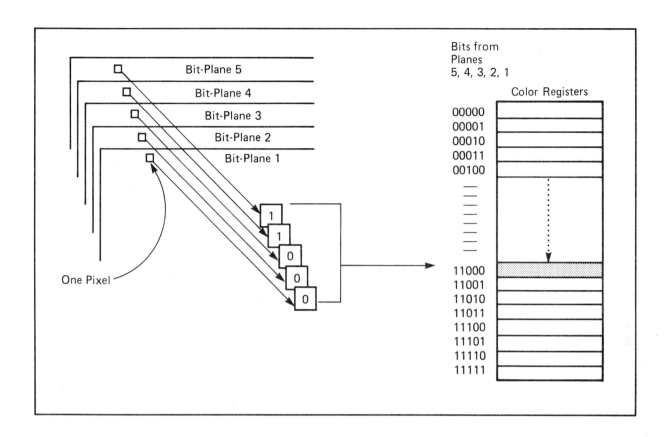

Figure 3-3: How Bit-planes Select a Color

Values in the highest numbered bit-plane have the highest significance in the binary number. As shown in Figure 3-4, the value in each pixel in the highest-numbered bit-plane forms the leftmost digit of the number. The value in the next highest-numbered bit-plane forms the next bit, and so on.

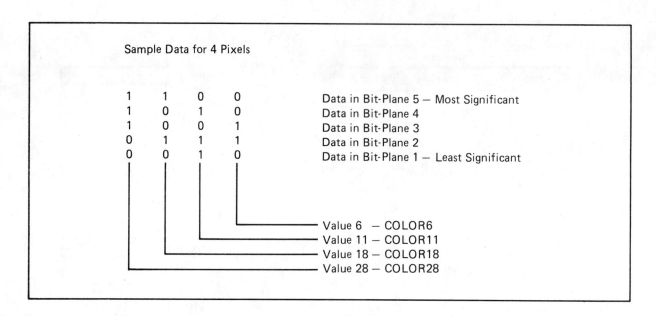

Sample Data for 4 Pixels

```
1   1   0   0     Data in Bit-Plane 5 — Most Significant
1   0   1   0     Data in Bit-Plane 4
1   0   0   1     Data in Bit-Plane 3
0   1   1   1     Data in Bit-Plane 2
0   0   1   0     Data in Bit-Plane 1 — Least Significant


                              Value 6  — COLOR6
                              Value 11 — COLOR11
                              Value 18 — COLOR18
                              Value 28 — COLOR28
```

Figure 3-4: Significance of Bit-Plane Data in Selecting Colors

You also have the choice of defining two separate playfields, each formed from up to three bit-planes. Each of the two playfields uses a separate set of eight different colors. This is called *dual-playfield mode.*

Forming a Basic Playfield

To get you started, this section describes how to directly access hardware registers to form a single basic playfield that is the same size as the video screen. Here, "same size" means that the playfield is the same size as the actual display window. This will leave a small border between the playfield and the edge of the video screen. The playfield usually does not extend all the way to the edge of the physical display.

To form a playfield, you need to define these characteristics:

- Height and width of the playfield and size of the display window (that is, how much of the playfield actually appears on the screen).

- Color of each pixel in the playfield.

- Horizontal resolution.

- Vertical resolution, or interlacing.

- Data fetch and modulo, which tell the system how much data to put on a horizontal line and how to fetch data from memory to the screen.

In addition, you need to allocate memory to store the playfield, set pointers to tell the system where to find the data in memory, and (optionally) write a Copper routine to handle redisplay of the playfield.

HEIGHT AND WIDTH OF THE PLAYFIELD

To create a playfield that is the same size as the screen, you can use a width of either 320 pixels or 640 pixels, depending upon the resolution you choose. The height is either 200 or 400 lines for NTSC, 256 or 512 lines for PAL, depending upon whether or not you choose interlaced mode.

BIT-PLANES AND COLOR

You define playfield color by:

1. Deciding how many colors you need and how you want to color each pixel.

2. Loading the colors into the color registers.

3. Allocating memory for the number of bit-planes you need and setting a pointer to each bit-plane.

4. Writing instructions to place a value in each bit in the bit-planes to give you the correct color.

Table 3-1 shows how many bit-planes to use for the color selection you need.

Table 3-1: Colors in a Single Playfield

Number of Colors	Number of Bit-Planes
1 - 2	1
3 - 4	2
5 - 8	3
9 - 16	4
17 - 32	5

The Color Table

The color table contains 32 registers, and you may load a different color into each of the registers. Here is a condensed view of the contents of the color table:

Table 3-2: Portion of the Color Table

Register Name	Contents	Meaning
COLOR00	12 bits	User-defined color for the background area and borders.
COLOR01	12 bits	User-defined color number 1 (For example, the alternate color selection for a two-color playfield).
COLOR02	12 bits	User-defined color number 2.
.	.	
.	.	
.	.	
COLOR31	12 bits	User-defined color number 31.

COLOR00 is always reserved for the background color. The background color shows in any area on the display where there is no other object present and is also displayed outside the defined display window, in the border area.

NOTE

If you are using the optional genlock board for video input from a camera, VCR, or laser disk, the background color will be replaced by the incoming video display.

Twelve bits of color selection allow you to define, for each of the 32 registers, one of 4,096 possible colors, as shown in Table 3-3.

Table 3-3: Contents of the Color Registers

Bits

Bits 15 - 12	Unused
Bits 11 - 8	Red
Bits 7 - 4	Green
Bits 3 - 0	Blue

Table 3-4 shows some sample color register bit assignments and the resulting colors. At the end of the chapter is a more extensive list.

Table 3-4: Sample Color Register Contents

Contents of the Color Register	Resulting Color
$FFF	White
$6FE	Sky blue
$DB9	Tan
$000	Black

Some sample instructions for loading the color registers are shown below:

```
LEA      CUSTOM,a0               ; Get base address of custom hardware...
MOVE.W   #$FFF,COLOR00(a0)       ; Load white into color register 0
MOVE.W   #$6FE,COLOR01(a0)       ; Load sky blue into color register 1
```

NOTE

The color registers are write-only. Only by looking at the screen can you find out the contents of each color register. As a standard practice, then, for these and certain other write-only registers, you may wish to keep a "back-up" RAM copy. As you write to the color register itself, you should update this RAM copy. If you do so, you will always know the value each register contains.

Selecting the Number of Bit-Planes

After deciding how many colors you want and how many bit-planes are required to give you those colors, you tell the system how many bit-planes to use.

You select the number of bit-planes by writing the number into the register BPLCON0 (for Bit Plane Control Register 0) The relevant bits are bits 14, 13, and 12, named BPU2, BPU1, and BPU0 (for "Bit Planes Used"). Table 3-5 shows the values to write to these bits and how the system assigns bit-plane numbers.

Table 3-5: Setting the Number of Bit-Planes

Value	Number of Bit-Planes	Name(s) of Bit-Planes
000	None *	
001	1	PLANE 1
010	2	PLANES 1 and 2
011	3	PLANES 1 - 3
100	4	PLANES 1 - 4
101	5	PLANES 1 - 5
110	6	PLANES 1 - 6 **
111		Value not used.

*   Shows only a background color; no playfield is visible.

**   Sixth bit-plane is used only in dual-playfield mode and in hold-and-modify mode (described in the section called "Advanced Topics").

NOTE

The bits in the BPLCON0 register cannot be set independently. To set any one bit, you must reload them all.

The following example shows how to tell the system to use two low-resolution bit-planes.

```
MOVE.W  #$2200,BPLCON0+CUSTOM   ; Write to it
```

Because register BPLCON0 is used for setting other characteristics of the display and the bits are not independently settable, the example above also sets other parameters (all of these parameters are described later in the chapter).

- Hold-and-modify mode is turned off.

- Single-playfield mode is set.

- Composite video color is enabled. (Not applicable in all models.)

- Genlock audio is disabled.

- Light pen is disabled.

- Interlaced mode is disabled.

- External resynchronization is disabled. (genlock)

SELECTING HORIZONTAL AND VERTICAL RESOLUTION

Standard home television screens are best suited for low-resolution displays. Low-resolution mode provides 320 pixels for each horizontal line. High-resolution monochrome and RGB monitors can produce displays in high-resolution mode, which provides 640 pixels for each horizontal line. If you define an object in low-resolution mode and then display it in high-resolution mode, the object will be only half as wide.

To set horizontal resolution mode, you write to bit 15, HIRES, in register BPLCON0:

> High-resolution mode — write 1 to bit 15.
> Low-resolution mode — write 0 to bit 15.

Note that in high-resolution mode, you can have up to four bit-planes in the playfield and, therefore, up to 16 colors.

Interlaced mode allows twice as much data to be displayed in the same vertical area as in non-interlaced mode. This is accomplished by doubling the number of lines appearing on the video screen. The following table shows the number of lines required to fill a normal, non-overscan screen.

Table 3-6: Lines in a Normal Playfield

	NTSC	PAL
Non-interlaced	200	256
Interlaced	400	512

In interlaced mode, the scanning circuitry vertically offsets the start of every other field by half a scan line.

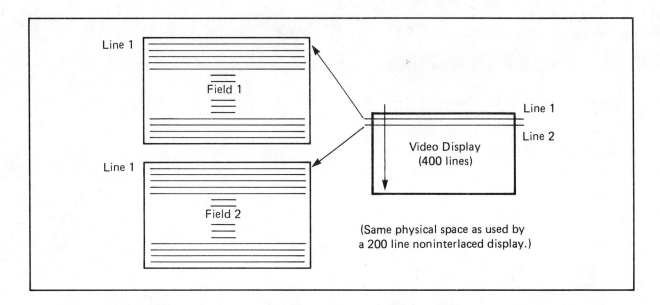

Figure 3-5: Interlacing

Even though interlaced mode requires a modest amount of extra work in setting registers (as you will see later on in this section), it provides fine tuning that is needed for certain graphics effects. Consider the diagonal line in Figure 3-6 as it appears in non-interlaced and interlaced modes. Interlacing eliminates much of the jaggedness or "staircasing" in the edges of the line.

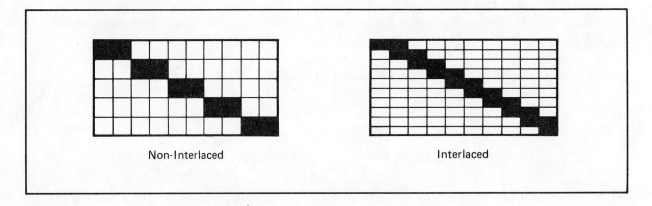

Figure 3-6: Effect of Interlaced Mode on Edges of Objects

When you use the special blitter DMA channel to draw lines or polygons onto an interlaced playfield, the playfield is treated as one display, rather than as odd and even fields. Therefore, you still get the smoother edges provided by interlacing.

To set interlaced or non-interlaced mode, you write to bit 2, LACE, in register BPLCON0:

> Interlaced mode — write 1 to bit 2.
> Non-interlaced mode — write 0 to bit 2.

As explained above in "Setting the Number of Bit-Planes," bits in BPLCON0 are not independently settable.

The following example shows how to specify high-resolution and interlaced modes.

```
MOVE.W  #$A204,BPLCON0+CUSTOM   ; Write to it
```

The example above also sets the following parameters that are also controlled through register BPLCON0:

- High-resolution mode is enabled.

- Two bit-planes are used.

- Hold-and-modify mode is disabled.

- Single-playfield mode is enabled.

- Composite video color is enabled.

- Genlock audio is disabled.

- Light pen is disabled.

- Interlaced mode is enabled.

- External resynchronization is disabled.

The amount of memory you need to allocate for each bit-plane depends upon the resolution modes you have selected, because high-resolution or interlaced playfields contain more data and require larger bit-planes.

ALLOCATING MEMORY FOR BIT-PLANES

After you set the number of bit-planes and specify resolution modes, you are ready to allocate memory. A bit-plane consists of an end-to-end sequence of words at consecutive memory locations. When operating under the Amiga operating system, use a system call such as AllocMem() to remove a block of memory from the free list and make it available to the program. If the machine has been taken over, simply reserve an area of memory for the bit-planes. Next, set the bit plane pointer registers (BPLxPTH/BPLxPTL) to point to the starting memory address of each bit-plane you are using. The starting address is the memory word that contains the bits of the upper left-hand corner of the bit-plane.

Table 3-6 shows how much memory is needed for basic playfields. You may need to balance your color and resolution requirements against the amount of available memory you have.

Table 3-7: Playfield Memory Requirements, NTSC

Picture Size	Modes	Number of Bytes per Bit-Plane
320 X 200	Low-resolution, non-interlaced	8,000
320 X 400	Low-resolution, interlaced	16,000
640 X 200	High-resolution, non-interlaced	16,000
640 X 400	High-resolution, interlaced	32,000

Table 3-8: Playfield Memory Requirements, PAL

Picture Size	Modes	Number of Bytes per Bit-Plane
320 X 256	Low-resolution, non-interlaced	8,192
320 X 512	Low-resolution, interlaced	16,384
640 X 256	High-resolution, non-interlaced	16,384
640 X 512	High-resolution, interlaced	32,768

NTSC EXAMPLE OF BIT PLANE SIZE

For example, using a normal, NTSC, low-resolution, non-interlaced display with 320 pixels across each display line and a total of 200 display lines, each line of the bit-plane requires 40 bytes (320 bits divided by 8 bits per byte = 40). Multiply the 200 lines times 40 bytes per line to get 8,000 bytes per bit-plane as given above.

A low-resolution, non-interlaced playfield made up of two bit-planes requires 16,000 bytes of memory area. The memory for each bit-plane must be continuous, so you need to have two 8,000-byte blocks of available memory. Figure 3-7 shows an 8,000-byte memory area organized as 200 lines of 40 bytes each, providing 1 bit for each pixel position in the display plane.

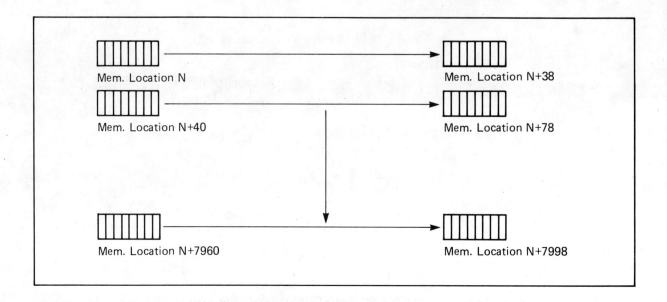

Figure 3-7: Memory Organization for a Basic Bit-Plane

Access to bit-planes in memory is provided by two address registers, BPLxPTH and BPLxPTL, for each bit-plane (12 registers in all). The "x" position in the name holds the bit-plane number; for example BPL1PTH and BPL1PTL hold the starting address of PLANE 1. Pairs of registers with names ending in PTH and PTL contain 19-bit addresses. 68000 programmers may treat these as one 32-bit address and write to them as one long word. You write to the high-order word, which is the register whose name ends in "PTH."

The example below shows how to set the bit-plane pointers. Assuming two bit-planes, one at $21000 and the other at $25000, the processor sets BPL1PT to $21000 and BPL2PT to $25000. Note that this is usually the Copper's task.

```
;
; Since the bit plane pointer registers are mapped as full 680x0 long-word
; data, we can store the addresses with a 32-bit move...
;
        LEA     CUSTOM,a0               ; Get base address of custom hardware...
        MOVE.L  $21000,BPL1PTH(a0)      ; Write bit-plane 1 pointer
        MOVE.L  $25000,BPL2PTH(a0)      ; Write bit-plane 2 pointer
```

Note that the memory requirements given here are for the playfield only. You may need to allocate additional memory for other parts of the display — sprites, audio, animation — and for your application programs. Memory allocation for other parts of the display is discussed in the chapters describing those topics.

CODING THE BIT-PLANES FOR CORRECT COLORING

After you have specified the number of bit-planes and set the bit-plane pointers, you can actually write the color register codes into the bit-planes.

A One- or Two-Color Playfield

For a one-color playfield, all you need do is write "0"s in all the bits of the single bit-plane as shown in the example below. This code fills a low-resolution bit-plane with the background color (COLOR00) by writing all "0"s into its memory area. The bit-plane starts at $21000 and is 8,000 bytes long.

```
        LEA     $21000,a0       ; Point at bit-plane
        MOVE.W  #2000,d0        ; Write 2000 longwords = 8000 bytes
LOOP:   MOVE.L  #0,(a0)+        ; Write out a zero
        DBRA    d0,LOOP         ; Decrement counter and loop until done...
```

For a two-color playfield, you define a bit-plane that has "0"s where you want the background color and "1"s where you want the color in register 1. The following example code is identical to the last example, except the bit-plane is filled with $FF00FF00 instead of all 0's. This will produce two colors.

```
        LEA     $21000,a0       ; Point at bit-plane
        MOVE.W  #2000,d0        ; Write 2000 longwords = 8000 bytes
LOOP:   MOVE.L  #$FF00FF00,(a0)+    ; Write out $FF00FF00
        DBRA    d0,LOOP         ; Decrement counter and loop until done...
```

A Playfield of Three or More Colors

For three or more colors, you need more than one bit-plane. The task here is to define each bit-plane in such a way that when they are combined for display, each pixel contains the correct combination of bits. This is a little more complicated than a playfield of one bit-plane. The following examples show a four-color playfield, but the basic idea and procedures are the same for playfields containing up to 32 colors.

Figure 3-8 shows two bit-planes forming a four-color playfield:

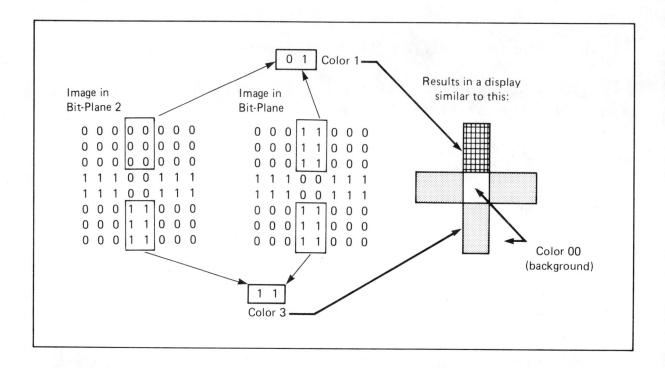

Figure 3-8: Combining Bit-planes

You place the correct "1"'s and "0"'s in both bit-planes to give each pixel in the picture above the correct color.

In a single playfield you can combine up to five bit-planes in this way. Using five bit-planes allows a choice of 32 different colors for any single pixel. The playfield color selection charts at the end of this chapter summarize the bit combinations for playfields made from four and five bit-planes.

DEFINING THE SIZE OF THE DISPLAY WINDOW

After you have completely defined the playfield, you need to define the size of the display window, which is the actual size of the on-screen display. Adjustment of display window size affects the entire display area, including the border and the sprites, not just the playfield. You cannot display objects outside of the defined display window. Also, the size of the border around the playfield depends on the size of the display window.

The basic playfield described in this section is the same size as the screen display area and also the same size as the display window. This is not always the case; often the display window is smaller than the actual "big picture" of the playfield as defined in memory (the raster). A display window that is smaller than the playfield allows you to display some segment of a large playfield or scroll the playfield through the window. You can also define display windows larger than the basic playfield. These larger playfields and different-sized display windows are described in the section below called "Bit-Planes and Display Windows of All Sizes."

You define the size of the display window by specifying the vertical and horizontal positions at which the window starts and stops and writing these positions to the display window registers. The resolution of vertical start and stop is one scan line. The resolution of horizontal start and stop is one low-resolution pixel. Each position on the screen defines the horizontal and vertical position of some pixel, and this position is specified by the x and y coordinates of the pixel. This document shows the x and y coordinates in this form: (x,y). Although the coordinates begin at (0,0) in the upper left-hand corner of the screen, the first horizontal position normally used is $81 and the first vertical position is $2C. The horizontal and vertical starting positions are the same both for NTSC and for PAL.

The hardware allows you to specify a starting position before ($81,$2C), but part of the display may not be visible. The difference between the absolute starting position of (0,0) and the normal starting position of ($81,$2C) is the result of the way many video display monitors are designed. To overcome the distortion that can occur at the extreme edges of the screen, the scanning beam sweeps over a larger area than the front face of the screen can display. A starting position of ($81,$2C) centers a normal size display, leaving a border of eight low-resolution pixels around the display window. Figure 3-9 shows the relationship between the normal display window, the visible screen area, and the area actually covered by the scanning beam.

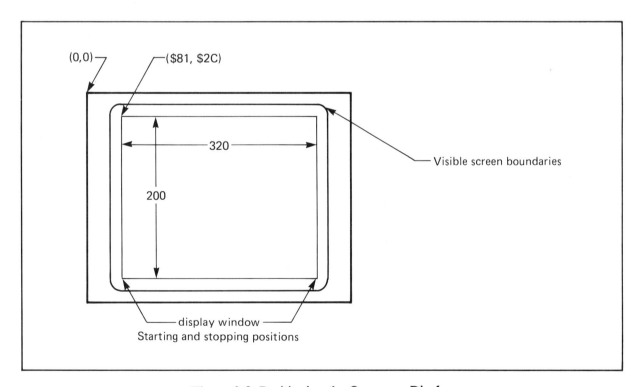

Figure 3-9: Positioning the On-screen Display

Setting the Display Window Starting Position

A horizontal starting position of approximately $81 and a vertical starting position of approximately $2C centers the display on most standard television screens. If you select high-resolution mode (640 pixels horizontally) or interlaced mode (400 lines NTSC, 512 PAL) the starting position does not change. The starting position is always interpreted in low-resolution, non-interlaced mode. In other words, you select a starting position that represents the correct coordinates in low-resolution, non-interlaced mode.

The register DIWSTRT (for "Display Window Start") controls the display window starting position. This register contains both the horizontal and vertical components of the display window starting positions, known respectively as HSTART and VSTART. The following example sets DIWSTRT for a basic playfield. You write $2C for VSTART and $81 for HSTART.

```
LEA     CUSTOM,a0                ; Get base address of custom hardware...
MOVE.W  #$2C81,DIWSTRT(a0)       ; Display window start register...
```

Setting the Display Window Stopping Position

You also need to set the display window stopping position, which is the lower right-hand corner of the display window. If you select high-resolution or interlaced mode, the stopping position does not change. Like the starting position, it is interpreted in low-resolution, non-interlaced mode.

The register DIWSTOP (for Display Window Stop) controls the display window stopping position. This register contains both the horizontal and vertical components of the display window stopping positions, known respectively as HSTOP and VSTOP. The instructions below show how to set HSTOP and VSTOP for the basic playfield, assuming a starting position of ($81,$2C). Note that the HSTOP value you write is the actual value minus 256 ($100). The HSTOP position is restricted to the right-hand side of the screen. The normal HSTOP value is ($1C1) but is written as ($C1). HSTOP is the same both for NTSC and for PAL.

The VSTOP position is restricted to the lower half of the screen. This is accomplished in the hardware by forcing the MSB of the stop position to be the complement of the next MSB. This allows for a VSTOP position greater than 256 ($100) using only 8 bits. Normally, the VSTOP is set to ($F4) for NTSC, ($2C) for PAL.

> The normal NTSC DIWSTRT is ($2C81).
> The normal NTSC DIWSTOP is ($F4C1).
>
> The normal PAL DIWSTRT is ($2C81).
> The normal PAL DIWSTOP is ($2CC1).

The following example sets DIWSTOP for a basic playfield to $F4 for the vertical position and $C1 for the horizontal position.

```
LEA     CUSTOM,a0            ; Get base address of custom hardware...
MOVE.W  #$F4C1,DIWSTOP(a0)   ; Display window stop register...
```

Table 3-9: DIWSTRT AND DIWSTOP Summary.

| | ---Nominal Values--- | | ---Possible Values--- | |
	NTSC	PAL	MIN	MAX
DIWSTRT:				
VSTART	$2C	$2C	$00	$FF
HSTART	$81	$81	$00	$FF
DIWSTOP:				
VSTOP	$F4	$2C (=$12C)	$80	$7F (=$17F)
HSTOP	$C1	$C1	$00 (=$100)	$FF (=$1FF)

TELLING THE SYSTEM HOW TO FETCH AND DISPLAY DATA

After defining the size and position of the display window, you need to give the system the on-screen location for data fetched from memory. To do this, you describe the horizontal positions where each line starts and stops and write these positions to the data-fetch registers. The data-fetch registers have a four-pixel resolution (unlike the display window registers, which have a one-pixel resolution). Each position specified is four pixels from the last one. Pixel 0 is position 0; pixel 4 is position 1, and so on.

The data-fetch start and display window starting positions interact with each other. It is recommended that data-fetch start values be restricted to a programming resolution of 16 pixels (8 clocks in low-resolution mode, 4 clocks in high-resolution mode). The hardware requires some time after the first data fetch before it can actually display the data. As a result, there is a difference between the value of window start and data-fetch start of 4.5 color clocks.

> The normal low-resolution DDFSTRT is ($0038).
> The normal high-resolution DDFSTRT is ($003C).

Recall that the hardware resolution of display window start and stop is twice the hardware resolution of data fetch:

$$\frac{\$81}{2} - 8.5 = \$38$$

$$\frac{\$81}{2} - 4.5 = \$3C$$

The relationship between data-fetch start and stop is

$$DDFSTRT = DDFSTOP - (8*(word\ count - 1))\ for\ low\ resolution$$

$$DDFSTRT = DDFSTOP - (4*(word\ count - 2))\ for\ high\ resolution$$

The normal low-resolution DDFSTOP is ($00D0). The normal high-resolution DDFSTOP is ($00D4).

The following example sets data-fetch start to $0038 and data-fetch stop to $00D0 for a basic playfield.

```
LEA     CUSTOM,a0             ; Point to base hardware address
MOVE.W  #$0038,DDFSTRT(a0)    ; Write to DDFSTRT
MOVE.W  #$00D0,DDFSTOP(a0)    ; Write to DDFSTOP
```

You also need to tell the system exactly which bytes in memory belong on each horizontal line of the display. To do this, you specify the modulo value. Modulo refers to the number of bytes in memory between the last word on one horizontal line and the beginning of the first word on the next line. Thus, the modulo enables the system to convert bit-plane data stored in linear form (each data byte at a sequentially increasing memory address) into rectangular form (one "line" of sequential data followed by another line). For the basic playfield, where the playfield in memory is the same size as the display window, the modulo is zero because the memory area contains exactly the same number of bytes as you want to display on the screen. Figures 3-10 and 3-11 show the basic bit-plane layout in memory and how to make sure the correct data is retrieved.

The bit-plane address pointers (BPLxPTH and BPLxPTL) are used by the system to fetch the data to the screen. These pointers are dynamic; once the data fetch begins, the pointers are continuously incremented to point to the next *word* to be fetched (data is fetched two bytes at a time). When the end-of-line condition is reached (defined by the data-fetch register, DDFSTOP) the modulo is added to the bit-plane pointers, adjusting the pointer to the first word to be fetched for the next horizontal line.

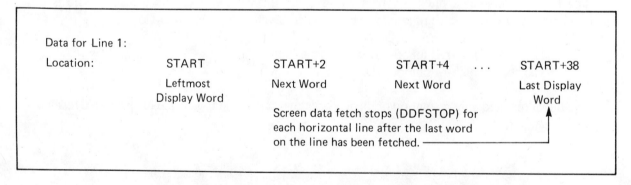

Figure 3-10: Data Fetched for the First Line When Modulo = 0

After the first line is fetched, the bit-plane pointers BPLxPTH and BPLxPTL contain the value START+40. The modulo (in this case, 0) is added to the current value of the pointer, so when the pointer begins the data fetch for the next line, it fetches the data you want on that line. The data for the next line begins at memory location START+40.

```
Data for Line 2:

Location:          START+40        START+42        START+44   ...   START+78

                   Leftmost        Next Word       Next Word         Last Display
                   Display Word                                      Word
```

Figure 3-11: Data Fetched for the Second Line When Modulo = 0

Note that the pointers always contain an even number, because data is fetched from the display a *word* at a time.

There are two modulo registers—BPL1MOD for the odd-numbered bit-planes and BPL2MOD for the even-numbered bit-planes. This allows for differing modulos for each playfield in dual-playfield mode. For normal applications, both BPL1MOD and BPL2MOD will be the same.

The following example sets the modulo to 0 for a low-resolution playfield with one bit-plane. The bit-plane is odd-numbered.

```
        MOVE.W  #0,BPL1MOD+CUSTOM       ; Set modulo to 0
```

Data Fetch in High-resolution Mode

When you are using high-resolution mode to display the basic playfield, you need to fetch 80 bytes for each line, instead of 40.

Modulo in Interlaced Mode

For interlaced mode, you must redefine the modulo, because interlaced mode uses two separate scannings of the video screen for a single display of the playfield. During the first scanning, the odd-numbered lines are fetched to the screen; and during the second scanning, the even-numbered lines are fetched.

The bit-planes for a full-screen-sized, interlaced display are 400 NTSC (512 PAL), rather than 200 NTSC (256 PAL), lines long. Assuming that the playfield in memory is the normal 320 pixels wide, data for the interlaced picture begins at the following locations (these are all byte addresses):

Line 1   START
Line 2   START+40
Line 3   START+80
Line 4   START+120

and so on. Therefore, you use a modulo of 40 to skip the lines in the other field. For odd fields, the bit-plane pointers begin at START. For even fields, the bit-plane pointers begin at START+40.

You can use the Copper to handle resetting of the bit-plane pointers for interlaced displays.

DISPLAYING AND REDISPLAYING THE PLAYFIELD

You start playfield display by making certain that the bit-plane pointers are set and bit-plane DMA is turned on. You turn on bit-plane DMA by writing a 1 to bit BPLEN in the DMACON (for DMA control) register. See Chapter 7, "System Control Hardware," for instructions on setting this register.

Each time the playfield is redisplayed, you have to reset the bit-plane pointers. Resetting is necessary because the pointers have been incremented to point to each successive word in memory and must be repointed to the first word for the next display. You write Copper instructions to handle the redisplay or perform this operation as part of a vertical blanking task.

ENABLING THE COLOR DISPLAY

The stock A1000 has a color composite output and requires bit 9 set in BPLCON0 to create a color composite display signal. Without the addition of specialized hardware, the A500 and A2000 cannot generate color composite output.

NOTE

The color burst enable does not affect the RGB video signal. RGB video is correctly generated regardless of the output of the composite video signal.

BASIC PLAYFIELD SUMMARY

The steps for defining a basic playfield are summarized below:

1. **Define Playfield Characteristics**

   a. Specify height in lines:

      - For NTSC:

         * 200 for non-interlaced mode.

         * 400 for interlaced mode.

      - For PAL:

         * 256 for non-interlaced mode.

         * 512 for interlaced mode.

   b. Specify width in pixels:

      - 320 for low-resolution mode.

      - 640 for high-resolution mode.

   c. Specify color for each pixel:

      - Load desired colors in color table registers.

      - Define color of each pixel in terms of the binary value that points at the desired color register.

      - Build bit-planes.

      - Set bit-plane registers:

         * Bits 12-14 in BPLCON0 - number of bit-planes (BPU2 - BPU0).

         * BPLxPTH - pointer to bit-plane starting position in memory (written as a long word).

d.   Specify resolution:

  • Low resolution:

    *   320 pixels in each horizontal line.

    *   Clear bit 15 in register BPLCON0 (HIRES).

  • High resolution:

    *   640 pixels in each horizontal line.

    *   Set bit 15 in register BPLCON0 (HIRES).

e.   Specify interlaced or non-interlaced mode:

  • Interlaced mode:

    *   400 vertical lines for NTSC, 512 for PAL.

    *   Set bit 2 in register BPLCON0 (LACE).

  • Non-interlaced mode:

    *   200 vertical lines for NTSC, 256 for PAL.

    *   Clear bit 2 in BPLCON0 (LACE).

2. **Allocate Memory**. To calculate data-bytes in the total bit-planes, use the following formula:

    Bytes per line * lines in playfield * number of bit-planes

3. **Define Size of Display Window**.

  • Write start position of display window in DIWSTRT:

    *   Horizontal position in bits 0 through 7 (low-order bits).

    *   Vertical position in bits 8 through 15 (high-order bits).

  • Write stop position of display window in DIWSTOP:

    *   Horizontal position in bits 0 through 7.

    *   Vertical position in bits 8 through 15.

4. **Define Data Fetch.** Set registers DDFSTRT and DDFSTOP:

   • For DDFSTRT, use the horizontal position as shown in "Setting the Display Window Starting Position."

   • For DDFSTOP, use the horizontal position as shown in "Setting the Display Window Stopping Position."

5. **Define Modulo.** Set registers BPL1MOD and BPL2MOD. Set modulo to 0 for non-interlaced, 40 for interlaced.

6. **Write Copper Instructions To Handle Redisplay.**

7. **Enable Color Display.** For the A1000: set bit 9 in BPLCON0 to enable the color display on a composite video monitor. RGB video is not affected. Only the A1000 has color composite video output, other machines cannot enable this feature using standard hardware.

EXAMPLES OF FORMING BASIC PLAYFIELDS

The following examples show how to set the registers and write the coprocessor lists for two different playfields.

The first example sets up a 320 x 200 playfield with one bit-plane, which is located at $21000. Also, a Copper list is set up at $20000.

This example relies on the include file "hw_examples.i", which is found in Appendix J.

```
        LEA      CUSTOM,a0              ; a0 points at custom chips
        MOVE.W   #$1200,BPLCON0(a0)     ; One bit-plane, enable composite color
        MOVE.W   #0,BPLCON1(a0)         ; Set horizontal scroll value to 0
        MOVE.W   #0,BPL1MOD(a0)         ; Set modulo to 0 for all odd bit-planes
        MOVE.W   #$0038,DDFSTRT(a0)     ; Set data-fetch start to $38
        MOVE.W   #$00D0,DDFSTOP(a0)     ; Set data-fetch stop to $D0
        MOVE.W   #$2C81,DIWSTRT(a0)     ; Set DIWSTRT to $2C81
        MOVE.W   #$F4C1,DIWSTOP(a0)     ; Set DIWSTOP to $F4C1
        MOVE.W   #$0F00,COLOR00(a0)     ; Set background color to red
        MOVE.W   #$0FF0,COLOR01(a0)     ; Set color register 1 to yellow
;
;   Fill bit-plane with $FF00FF00 to produce stripes
;
        MOVE.L   #$21000,a1     ; Point at beginning of bit-plane
        MOVE.L   #$FF00FF00,d0  ; We will write $FF00FF00 long words
        MOVE.W   #2000,d1       ; 2000 long words = 8000 bytes
;
LOOP:   MOVE.L   d0,(a1)+       ; Write a long word
        DBRA     d1,LOOP        ; Decrement counter and loop until done...
;
;   Set up Copper list at $20000
;
        MOVE.L   #$20000,a1     ; Point at Copper list destination
        LEA      COPPERL(pc),a2 ; Point a2 at Copper list data
```

```
CLOOP:  MOVE.L   (a2),(a1)+        ; Move a word
        CMPI.L   #$FFFFFFFE,(a2)+           ; Check for last longword of Copper list
        BNE      CLOOP             ; Loop until entire copper list is moved
;
;   Point Copper at Copper list
;
        MOVE.L   #$20000,COP1LCH(a0)       ; Write to Copper location register
        MOVE.W   COPJMP1(a0),d0    ; Force copper to $20000
;
;   Start DMA
;
        MOVE.W   #(DMAF_SETCLR!DMAF_COPPER!DMAF_RASTER!DMAF_MASTER),DMACON(a0)
                          ; Enable bit-plane and Copper DMA
        BRA      ....     ; Go do next task
;
;   This is the data for the Copper list.
;
COPPERL:
        DC.W     BPL1PTH,$0002    ; Move $0002 to address $0E0    (BPL1PTH)
        DC.W     BPL1PTL,$1000    ; Move $1000 to address $0E2    (BPL1PTL)
        DC.W     $FFFF,$FFFE      ; End of Copper list
;
```

The second example sets up a high-resolution, interlaced display with one bit-plane. This example also relies on the include file "hw_examples.i", which is found in Appendix J.

```
        LEA      CUSTOM,a0                 ; Address of custom chips
        MOVE.W   #$9204,BPLCON0(a0)        ; Hires, one bit-plane, interlaced
        MOVE.W   #0,BPLCON1(a0)            ; Horizontal scroll value = 0
        MOVE.W   #80,BPL1MOD(a0)           ; Modulo = 80 for odd bit-planes
        MOVE.W   #80,BPL2MOD(a0)           ; Ditto for even bit-planes
        MOVE.W   #$003C,DDFSTRT(a0)        ; Set data-fetch start for hires
        MOVE.W   #$00D4,DDFSTOP(a0)        ; Set data-fetch stop
        MOVE.W   #$2C81,DIWSTRT(a0)        ; Set display window start
        MOVE.W   #$F4C1,DIWSTOP(a0)        ; Set display window stop
;
;   Set up color registers
;
        MOVE.W   #$000F,COLOR00(a0)        ; Background color = blue
        MOVE.W   #$0FFF,COLOR01(a0)        ; Foreground color = white
;
;   Set up bit-plane at $20000
;
        LEA      $20000,a1        ; Point a1 at bit-plane
        LEA      CHARLIST(pc),a2  ; a2 points at character data
        MOVE.W   #400,d1          ; Write 400 lines of data
        MOVE.W   #20,d0           ; Write 20 long words per line
L1:
        MOVE.L   (a2),(a1)+       ; Write a long word
        DBRA     d0,L1            ; Decrement counter and loop until full...
;
        MOVE.W   #20,d0           ; Reset long word counter
        ADDQ.L   #4,a2            ; Point at next word in char list
        CMPI.L   #$FFFFFFFF,(a2)  ; End of char list?
        BNE      L2
        LEA      CHARLIST(pc),a2  ; Yes, reset a2 to beginning of list
L2:     DBRA     d1,L1            ; Decrement line counter and loop until done...
;
;   Start DMA
;
```

```
        MOVE.W   #(DMAF_SETCLR!DMAF_RASTER!DMAF_MASTER),DMACON(a0)
                                   ; Enable bit-plane DMA only, no Copper


; Because this example has no Copper list, it sits in a
; loop waiting for the vertical blanking interval.  When it
; comes, you check the LOF ( long frame ) bit in VPOSR.  If
; LOF = 0, this is a short frame and the bit-plane pointers
; are set to point to $20050.  If LOF = 1, then this is a
; long frame and the bit-plane pointers are set to point to
; $20000.  This keeps the long and short frames in the
; right relationship to each other.


VLOOP:  MOVE.W   INTREQR(a0),d0          ; Read interrupt requests
        AND.W    #$0020,d0              ; Mask off all but vertical blank
        BEQ      VLOOP                 ; Loop until vertical blank comes
        MOVE.W   #$0020,INTREQ(a0)     ; Reset vertical interrupt
        MOVE.W   VPOSR(a0),d0          ; Read LOF bit into d0 bit 15
        BPL      VL1                   ; If LOF = 0, jump
        MOVE.L   #$20000,BPL1PTH(a0)   ; LOF = 1, point to $20000
        BRA      VLOOP                 ; Back to top
VL1:
        MOVE.L   #$20050,BPL1PTH(a0)   ; LOF = 0, point to $20050
        BRA      VLOOP                 ; Back to top
;
;   Character list
;
CHARLIST:
        DC.L     $18FC3DF0,$3C6666D8,$3C66C0CC,$667CC0CC
        DC.L     $7E66C0CC,$C36666D8,$C3FC3DF0,$00000000
        DC.L     $FFFFFFFF
```

Forming a Dual-playfield Display

For more flexibility in designing your background display, you can specify two playfields instead of one. In dual-playfield mode, one playfield is displayed directly in front of the other. For example, a computer game display might have some action going on in one playfield in the background, while the other playfield is showing a control panel in the foreground. You can then change either the foreground or the background without having to redesign the entire display. You can also move the two playfields independently.

A dual-playfield display is similar to a single-playfield display, differing only in these aspects:

- Each playfield in a dual display is formed from one, two or three bit-planes.

- The colors in each playfield (up to seven plus transparent) are taken from different sets of color registers.

- You must set a bit to activate dual-playfield mode.

Figure 3-12 shows a dual-playfield display.

In Figure 3-12, one of the colors in each playfield is "transparent" (color 0 in playfield 1 and color 8 in playfield 2). You can use transparency to allow selected features of the background playfield to show through.

In dual-playfield mode, each playfield is formed from up to three bit-planes. Color registers 0 through 7 are assigned to playfield 1, depending upon how many bit-planes you use. Color registers 8 through 15 are assigned to playfield 2.

Bit-Plane Assignment in Dual-playfield Mode

The three odd-numbered bit-planes (1, 3, and 5) are grouped together by the hardware and may be used in playfield 1. Likewise, the three even-numbered bit-planes (2, 4, and 6) are grouped together and may be used in playfield 2. The bit-planes are assigned alternately to each playfield, as shown in Figure 3-13.

NOTE

In high-resolution mode, you can have up to two bit-planes in each playfield — bit-planes 1 and 3 in playfield 1 and bit-planes 2 and 4 in playfield 2.

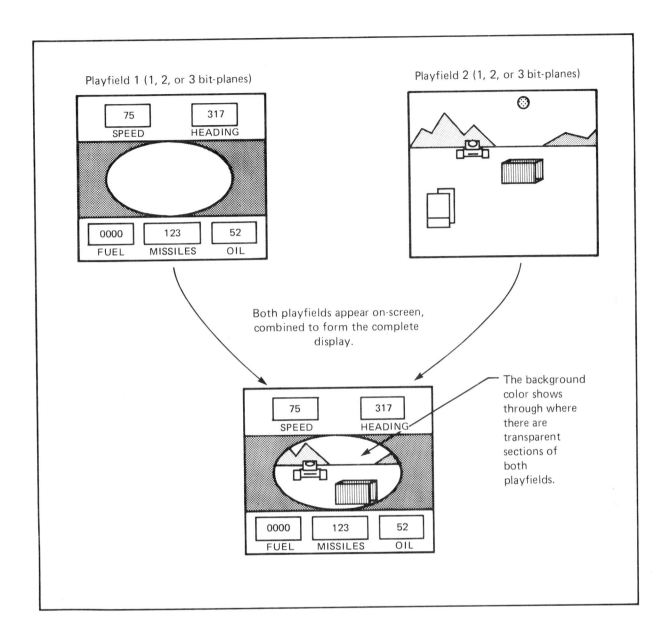

Playfield 1 (1, 2, or 3 bit-planes)

| 75 | 317 |
| SPEED | HEADING |

0000   123   52
FUEL MISSILES OIL

Playfield 2 (1, 2, or 3 bit-planes)

Both playfields appear on-screen, combined to form the complete display.

| 75 | 317 |
| SPEED | HEADING |

0000   123   52
FUEL MISSILES OIL

The background color shows through where there are transparent sections of both playfields.

Figure 3-12: A Dual-playfield Display

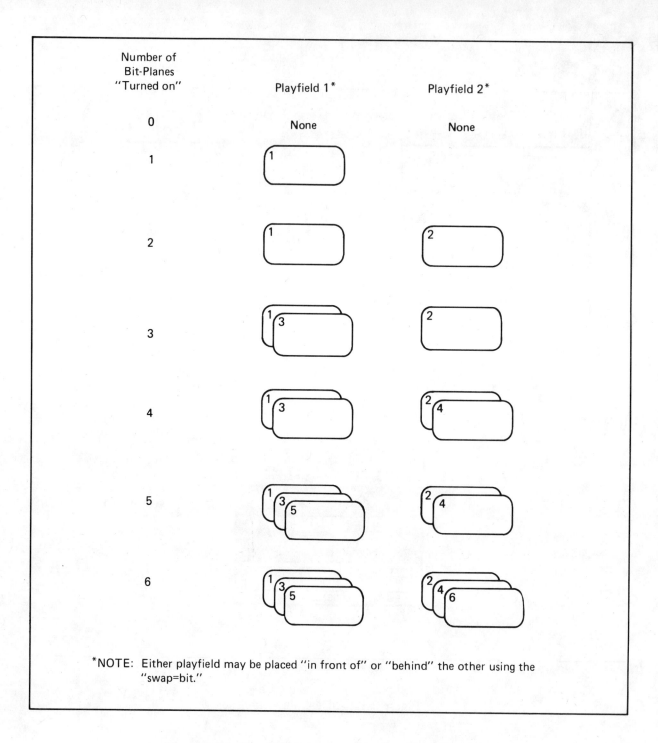

Figure 3-13: How Bit-Planes Are Assigned to Dual Playfields

COLOR REGISTERS IN DUAL-PLAYFIELD MODE

When you are using dual playfields, the hardware interprets color numbers for playfield 1 from the bit combinations of bit-planes 1, 3, and 5. Bits from PLANE 5 have the highest significance and form the most significant digit of the color register number. Bits from PLANE 0 have the lowest significance. These bit combinations select the first eight color registers from the color palette as shown in Table 3-10.

Table 3-10: Playfield 1 Color Registers — Low-resolution Mode

PLAYFIELD 1

Bit Combination	Color Selected
000	Transparent mode
001	COLOR1
010	COLOR2
011	COLOR3
100	COLOR4
101	COLOR5
110	COLOR6
111	COLOR7

The hardware interprets color numbers for playfield 2 from the bit combinations of bit-planes 2, 4, and 6. Bits from PLANE 6 have the highest significance. Bits from PLANE 2 have the lowest significance. These bit combinations select the color registers from the second eight colors in the color table as shown in Table 3-11.

Table 3-11: Playfield 2 Color Registers — Low-resolution Mode

PLAYFIELD 2

Bit Combination	Color Selected
000	Transparent mode
001	COLOR9
010	COLOR10
011	COLOR11
100	COLOR12
101	COLOR13
110	COLOR14
111	COLOR15

Combination 000 selects transparent mode, to show the color of whatever object (the other playfield, a sprite, or the background color) may be "behind" the playfield.

Table 3-12 shows the color registers for high-resolution, dual-playfield mode.

Table 3-12: Playfields 1 and 2 Color Registers — High-resolution Mode

PLAYFIELD 1

Bit Combination	Color Selected
00	Transparent mode
01	COLOR1
10	COLOR2
11	COLOR3

PLAYFIELD 2

Bit Combination	Color Selected
00	Transparent mode
01	COLOR9
10	COLOR10
11	COLOR11

DUAL-PLAYFIELD PRIORITY AND CONTROL

Either playfield 1 or 2 may have priority; that is, either one may be displayed in front of the other. Playfield 1 normally has priority. The bit known as PF2PRI (bit 6) in register BPLCON2 is used to control priority. When PF2PRI = 1, playfield 2 has priority over playfield 1. When PF2PRI = 0, playfield 1 has priority.

You can also control the relative priority of playfields and sprites. Chapter 7, "System Control Hardware," shows you how to control the priority of these objects.

You can control the two playfields separately as follows:

- They can have different-sized representations in memory, and different portions of each one can be selected for display.

- They can be scrolled separately.

NOTE

You must take special care when scrolling one playfield and holding the other stationary. When you are scrolling low-resolution playfields, you must fetch one word more than the width of the playfield you are trying to scroll (two words more in high-resolution mode) in order to provide some data to display when the actual scrolling takes place. Only one data-fetch start register and one data-fetch stop register are available, and these are shared by both playfields. If you want to scroll one playfield and hold the other, you must adjust the data-fetch start and data-fetch stop to handle the playfield being scrolled. Then, you must adjust the modulo and the bit-plane pointers of the playfield that is *not* being scrolled to maintain its position on the display. In low-resolution mode, you adjust the pointers by -2 and the modulo by -2. In high-resolution mode, you adjust the pointers by -4 and the modulo by -4.

ACTIVATING DUAL-PLAYFIELD MODE

Writing a 1 to bit 10 (called DBLPF) of the bit-plane control register BPLCON0 selects dual-playfield mode. Selecting dual-playfield mode changes both the way the hardware groups the bit-planes for color interpretation—all odd-numbered bit-planes are grouped together and all even-numbered bit-planes are grouped together, and the way hardware can move the bit-planes on the screen.

DUAL PLAYFIELD SUMMARY

The steps for defining dual playfields are almost the same as those for defining the basic playfield. Only in the following steps does the dual-playfield creation process differ from that used for the basic playfield:

- **Loading colors into the registers.** Keep in mind that color registers 0-7 are used by playfield 1 and registers 8 through 15 are used by playfield 2 (if there are three bit-planes in each playfield).

- **Building bit-planes.** Recall that playfield 1 is formed from PLANES 1, 3, and 5 and playfield 2 from PLANES 2, 4, and 6.

- **Setting the modulo registers.** Write the modulo to both BPL1MOD and BPL2MOD as you will be using both odd- and even-numbered bit-planes.

These steps are added:

- **Defining priority.** If you want playfield 2 to have priority, set bit 6 (PF2PRI) in BPLCON2 to 1.

- **Activating dual-playfield mode.** Set bit 10 (DBLPF) in BPLCON0 to 1.

Bit-planes and Display Windows of All Sizes

You have seen how to form single and dual playfields in which the playfield in memory is the same size as the display window. This section shows you how to define and use a playfield whose big picture in memory is larger than the display window, how to define display windows that are larger or smaller than the normal playfield size, and how to move the display window in the big picture.

WHEN THE BIG PICTURE IS LARGER THAN THE DISPLAY WINDOW

If you design a memory picture larger than the display window, you must choose which part of it to display. Displaying a portion of a larger playfield differs in the following ways from displaying the basic playfields described up to now:

- If the big picture in memory is larger than the display window, you must respecify the modulos. The modulo must be some value other than 0.

- You must allocate more memory for the larger memory picture.

Specifying the Modulo

For a memory picture wider than the display window, you need to respecify the modulo so that the correct data words are fetched for each line of the display. As an example, assume the display window is the standard 320 pixels wide, so 40 bytes are to be displayed on each line. The big picture in memory, however, is exactly twice as wide as the display window, or 80 bytes wide. Also, assume that you wish to display the left half of the big picture. Figure 3-14 shows the relationship between the big picture and the picture to be displayed.

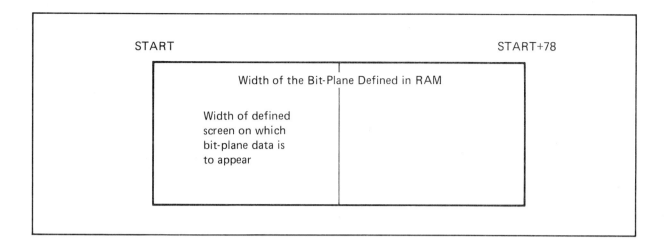

START   START+78

Width of the Bit-Plane Defined in RAM

Width of defined
screen on which
bit-plane data is
to appear

Figure 3-14: Memory Picture Larger than the Display

Because 40 bytes are to be fetched for each line, the data fetch for line 1 is as shown in Figure 3-15.

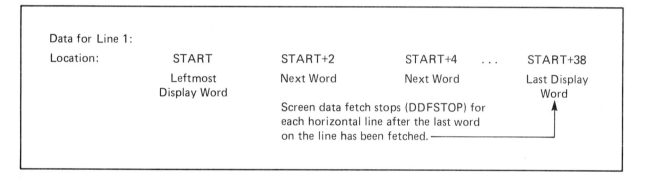

Data for Line 1:

Location: START   START+2   START+4   . . .   START+38

                    Leftmost   Next Word   Next Word   Last Display
                    Display Word   Word

                                     Screen data fetch stops (DDFSTOP) for
                                     each horizontal line after the last word
                                     on the line has been fetched. ────────────┘

Figure 3-15: Data Fetch for the First Line When Modulo = 40

At this point, BPLxPTH and BPLxPTL contain the value START+40. The modulo, which is 40, is added to the current value of the pointer so that when it begins the data fetch for the next line, it fetches the data that you intend for that line. The data fetch for line 2 is shown in Figure 3-16.

```
Data for Line 2:
Location:          START+80           START+82          START+84   ...   START+118
                   Leftmost           Next Word         Next Word        Last Display
                   Display Word                                          Word
```

Figure 3-16: Data Fetch for the Second Line When Modulo = 40

To display the right half of the big picture, you set up a vertical blanking routine to start the bit-plane pointers at location START+40 rather than START with the modulo remaining at 40. The data layout is shown in Figures 3-17 and 3-18.

```
Data for Line 1:
Location:          START+40           START+42          START+44   ...   START+78
                   Leftmost           Next Word         Next Word        Last Display
                   Display Word                                          Word
```

Figure 3-17: Data Layout for First Line—Right Half of Big Picture

Now, the bit-plane pointers contain the value START+80. The modulo (40) is added to the pointers so that when they begin the data fetch for the second line, the correct data is fetched.

```
Data for Line 2:
Location:          START+120          START+122         START+124  ...   START+158
                   Leftmost           Next Word         Next Word        Last Display
                   Display Word                                          Word
```

Figure 3-18: Data Layout for Second Line—Right Half of Big Picture

Remember, in high-resolution mode, you need to fetch twice as many bytes as in low-resolution mode. For a normal-sized display, you fetch 80 bytes for each horizontal line instead of 40.

Specifying the Data Fetch

The data-fetch registers specify the beginning and end positions for data placement on each horizontal line of the display. You specify data fetch in the same way as shown in the section called "Forming a Basic Playfield."

Memory Allocation

For larger memory pictures, you need to allocate more memory. Here is a formula for calculating memory requirements in general:

$$bytes\ per\ line\ *\ lines\ in\ playfield\ *\ \#\ of\ bit\text{-}planes$$

Thus, if the wide playfield described in this section is formed from two bit-planes, it requires:

$$80\ *\ 200\ *\ 2 = 32,000\ bytes\ of\ memory$$

Recall that this is the memory requirement for the playfield alone. You need more memory for any sprites, animation, audio, or application programs you are using.

Selecting the Display Window Starting Position

The display window starting position is the horizontal and vertical coordinates of the upper left-hand corner of the display window. One register, DIWSTRT, holds both the horizontal and vertical coordinates, known as HSTART and VSTART. The eight bits allocated to HSTART are assigned to the first 256 positions, counting from the leftmost possible position. Thus, you can start the display window at any pixel position within this range.

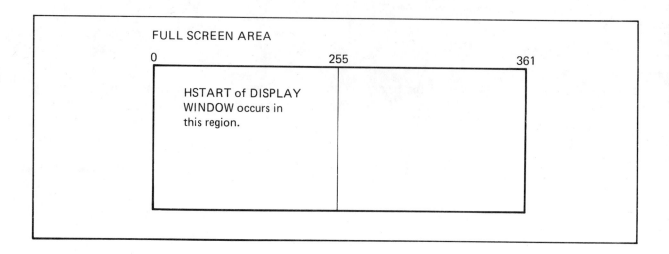

FULL SCREEN AREA

0   255   361

HSTART of DISPLAY
WINDOW occurs in
this region.

Figure 3-19: Display Window Horizontal Starting Position

The eight bits allocated to VSTART are assigned to the first 256 positions counting down from **the top of the display.**

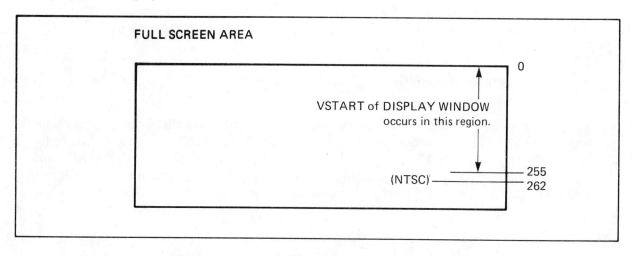

FULL SCREEN AREA

0

VSTART of DISPLAY WINDOW
occurs in this region.

255

(NTSC)
262

Figure 3-20: Display Window Vertical Starting Position

Recall that you select the values for the starting position as if the display were in low-resolution, non-interlaced mode. Keep in mind, though, that for interlaced mode the display window should be an even number of lines in height to allow for equal-sized odd and even fields.

To set the display window starting position, write the value for HSTART into bits 0 through 7 and the value for VSTART into bits 8 through 15 of DIWSTRT.

Selecting the Stopping Position

The stopping position for the display window is the horizontal and vertical coordinates of the lower right-hand corner of the display window. One register, DIWSTOP, contains both coordinates, known as HSTOP and VSTOP.

See the notes in the "Forming a Basic Playfield" section for instructions on setting these registers.

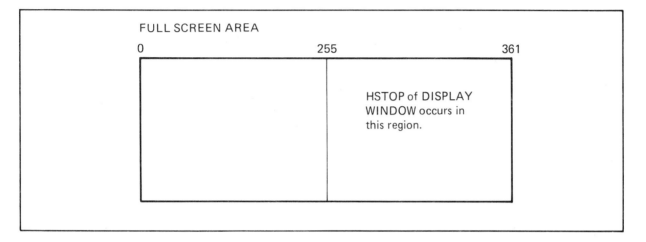

Figure 3-21: Display Window Horizontal Stopping Position

Select a value that represents the correct position in low-resolution, non-interlaced mode.

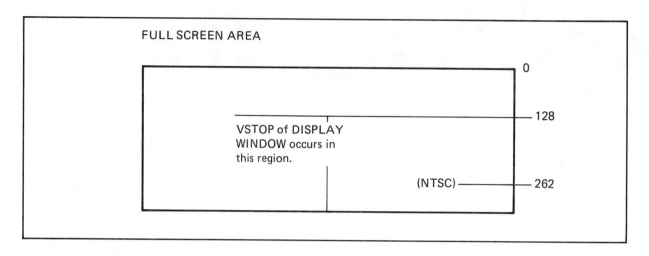

Figure 3-22: Display Window Vertical Stopping Position

To set the display window stopping position, write HSTOP into bits 0 through 7 and VSTOP into bits 8 through 15 of DIWSTOP.

MAXIMUM DISPLAY WINDOW SIZE

The maximum size of a playfield display is determined by the maximum number of lines and the maximum number of columns. Vertically, the restrictions are simple. No data can be displayed in the vertical blanking area. The following table shows the allowable vertical display area.

Table 3-13: Maximum Allowable Vertical Screen Video

Vertical Blank	NTSC	PAL
Start	0	0
Stop	$15 (21)	$1D (29)

	NTSC Normal	NTSC Interlaced	PAL Normal	PAL Interlaced
Displayable lines of screen video	241	483 =525-(21*2)	283	567 =625-(29*2)

Horizontally, the situation is similar. Strictly speaking, the hardware sets a rightmost limit to DDFSTOP of ($D8) and a leftmost limit to DDFSTRT of ($18). This gives a maximum of 25 words fetched in low-resolution mode. In high-resolution mode the maximum here is 49 words, because the rightmost limit remains ($D8) and only one word is fetched at this limit. However, horizontal blanking actually limits the displayable video to 368 low-resolution pixels (23 words). These numbers are the same both for NTSC and for PAL. In addition, it should be noted that using a data-fetch start earlier than ($38) will disable some sprites.

Table 3-14: Maximum Allowable Horizontal Screen Video

	LoRes	HiRes
DDFSTRT (standard)	$0038	$003C
DDFSTOP (standard)	$00D0	$00D4
DDFSTRT (hw limits)	$0018	$0018
DDFSTOP (hw limits)	$00D8	$00D8
max words fetched	25	49
max display pixels	368 (low res)	

Moving (Scrolling) Playfields

If you want a background display that moves, you can design a playfield larger than the display window and scroll it. If you are using dual playfields, you can scroll them separately.

In vertical scrolling, the playfield appears to move smoothly up or down on the screen. All you need do for vertical scrolling is progressively increase or decrease the starting address for the bit-plane pointers by the size of a horizontal line in the playfield. This has the effect of showing a lower or higher part of the picture each field time.

In horizontal scrolling the playfield appears to move from right-to-left or left-to-right on the screen. Horizontal scrolling works differently from vertical scrolling — you must arrange to fetch one more word of data for each display line and delay the display of this data.

For either type of scrolling, resetting of pointers or data-fetch registers can be handled by the Copper during the vertical blanking interval.

VERTICAL SCROLLING

You can scroll a playfield upward or downward in the window. Each time you display the playfield, the bit-plane pointers start at a progressively higher or lower place in the big picture in memory. As the value of the pointer increases, more of the lower part of the picture is shown and the picture appears to scroll upward. As the value of the pointer decreases, more of the upper part is shown and the picture scrolls downward. On an NTSC system, with a display that has 200 vertical lines, each step can be as little as 1/200th of the screen. In interlaced mode each step could be 1/400th of the screen if clever manipulation of the pointers is used, but it is recommended that scrolling be done two lines at a time to maintain the odd/even field relationship. Using a PAL system with 256 lines on the display, the step can be 1/256th of a screen, or 1/512th of a screen in interlace.

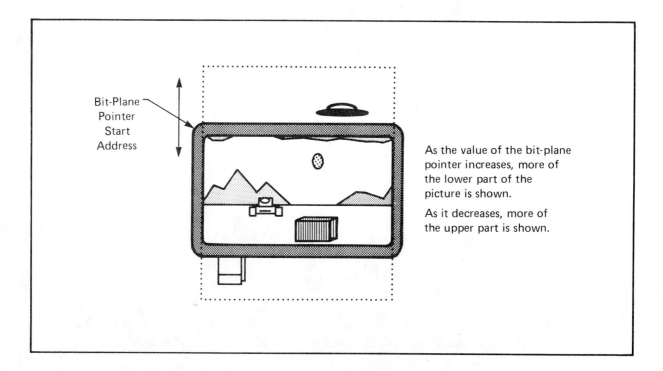

Figure 3-23: Vertical Scrolling

To set up a playfield for vertical scrolling, you need to form bit-planes tall enough to allow for the amount of scrolling you want, write software to calculate the bit-plane pointers for the scrolling you want, and allow for the Copper to use the resultant pointers.

Assume you wish to scroll a playfield upward one line at a time. To accomplish this, before each field is displayed, the bit-plane pointers have to increase by enough to ensure that the pointers begin one line lower each time. For a normal-sized, low-resolution display in which the modulo is 0, the pointers would be incremented by 40 bytes each time.

HORIZONTAL SCROLLING

You can scroll playfields horizontally from left to right or right to left on the screen. You control the speed of scrolling by specifying the amount of delay in pixels. Delay means that an extra word of data is fetched but not immediately displayed. The extra word is placed just to the left of the window's leftmost edge and before normal data fetch. As the display shifts to the right, the bits in this extra word appear on-screen at the left-hand side of the window as bits on the right-hand side disappear off-screen. For each pixel of delay, the on-screen data shifts one pixel to the right each display field. The greater the delay, the greater the speed of scrolling. You can have up to 15 pixels of delay. In high-resolution mode, scrolling is in increments of 2 pixels. Figure 3-24 shows how the delay and extra data fetch combine to cause the scrolling effect.

To set up a playfield for horizontal scrolling, you need to

- Define bit-planes wide enough to allow for the scrolling you need.

- Set the data-fetch registers to correctly place each horizontal line, including the extra word, on the screen.

- Set the delay bits.

- Set the modulo so that the bit-plane pointers begin at the correct word for each line.

- Write Copper instructions to handle the changes during the vertical blanking interval.

Specifying Data Fetch in Horizontal Scrolling

The normal data-fetch start for non-scrolled displays is ($38). If horizontal scrolling is desired, then the data fetch must start one word sooner (DDFSTRT = $0030). Incidentally, this will disable sprite 7. DDFSTOP remains unchanged. Remember that the settings of the data-fetch registers affect both playfields.

Specifying the Modulo in Horizontal Scrolling

As always, the modulo is two counts less than the difference between the address of the next word you want to fetch and the address of the last word that was fetched. As an example for horizontal scrolling, let us assume a 40-byte display in an 80-byte "big picture." Because horizontal scrolling requires a data fetch of two extra bytes, the data for each line will be 42 bytes long.

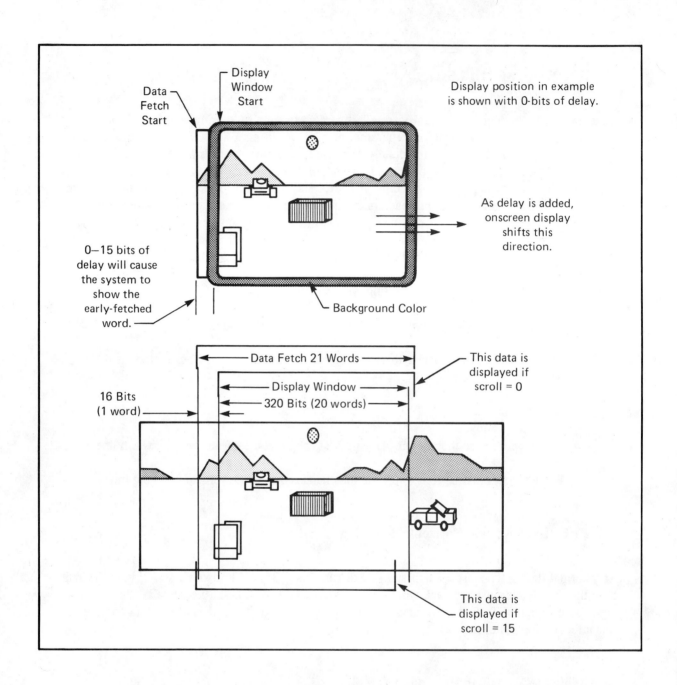

Figure 3-24: Horizontal Scrolling

NOTE

Fetching an extra word for scrolling will disable some sprites.

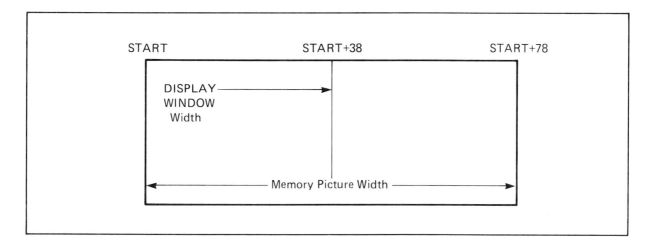

Figure 3-25: Memory Picture Larger Than the Display Window

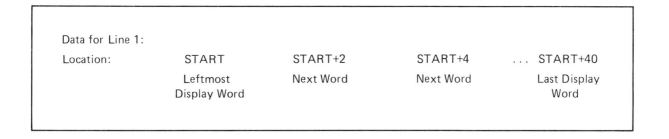

Figure 3-26: Data for Line 1 - Horizontal Scrolling

At this point, the bit-plane pointers contain the value START+42. Adding the modulo of 38 gives the correct starting point for the next line.

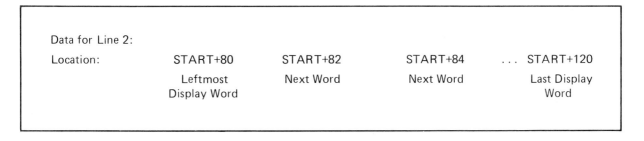

Figure 3-27: Data for Line 2—Horizontal Scrolling

In the BPLxMOD registers you set the modulo for each bit-plane used.

Specifying Amount of Delay

The amount of delay in horizontal scrolling is controlled by bits 7-0 in BPLCON1. You set the delay separately for each playfield; bits 3-0 for playfield 1 (bit-planes 1, 3, and 5) and bits 7-4 for playfield 2 (bit-planes 2, 4, and 6).

NOTE

Always set all six bits, even if you have only one playfield. Set 3-0 and 7-4 to the same value if you are using only one playfield.

The following example sets the horizontal scroll delay to 7 for both playfields.

```
MOVE.W   #$77,BPLCON1+CUSTOM
```

SCROLLED PLAYFIELD SUMMARY

The steps for defining a scrolled playfield are the same as those for defining the basic playfield, except for the following steps:

- **Defining the data fetch.** Fetch one extra word per horizontal line and start it 16 pixels before the normal (unscrolled) data-fetch start.

- **Defining the modulo.** The modulo is two counts less than when there is no scrolling.

These steps are added:

- **For vertical scrolling, reset the bit-plane pointers for the amount of the scrolling increment.** Reset BPLxPTH and BPLxPTL during the vertical blanking interval.

- **For horizontal scrolling, specify the delay.** Set bits 7-0 in BPLCON1 for 0 to 15 bits of delay.

Advanced Topics

This section describes features that are used less often or are optional.

INTERACTIONS AMONG PLAYFIELDS AND OTHER OBJECTS

Playfields share the display with sprites. Chapter 7, "System Control Hardware," shows how playfields can be given different video display priorities relative to the sprites and how playfields can collide with (overlap) the sprites or each other.

HOLD-AND-MODIFY MODE

This is a special mode that allows you to produce up to 4,096 colors on the screen at the same time. Normally, as each value formed by the combination of bit-planes is selected, the data contained in the selected color register is loaded into the color output circuit for the pixel being written on the screen. Therefore, each pixel is colored by the contents of the selected color register.

In hold-and-modify mode, however, the value in the color output circuitry is held, and one of the three components of the color (red, green, or blue) is modified by bits coming from certain preselected bit-planes. After modification, the pixel is written to the screen.

The hold-and-modify mode allows very fine gradients of color or shading to be produced on the screen. For example, you might draw a set of 16 vases, each a different color, using all 16 colors in the color palette. Then, for each vase, you use hold-and-modify to very finely shade or highlight or add a completely different color to each of the vases. Note that a particular hold-and-modify pixel can only change one of the three color values at a time. Thus, the effect has a limited control.

In hold and modify mode, you use all six bit-planes. Planes 5 and 6 are used to modify the way bits from planes 1 - 4 are treated, as follows:

- If the 6-5 bit combination from planes 6 and 5 for any given pixel is 00, normal color selection procedure is followed. Thus, the bit combinations from planes 4 - 1, in that order of significance, are used to choose one of 16 color registers (registers 0 - 15).

  If only five bit-planes are used, the data from the sixth plane is automatically supplied with the value as 0.

- If the 6-5 bit combination is 01, the color of the pixel immediately to the left of this pixel is duplicated and then modified. The bit-combinations from planes 4 - 1 are used to replace the four "blue" bits in the corresponding color register.

- If the 6-5 bit combination is 10, the color of the pixel immediately to the left of this pixel is duplicated and then modified. The bit-combinations from planes 4 - 1 are used to replace the four "red" bits.

- If the 6-5 bit combination is 11, the color of the pixel immediately to the left of this pixel is duplicated and then modified. The bit-combinations from planes 4 - 1 are used to replace the four "green" bits.

Using hold-and-modify mode, it is possible to get by with defining only *one* color register, which is COLOR0, the color of the background. You treat the entire screen as a modification of that original color, according to the scheme above.

Bit 11 of register BPLCON0 selects hold-and-modify mode. The following bits in BPLCON0 must be set for hold-and-modify mode to be active:

- Bit HOMOD, bit 11, is 1.

- Bit DBLPF, bit 10, is 0 (single-playfield mode specified).

- Bit HIRES, bit 15, is 0 (low-resolution mode specified).

- Bits BPU2, BPU1, and BPU0 - bits 14, 13, and 12, are 101 or 110 (five or six bit-planes active).

The following example code generates a six-bit-plane display with hold-and-modify mode turned on. All 32 color registers are loaded with black to prove that the colors are being generated by hold-and-modify. The equates are the usual and are not repeated here.

```
;   First, set up the control registers.
;
        LEA     CUSTOM,a0               ; Point a0 at custom chips
        MOVE.W  #$6A00,BPLCON0(a0)      ; Six bit-planes, hold-and-modify mode
        MOVE.W  #0,BPLCON1(a0)          ; Horizontal scroll = 0
        MOVE.W  #0,BPL1MOD(a0)          ; Modulo for odd bit-planes = 0
        MOVE.W  #0,BPL2MOD(a0)          ; Ditto for even bit-planes
        MOVE.W  #$0038,DDFSTRT(a0)      ; Set data-fetch start
        MOVE.W  #$00D0,DDFSTOP(a0)      ; Set data-fetch stop
        MOVE.W  #$2C81,DIWSTRT(a0)      ; Set display window start
        MOVE.W  #$F4C1,DIWSTOP(a0)      ; Set display window stop
;
; Set all color registers = black to prove that hold-and-modify mode is working.
;
        MOVE.W  #32,d0                  ; Initialize counter
        LEA     CUSTOM+COLOR00,a1       ; Point a1 at first color register
CREGLOOP:
        MOVE.W  #$0000,(a1)+            ; Write black to a color register
        DBRA    d0,CREGLOOP             ; Decrement counter and loop til done...
;
; Fill six bit-planes with an easily recognizable pattern.
;
; NOTE:  This is just for example use.  Normally these bit planes would
;        need to be allocated from the system MEMF_CHIP memory pool.
;
```

```
        MOVE.W   #2000,d0              ; 2000 longwords per bit-plane
        MOVE.L   #$21000,a1            ; Point a1 at bit-plane 1
        MOVE.L   #$23000,a2            ; Point a2 at bit-plane 2
        MOVE.L   #$25000,a3            ; Point a3 at bit-plane 3
        MOVE.L   #$27000,a4            ; Point a4 at bit-plane 4
        MOVE.L   #$29000,a5            ; Point a5 at bit-plane 5
        MOVE.L   #$2B000,a6            ; Point a6 at bit-plane 6
FPLLOOP:
        MOVE.L   #$55555555,(a1)+      ; Fill bit-plane 1 with $55555555
        MOVE.L   #$33333333,(a2)+      ; Fill bit-plane 2 with $33333333
        MOVE.L   #$0F0F0F0F,(a3)+      ; Fill bit-plane 3 with $0F0F0F0F
        MOVE.L   #$00FF00FF,(a4)+      ; Fill bit-plane 4 with $00FF00FF
        MOVE.L   #$CF3CF3CF,(a5)+      ; Fill bit-plane 5 with $CF3CF3CF
        MOVE.L   #$3CF3CF3C,(a6)+      ; Fill bit-plane 6 with $3CF3CF3C
        DBRA     d0,FPLLOOP            ; Decrement counter and loop til done...
;
;  Set up a Copper list at $20000.
;
;  NOTE:  As with the bit planes, the copper list location should be allocated
;         from the system MEMF_CHIP memory pool.
;
        MOVE.L   #$20000,a1           ; Point a1 at Copper list destination
        LEA      COPPERL(pc),a2       ; Point a2 at Copper list image
CLOOP:  MOVE.L   (a2),(a1)+           ; Move a long word...
        CMPI.L   #$FFFFFFFE,(a2)+     ; Check for end of Copper list
        BNE      CLOOP               ; Loop until entire Copper list moved
;
;  Point Copper at Copper list.
;
        MOVE.L   #$20000,COP1LCH(a0)  ; Load Copper jump register
        MOVE.W   COPJMP1(a0),d0       ; Force load into Copper P.C.
;
;  Start DMA.
;
        MOVE.W   #$8380,DMACON(a0)    ; Enable bit-plane and Copper DMA

        BRA      .....next stuff to do.....
;
;  Copper list for six bit-planes.  Bit-plane 1 is at $21000; 2 is at $23000;
;  3 is at $25000; 4 is at $27000; 5 is at $29000; 6 is at $2B000.
;
;  NOTE:  These bit-plane addresses are for example purposes only.
;         See note above.
;
COPPERL:
        DC.W     BPL1PTH,$0002    ; Bit-plane 1 pointer = $21000
        DC.W     BPL1PTL,$1000
        DC.W     BPL2PTH,$0002    ; Bit-plane 2 pointer = $23000
        DC.W     BPL2PTL,$3000
        DC.W     BPL3PTH,$0002    ; Bit-plane 3 pointer = $25000
        DC.W     BPL3PTL,$5000
        DC.W     BPL4PTH,$0002    ; Bit-plane 4 pointer = $27000
        DC.W     BPL4PTL,$7000
        DC.W     BPL5PTH,$0002    ; Bit-plane 5 pointer = $29000
        DC.W     BPL5PTL,$9000
        DC.W     BPL6PTH,$0002    ; Bit-plane 6 pointer = $2B000
        DC.W     BPL6PTL,$B000
        DC.W     $FFFF,$FFFE      ; Wait for the impossible, i.e., quit
```

FORMING A DISPLAY WITH SEVERAL DIFFERENT PLAYFIELDS

The graphics library provides the ability to split the screen into several "ViewPorts", each with its own colors and resolutions. See the *Amiga ROM Kernel Manual* for more information.

USING AN EXTERNAL VIDEO SOURCE

An optional board that provides *genlock* is available for the Amiga. Genlock allows you to bring in your graphics display from an external video source (such as a VCR, camera, or laser disk player). When you use genlock, the background color is replaced by the display from this external video source. For more information, see the instructions furnished with the optional board.

SUMMARY OF PLAYFIELD REGISTERS

This section summarizes the registers used in this chapter and the meaning of their bit settings. The color registers are summarized in the next section. See Appendix A for a summary of all registers.

BPLCON0 - Bit Plane Control

NOTE
Bits in this register cannot be independently set.

Bit 0 - unused

Bit 1 - ERSY (external synchronization enable)
    1 = External synchronization enabled (allows genlock synchronization to occur)
    0 = External synchronization disabled

Bit 2 - LACE (interlace enable)
    1 = interlaced mode enabled
    0 = non-interlaced mode enabled

Bit 3 - LPEN (light pen enable)

Bits 4-7 not used (make 0)

Bit 8 - GAUD (genlock audio enable)
    1 = Genlock audio enabled
    0 = Genlock audio disabled (in blanking periods, this bit goes out on the pixel switch ZD)

Bit 9 - COLOR_ON (color enable)
    1 = composite video color-burst enabled
    0 = composite video color-burst disabled

Bit 10 - DBLPF (double-playfield enable)
    1 = dual playfields enabled
    0 = single playfield enabled

Bit 11 - HOMOD (hold-and-modify enable)
    1 = hold-and-modify enabled
    0 = hold-and-modify disabled

Bits 14, 13, 12 - BPU2, BPU1, BPU0
    Number of bit-planes used.

    000 = only a background color
    001 = 1 bit-plane, PLANE 1
    010 = 2 bit-planes, PLANES 1 and 2
    011 = 3 bit-planes, PLANES 1 - 3
    100 = 4 bit-planes, PLANES 1 - 4
    101 = 5 bit-planes, PLANES 1 - 5
    110 = 6 bit-planes, PLANES 1 - 6
    111 not used

Bit 15 - HIRES (high-resolution enable)
    1 = high-resolution mode
    0 = low-resolution mode

BPLCON1 - Bit-plane Control

Bits 3-0 - PF1H(3-0)
    Playfield 1 delay

Bits 7-4 - PF2H(3-0)
    Playfield 2 delay

Bits 15-8 not used

BPLCON2 - Bit-plane Control

Bit 6 - PF2PRI

1 = Playfield 2 has priority

0 = Playfield 1 has priority

Bits 0-5 Playfield sprite priority

Bits 7-15 not used

DDFSTRT - Data-fetch Start
(Beginning position for data fetch)

Bits 15-8 - not used

Bits 7-2 - pixel position H8-H3
   Bit H3 only respected in HiRes Mode.

Bits 1-0 - not used

DDFSTOP - Data-fetch Stop
(Ending position for data fetch)

Bits 15-8 - not used

Bits 7-2 - pixel position H8-H3
   Bit H3 only respected in HiRes Mode.

Bits 1-0 - not used

BPLxPTH - Bit-plane Pointer
(Bit-plane pointer high word, where x is the bit-plane number)

BPLxPTL - Bit-plane Pointer
(Bit-plane pointer low word, where x is the bit-plane number)

DIWSTRT - Display Window Start
(Starting vertical and horizontal coordinates)

Bits 15-8 - VSTART (V7-V0)

Bits 7-0 - HSTART (H7-H0)

DIWSTOP - Display Window Stop
(Ending vertical and horizontal coordinates)

Bits 15-8 - VSTOP (V7-V0)

Bits 7-0 - HSTOP (H7-H0)

BPL1MOD - Bit-plane Modulo
(Odd-numbered bit-planes, playfield 1)

BPL2MOD - Bit-plane Modulo
(Even-numbered bit-planes, playfield 2)

Summary of Color Selection

This section contains summaries of playfield color selection including color register contents, example colors, and the differences in color selection in high-resolution and low-resolution modes.

COLOR REGISTER CONTENTS

Table 3-15 shows the contents of each color register. All color registers are write-only.

Table 3-15: Color Register Contents

Bits	Contents
15-12	(Unused - set to 0)
11-8	Red
7-4	Green
3-0	Blue

SOME SAMPLE COLOR REGISTER CONTENTS

Table 3-16 shows a variety of colors and the hexadecimal values to load into the color registers for these colors.

Table 3-16: Some Register Values and Resulting Colors

Value	Color	Value	Color
$FFF	White	$1FB	Light aqua
$D00	Brick red	$6FE	Sky blue
$F00	Red	$6CE	Light blue
$F80	Red-orange	$00F	Blue
$F90	Orange	$61F	Bright blue
$FB0	Golden orange	$06D	Dark blue
$FD0	Cadmium yellow	$91F	Purple
$FF0	Lemon yellow	$C1F	Violet
$BF0	Lime green	$F1F	Magenta
$8E0	Light green	$FAC	Pink
$0F0	Green	$DB9	Tan
$2C0	Dark green	$C80	Brown
$0B1	Forest green	$A87	Dark brown
$0BB	Blue green	$CCC	Light grey
$0DB	Aqua	$999	Medium grey
		$000	Black

COLOR SELECTION IN LOW-RESOLUTION MODE

Table 3-17 shows playfield color selection in low-resolution mode. If the bit-combinations from the playfields are as shown, the color is taken from the color register number indicated.

Table 3-17: Low-resolution Color Selection

| Single Playfield | | Dual Playfields | |
Normal Mode (Bit-planes 5,4,3,2,1)	Hold-and-modify Mode (Bit-planes 4,3,2,1)		Color Register Number
		Playfield 1 **Bit-planes 5,3,1**	
00000	0000	000	0 *
00001	0001	001	1
00010	0010	010	2
00011	0011	011	3
00100	0100	100	4
00101	0101	101	5
00110	0100	110	6
00111	0111	111	7
		Playfield 2 **Bit-planes 6,4,2**	
01000	1000	000 **	8
01001	1001	001	9
01010	1010	010	10
01011	1011	011	11
01100	1100	100	12
01101	1101	101	13
01110	1110	110	14
01111	1111	111	15
10000			16
10001			17
10010			18
10011			19
10100	NOT	NOT	20
10101	USED	USED	21
10110	IN	IN	22
10111	THIS	THIS	23
11000	MODE	MODE	24
11001			25
11010			26
11011			27
11100			28
11101			29
11110			30
11111			31

* Color register 0 always defines the background color.
** Selects "transparent" mode instead of selecting color register 8.

COLOR SELECTION IN HOLD-AND-MODIFY MODE

In hold-and-modify mode, the color register contents are changed as shown in Table 3-18. This mode is in effect only if bit 10 of BPLCON0 = 1.

Table 3-18: Color Selection in Hold-and-modify Mode

Bit-plane 6	Bit-plane 5		Result
0	0	Normal operation	(use color register itself)
0	1	Hold green and red	B = Bit-plane 4-1 contents
1	0	Hold green and blue	R = Bit-plane 4-1 contents
1	1	Hold blue and red	G = Bit-plane 4-1 contents

COLOR SELECTION IN HIGH-RESOLUTION MODE

Table 3-19 shows playfield color selection in high-resolution mode. If the bit-combinations from the playfields are as shown, the color is taken from the color register number indicated.

Table 3-19: High-resolution Color Selection

Single Playfield Bit-planes 4,3,2,1	Dual Playfields	Color Register Number
	Playfield 1 **Bit-planes 3,1**	
0000	00 *	0 **
0001	01	1
0010	10	2
0011	11	3
0100	|	4
0101	NOT USED	5
0110	IN THIS MODE	6
0111	|	7
	Playfield 2 **Bit-planes 4,2**	
1000	00 *	8
1001	01	9
1010	10	10
1011	11	11
1100	|	12
1101	NOT USED	13
1110	IN THIS MODE	14
1111	|	15

---

* Selects ''transparent'' mode.
** Color register 0 always defines the background color.

Chapter 4

SPRITE HARDWARE

Introduction

Sprites are hardware objects that are created and moved independently of the playfield display and independently of each other. Together with playfields, sprites form the graphics display of the Amiga. You can create more complex animation effects by using the blitter, which is described in the chapter called "Blitter Hardware." Sprites are produced on-screen by eight special-purpose sprite DMA channels. Basic sprites are 16 pixels wide and any number of lines high. You can choose from three colors for a sprite's pixels, and a pixel may also be transparent, showing any object behind the sprite. For larger or more complex objects, or for more color choices, you can combine sprites.

Sprite DMA channels can be reused several times within the same display field. Thus, you are not limited to having only eight sprites on the screen at the same time.

ABOUT THIS CHAPTER

This chapter discusses the following topics:

- Defining the size, shape, color, and screen position of sprites.

- Displaying and moving sprites.

- Combining sprites for more complex images, additional width, or additional colors.

- Reusing a sprite DMA channel multiple times within a display field to create more than eight sprites on the screen at one time.

Forming a Sprite

To form a sprite, you must first define it and then create a formal data structure in memory. You define a sprite by specifying its characteristics:

- On-screen width of up to 16 pixels.

- Unlimited height.

- Any shape.

- A combination of three colors, plus transparent.

- Any position on the screen.

SCREEN POSITION

A sprite's screen position is defined as a set of X,Y coordinates. Position (0,0), where X = 0 and Y = 0, is the upper left-hand corner of the display. You define a sprite's location by specifying the coordinates of its upper left-hand pixel. Sprite position is always defined as though the display modes were low-resolution and non-interlaced. The X,Y coordinate system and definition of a sprite's position are graphically represented in Figure 4-1. Notice that because of display overscan, position (0,0) (that is, X = 0, Y = 0) is not normally in a viewable region of the screen.

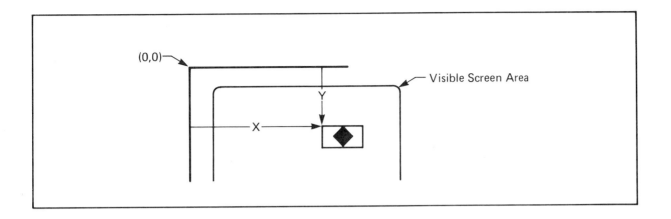

Figure 4-1: Defining Sprite On-screen Position

The amount of viewable area is also affected by the size of the playfield display window (defined by the values in DDFSTRT, DDFSTOP, DIWSTRT, DIWSTOP, etc.). See the "Playfield Hardware" chapter for more information about overscan and display windows.

Horizontal Position

A sprite's horizontal position (X value) can be at any pixel on the screen from 0 to 447. To be visible, however, an object must be within the boundaries of the playfield display window. In the examples in this chapter, a window with horizontal positions from pixel 64 to pixel 383 is used (that is, each line is 320 pixels long). Larger or smaller windows can be defined as required, but it is recommended that you read the "Playfield Hardware" chapter before attempting to do so. A larger area is actually scanned by the video beam but is not usually visible on the screen.

If you specify an X value for a sprite that takes it outside the display window, then part or all of the sprite may not appear on the screen. This is sometimes desirable; such a sprite is said to be "clipped."

To make a sprite appear in its correct on-screen horizontal position in the display window, simply add its left offset to the desired X value. In the example given above, this would involve adding 64 to the X value. For example, to make the upper leftmost pixel of a sprite appear at a position 94 pixels from the left edge of the screen, you would perform this calculation:

Desired X position + horizontal-offset of display window = 94 + 64 = 158

Thus, 158 becomes the X value, which will be written into the data structure.

NOTE

The X position represents the location of the *very first* (leftmost) pixel in the full 16-bit-wide sprite. This is always the case, even if the leftmost pixels are specified as transparent and do not appear on the screen.

If the sprite shown in Figure 4-2 were located at an X value of 158, the actual image would begin on-screen four pixels later at 162. The first four pixels in this sprite are transparent and allow the background to show through.

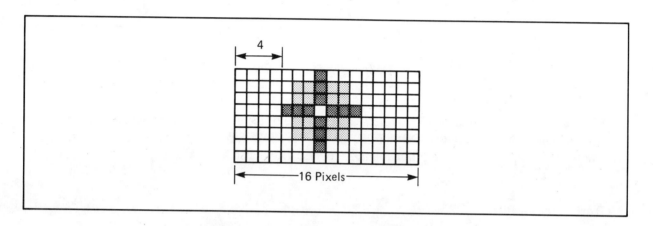

Figure 4-2: Position of Sprites

Vertical Position

You can select any position from line 0 to line 262 for the topmost edge of the sprite. In the examples in this chapter, an NTSC window with vertical positions from line 44 to line 243 is used. This allows the normal display height of 200 lines in non-interlaced mode. If you specify a vertical position (Y value) of less than 44 (i.e., above the top of the display window) the top edge of the sprite may not appear on screen.

To make a sprite appear in its correct on-screen vertical position, add the Y value to the desired position. Using the above numbers, add 44 to the desired Y position. For example, to make the upper leftmost pixel appear 25 lines below the top edge of the screen, perform this calculation:

Desired Y position + vertical-offset of the display window = 25 + 44 = 69

Thus, 69 is the Y value you will write into the data structure.

Clipped Sprites

As noted above, sprites will be partially or totally clipped if they pass across or beyond the boundaries of the display window. The values of 64 (horizontal) and 44 (vertical) are "normal" for a centered display on a standard NTSC video monitor. See Chapter 3, "Playfield Hardware", for more information on display offsets. Information on PAL displays will be found there. If you choose other values to establish your display window, your sprites will be clipped accordingly.

SIZE OF SPRITES

Sprites are 16 pixels wide and can be almost any height you wish — as short as one line or taller than the screen. You would probably move a very tall sprite vertically to display a portion of it at a time.

Sprite size is based on a pixel that is 1/320th of a screen's width, 1/200th of a NTSC screen's height, or 1/256 of a PAL screen's height. This pixel size corresponds to the low-resolution and non-interlaced modes of the normal full-size playfield. Sprites, however, are independent of playfield modes of display, so changing the resolution or interlace mode of the playfield has *no effect* on the size or resolution of a sprite.

SHAPE OF SPRITES

A sprite can have any shape that will fit within the 16-pixel width. You define a sprite's shape by specifying which pixels actually appear in each of the sprite's locations. For example, Figures 4-3 and 4-4 show a spaceship whose shape is marked by Xs. The first figure shows only the spaceship as you might sketch it out on graph paper. The second figure shows the spaceship within the 16-pixel width. The 0s around the spaceship mark the part of the sprite not covered by the spaceship and transparent when displayed.

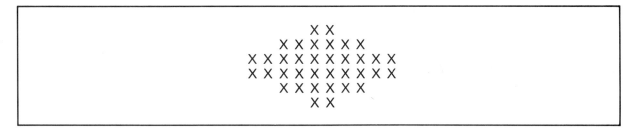

Figure 4-3: Shape of Spaceship

```
0 0 0 0 X X 0 0 0 0 0 0 0 0 0 0
0 0 X X X X X X 0 0 0 0 0 0 0 0
X X X X X X X X X X 0 0 0 0 0 0
X X X X X X X X X X 0 0 0 0 0 0
0 0 X X X X X X 0 0 0 0 0 0 0 0
0 0 0 0 X X 0 0 0 0 0 0 0 0 0 0
```

Figure 4-4: Sprite with Spaceship Shape Defined

In this example, the widest part of the shape is ten pixels and the shape is shifted to the left of the sprite. Whenever the shape is narrower than the sprite, you can control which part of the sprite is used to define the shape. This particular shape could also start at any of the pixels from 2-7 instead of pixel 1.

SPRITE COLOR

When sprites are used individually (that is, not ''attached'' as described under ''Attached Sprites'' later), each pixel can be one of three colors or transparent. Colors are selected in much the same manner as playfield colors. Figure 4-5 shows how the color of each pixel in a sprite is determined.

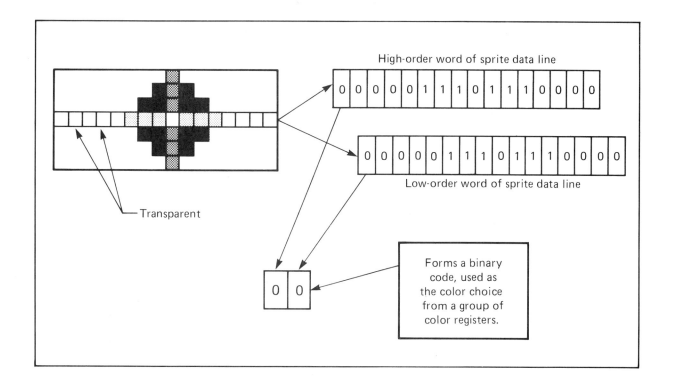

Figure 4-5: Sprite Color Definition

The 0s and 1s in the two data words that define each line of a sprite in the data structure form a binary number. This binary number points to one of the four color registers assigned to that particular sprite DMA channel. The eight sprites use system color registers 16 - 31. For purposes of color selection, the eight sprites are organized into pairs and each pair uses four of the color registers as shown in Figure 4-6.

NOTE

The color value of the first register in each group of four registers is ignored by sprites. When the sprite bits select this register, the "transparent" value is used.

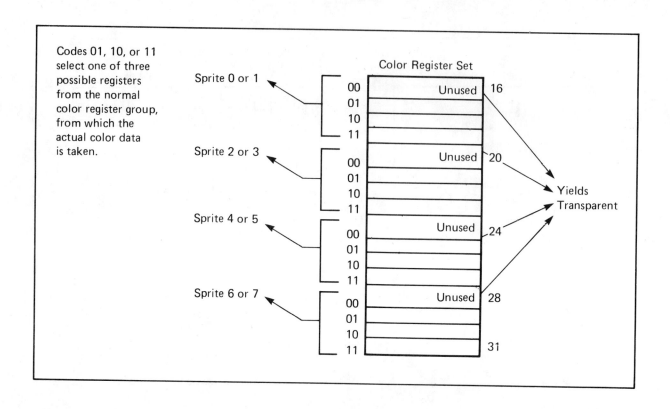

Figure 4-6: Color Register Assignments

If you require certain colors in a sprite, you will want to load the sprite's color registers with those colors. The "Playfield Hardware" chapter contains instructions on loading color registers.

The binary number 00 is special in this color scheme. A pixel whose value is 00 becomes transparent and shows the color of any other sprite or playfield that has lower video priority. An object with low priority appears "behind" an object with higher priority. Each sprite has a fixed video priority with respect to all the other sprites. You can vary the priority between sprites and playfields. (See Chapter 7, "System Control Hardware," for more information about sprite priority.)

DESIGNING A SPRITE

For design purposes, it is convenient to lay out the sprite on paper first. You can show the desired colors as numbers from 0 to 3. For example, the spaceship shown above might look like this:

```
0000122332210000
0001223333221000
0012223333222100
0001223333221000
0000122332210000
```

The next step is to convert the numbers 0-3 into binary numbers, which will be used to build the color descriptor words of the sprite data structure. The section below shows how to do this.

BUILDING THE DATA STRUCTURE

After defining the sprite, you need to build its data structure, which is a series of 16-bit words in a contiguous memory area. Some of the words contain position and control information and some contain color descriptions. To create a sprite's data structure, you need to:

- Write the horizontal and vertical position of the sprite into the first control word.

- Write the vertical stopping position into the second control word.

- Translate the decimal color numbers 0 - 3 in your sprite grid picture into binary color numbers. Use the binary values to build color descriptor (data) words and write these words into the data structure.

- Write the control words that indicate the end of the sprite data structure.

NOTE

Sprite data, like all other data accessed by the custom chips, must be loaded into Chip RAM. Be sure all of your sprite data structures are word aligned in Chip Memory.

Table 4-1 shows a sprite data structure with the memory location and function of each word:

Table 4-1: Sprite Data Structure

Memory Location	16-bit Word	Function
N	Sprite control word 1	Vertical and horizontal start position
N+1	Sprite control word 2	Vertical stop position
N+2	Color descriptor low word	Color bits for line 1
N+3	Color descriptor high word	Color bits for line 1
N+4	Color descriptor low word	Color bits for line 2
N+5	Color descriptor high word	Color bits for line 2
	.	
	.	
	.	
	End-of-data words	Two words indicating the next usage of this sprite

All memory addresses for sprites are word addresses. You will need enough contiguous memory to provide room for two words for the control information, two words for each horizontal line in the sprite, and two end-of-data words.

Because this data structure must be accessible by the special-purpose chips, you must ensure that this data is located within chip memory.

Figure 4-7 shows how the data structure relates to the sprite.

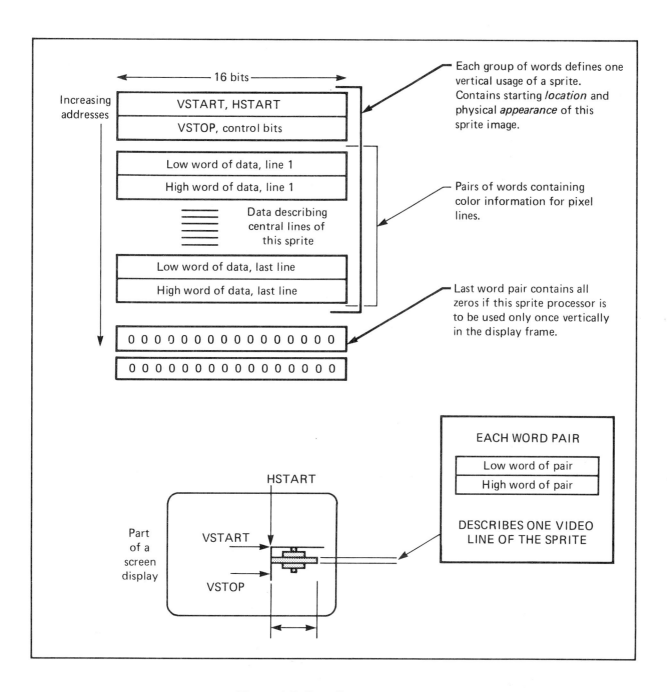

Figure 4-7: Data Structure Layout

Sprite Control Word 1 : SPRxPOS

This word contains the vertical (VSTART) and horizontal (HSTART) starting position for the sprite. This is where the topmost line of the sprite will be positioned.

> Bits 15-8 contain the low 8 bits of VSTART
> Bits 7-0 contain the high 8 bits of HSTART

Sprite Control Word 2 : SPRxCTL

This word contains the vertical stopping position of the sprite on the screen (i.e., the line AFTER the last displayed row of the sprite). It also contains some data having to do with sprite attachment, which is described later on.

SPRxCTL

Bits 15-8	The low eight bits of VSTOP
Bit 7	(Used in attachment)
Bits 6-3	Unused (make zero)
Bit 2	The VSTART high bit
Bit 1	The VSTOP high bit
Bit 0	The HSTART low bit

The value (VSTOP - VSTART) defines how many scan lines high the sprite will be when it is displayed.

Sprite Color Descriptor Words

It takes two color descriptor words to describe each horizontal line of a sprite; the high-order word and the low-order word. To calculate how many color descriptor words you need, multiply the height of the sprite in lines by 2. The bits in the high-order color descriptor word contribute the leftmost digit of the binary color selector number for each pixel; the low-order word contributes the rightmost digit.

To form the color descriptor words, you first need to form a picture of the sprite, showing the color of each pixel as a number from 0 - 3. Each number represents one of the colors in the sprite's color registers. For example, here is the spaceship sprite again:

```
00001223322210000
00012233333221000
00122233333222100
00012233333221000
00001223322210000
```

Next, you translate each of the numbers in this picture into a binary number. The first line in binary is shown below. The binary numbers are represented vertically with the low digit in the top line and the high digit right below it. This is how the two color descriptor words for each sprite line are written in memory.

```
0 0 0 0 1 0 0 1 1 0 0 1 0 0 0 0   ← Low Sprite Word
0 0 0 0 0 1 1 1 1 1 1 0 0 0 0 0   ← High Sprite Word
```

The first line above becomes the color descriptor low word for line 1 of the sprite. The second line becomes the color descriptor high word. In this fashion, you translate each line in the sprite into binary 0s and 1s. See Figure 4-7.

Each of the binary numbers formed by the combination of the two data words for each line refers to a specific color register in that particular sprite channel's segment of the color table. Sprite channel 0, for example, takes its colors from registers 17 - 19. The binary numbers corresponding to the color registers for sprite DMA channel 0 are shown in Table 4-2.

Table 4-2: Sprite Color Registers

Binary Number	Color Register Number
00	Transparent
01	17
10	18
11	19

Recall that binary 00 always means transparent and never refers to a color except background.

End-of-data Words

When the vertical position of the beam counter is equal to the VSTOP value in the sprite control words, the next two words fetched from the sprite data structure are written into the sprite control registers instead of being sent to the color registers. These two words are interpreted by the hardware in the same manner as the original words that were first loaded into the control registers. If the VSTART value contained in these words is lower than the current beam position, this sprite will not be reused in this display field. For consistency, the value 0 should be used for both words when ending the usage of a sprite. Sprite reuse is discussed later.

The following data structure is for the spaceship sprite. It will be located at V = 65 and H = 128 on the normally visible part of the screen.

```
SPRITE:
        DC.W    $6D60,$7200     ;VSTART, HSTART, VSTOP
        DC.W    $0990,$07E0     ;First pair of descriptor words
        DC.W    $13C8,$0FF0
        DC.W    $23C4,$1FF8
        DC.W    $13C8,$0FF0
        DC.W    $0990,$07E0
        DC.W    $0000,$0000     ;End of sprite data
```

Displaying a Sprite

After building the data structure, you need to tell the system to display it. This section describes the display of sprites in "automatic" mode. In this mode, once the sprite DMA channel begins to retrieve and display the data, the display continues until the VSTOP position is reached. Manual mode is described later on in this chapter.

The following steps are used in displaying the sprite:

1. Decide which of the eight sprite DMA channels to use (making certain that the chosen channel is available).

2. Set the sprite pointers to tell the system where to find the sprite data.

3. Turn on sprite direct memory access if it is not already on.

4. For each subsequent display field, during the vertical blanking interval, rewrite the sprite pointers.

CAUTION

If sprite DMA is turned off while a sprite is being displayed (that is, after VSTART but before VSTOP), the system will continue to display the line of sprite data that was most recently fetched. This causes a vertical bar to appear on the screen. It is recommended that sprite DMA be turned off only during vertical blanking or during some portion of the display where you are *sure* that no sprite is being displayed.

SELECTING A DMA CHANNEL AND SETTING THE POINTERS

In deciding which DMA channel to use, you should take into consideration the colors assigned to the sprite and the sprite's video priority.

The sprite DMA channel uses two pointers to read in sprite data and control words. During the vertical blanking interval before the first display of the sprite, you need to write the sprite's memory address into these pointers. The pointers for each sprite are called SPRxPTH and SPRxPTL, where "x" is the number of the sprite DMA channel. SPRxPTH contains the high three bits of the memory address of the first word in the sprite and SPRxPTL contains the low sixteen bits. The least significant bit of SPRxPTL is ignored, as sprite data must be word aligned. Thus, only fifteen bits of SPRxPTL are used. As usual, you can write a long word into SPRxPTH.

In the following example the processor initializes the data pointers for sprite 0. Normally, this is done by the Copper. The sprite is at address $20000.

```
MOVE.L  #$20000,SPR0PTH+CUSTOM  ;Write $20000 to sprite 0 pointer...
```

These pointers are dynamic; they are incremented by the sprite DMA channel to point first to the control words, then to the data words, and finally to the end-of-data words. After reading in the sprite control information and storing it in other registers, they proceed to read in the color descriptor words. The color descriptor words are stored in sprite data registers, which are used by the sprite DMA channel to display the data on screen. For more information about how the sprite DMA channels handle the display, see the "Hardware Details" section below.

RESETTING THE ADDRESS POINTERS

For one single display field, the system will automatically read the data structure and produce the sprite on-screen in the colors that are specified in the sprite's color registers. If you want the sprite to be displayed in subsequent display fields, you must rewrite the contents of the sprite pointers during each vertical blanking interval. This is necessary because during the display field, the pointers are incremented to point to the data which is being fetched as the screen display progresses.

The rewrite becomes part of the vertical blanking routine, which can be handled by instructions in the Copper lists.

SPRITE DISPLAY EXAMPLE

This example displays the spaceship sprite at location V = 65, H = 128. Remember to include the file "hw_examples.i", located in Appendix J.

```
; First, we set up a single bit-plane.
;
        LEA     CUSTOM,a0               ;Point a0 at custom chips
        MOVE.W  #$1200,BPLCON0(a0)      ;1 bit-plane color is on
        MOVE.W  #$0000,BPL1MOD(a0)      ;Modulo = 0
        MOVE.W  #$0000,BPLCON1(a0)      ;Horizontal scroll value = 0
        MOVE.W  #$0024,BPLCON2(a0)      ;Sprites have priority over playfields
        MOVE.W  #$0038,DDFSTRT(a0)      ;Set data-fetch start
        MOVE.W  #$00D0,DDFSTOP(a0)      ;Set data-fetch stop

; Display window definitions.

        MOVE.W  #$2C81,DIWSTRT(a0)      ;Set display window start
                                        ;Vertical start in high byte.
                                        ;Horizontal start * 2 in low byte.

        MOVE.W  #$F4C1,DIWSTOP(a0)      ;Set display window stop
                                        ;Vertical stop in high byte.
                                        ;Horizontal stop * 2 in low byte.
;
; Set up color registers.
;
        MOVE.W  #$0008,COLOR00(a0)      ;Background color = dark blue
        MOVE.W  #$0000,COLOR01(a0)      ;Foreground color = black
        MOVE.W  #$0FF0,COLOR17(a0)      ;Color 17 = yellow
        MOVE.W  #$00FF,COLOR18(a0)      ;Color 18 = cyan
        MOVE.W  #$0F0F,COLOR19(a0)      ;Color 19 = magenta
;
; Move Copper list to $20000.
;
        MOVE.L  #$20000,a1              ;Point A1 at Copper list destination
        LEA     COPPERL(pc),a2          ;Point A2 at Copper list source
CLOOP:
        MOVE.L  (a2),(a1)+              ;Move a long word
        CMP.L   #$FFFFFFFE,(a2)+        ;Check for end of list
        BNE     CLOOP                   ;Loop until entire list is moved
;
; Move sprite to $25000.
;
        MOVE.L  #$25000,a1              ;Point A1 at sprite destination
        LEA     SPRITE(pc),a2           ;Point A2 at sprite source
SPRLOOP:
        MOVE.L  (a2),(a1)+              ;Move a long word
        CMP.L   #$00000000,(a2)+        ;Check for end of sprite
        BNE     SPRLOOP                 ;Loop until entire sprite is moved
;
; Now we write a dummy sprite to $30000, since all eight sprites are activated
; at the same time and we're only going to use one.  The remaining sprites
; will point to this dummy sprite data.
;
        MOVE.L  #$00000000,$30000       ;Write it
;
; Point Copper at Copper list.
```

```
;
        MOVE.L  #$20000,COP1LC(a0)
;
; Fill bit-plane with $FFFFFFFF.
;
        MOVE.L  #$21000,a1                ;Point A1 at bit-plane
        MOVE.W  #1999,d0                  ;2000-1(for dbf) long words = 8000 bytes
FLOOP
        MOVE.L  #$FFFFFFFF,(a1)+          ;Move a long word of $FFFFFFFF
        DBF     d0,FLOOP                  ;Decrement, repeat until false.
;
; Start DMA.
;
        MOVE.W  d0,COPJMP1(a0)            ;Force load into Copper
                                          ;  program counter
        MOVE.W  #$83A0,DMACON(a0)         ;Bit-plane, Copper, and sprite DMA
        RTS                               ;..return to rest of program..


;
; This is a Copper list for one bit-plane, and 8 sprites.
; The bit-plane lives at $21000.
; Sprite 0 lives at $25000; all others live at $30000 (the dummy sprite).
;
COPPERL:
        DC.W    BPL1PTH,$0002             ;Bit plane 1 pointer = $21000
        DC.W    BPL1PTL,$1000
        DC.W    SPR0PTH,$0002             ;Sprite 0 pointer = $25000
        DC.W    SPR0PTL,$5000
        DC.W    SPR1PTH,$0003             ;Sprite 1 pointer = $30000
        DC.W    SPR1PTL,$0000
        DC.W    SPR2PTH,$0003             ;Sprite 2 pointer = $30000
        DC.W    SPR2PTL,$0000
        DC.W    SPR3PTH,$0003             ;Sprite 3 pointer = $30000
        DC.W    SPR3PTL,$0000
        DC.W    SPR4PTH,$0003             ;Sprite 4 pointer = $30000
        DC.W    SPR4PTL,$0000
        DC.W    SPR5PTH,$0003             ;Sprite 5 pointer = $30000
        DC.W    SPR5PTL,$0000
        DC.W    SPR6PTH,$0003             ;Sprite 6 pointer = $30000
        DC.W    SPR6PTL,$0000
        DC.W    SPR7PTH,$0003             ;Sprite 7 pointer = $30000
        DC.W    SPR7PTL,$0000
        DC.W    $FFFF,$FFFE               ;End of Copper list
;
; Sprite data for spaceship sprite.  It appears on the screen at V=65 and H=128.
;
SPRITE:
        DC.W    $6D60,$7200               ;VSTART, HSTART, VSTOP
        DC.W    $0990,$07E0               ;First pair of descriptor words
        DC.W    $13C8,$0FF0
        DC.W    $23C4,$1FF8
        DC.W    $13C8,$0FF0
        DC.W    $0990,$07E0
        DC.W    $0000,$0000               ;End of sprite data
```

Moving a Sprite

A sprite generated in automatic mode can be moved by specifying a different position in the data structure. For each display field, the data is reread and the sprite redrawn. Therefore, if you change the position data before the sprite is redrawn, it will appear in a new position and will seem to be moving.

You must take care that you are not moving the sprite (that is, changing control word data) at the same time that the system is using that data to find out where to display the object. If you do so, the system might find the start position for one field and the stop position for the following field as it retrieves data for display. This would cause a "glitch" and would mess up the screen. Therefore, you should change the content of the control words only during a time when the system is not trying to read them. Usually, the vertical blanking period is a safe time, so moving the sprites becomes part of the vertical blanking tasks and is handled by the Copper as shown in the example below.

As sprites move about on the screen, they can collide with each other or with either of the two playfields. You can use the hardware to detect these collisions and exploit this capability for special effects. In addition, you can use collision detection to keep a moving object within specified on-screen boundaries. Collision Detection is described in Chapter 7, "System Control Hardware."

In this example of moving a sprite, the spaceship is bounced around on the screen, changing direction whenever it reaches an edge.

The sprite position data, containing VSTART and HSTART, lives in memory at $25000. VSTOP is located at $25002. You write to these locations to move the sprite. Once during each frame, VSTART is incremented (or decremented) by 1 and HSTART by 2. Then a new VSTOP is calculated, which will be the new VSTART + 6.

```
        MOVE.B  #151,d0         ;Initialize horizontal count
        MOVE.B  #194,d1         ;Initialize vertical count
        MOVE.B  #64,d2          ;Initialize horizontal position
        MOVE.B  #44,d3          ;Initialize vertical position
        MOVE.B  #1,d4           ;Initialize horizontal increment value
        MOVE.B  #1,d5           ;Initialize vertical increment value
;
;Here we wait for the start of the screen updating.
;This ensures a glitch-free display.
;
        LEA     CUSTOM,a0       ;Set custom chip base pointer
VLOOP:
        MOVE.B  VHPOSR(a0),d6   ;Read Vertical beam position.
;Only insert the folllowing line if you are using a PAL machine.
;       CMP.B   #$20,d6         ;Compare with end of PAL screen.
        BNE.S   VLOOP           ;Loop if not end of screen.
;Alternatively you can use the following code:
;VLOOP:
```

```
;        MOVE.W  INTREQR(a0),d6        ;Read interrupt request word
;        AND.W   #$0020,d6             ;Mask off all but vertical blank bit
;        BEQ     VLOOP                 ;Loop until bit is a 1
;        MOVE.W  #$0020,INTREQ(a0)     ;Vertical bit is on, so reset it
;
;Please note that this will only work if you have turned OFF the Vertical
;blanking interupt enable (not recommended for long periods).

         ADD.B   d4,d2                 ;Increment horizontal value
         SUBQ.B  #1,d0                 ;Decrement horizontal counter
         BNE     L1
         MOVE.B  #151,d0               ;Count exhausted, reset to 151
         EOR.B   #$FE,d4               ;Negate the increment value
L1:      MOVE.B  d2,$25001             ;Write new HSTART value to sprite
         ADD.B   d5,d3                 ;Increment vertical value
         SUBQ.B  #1,d1                 ;Decrement vertical counter
         BNE     L2
         MOVE.B  #194,d1               ;Count exhausted, reset to 194
         EOR.B   #$FE,d5               ;Negate the increment value
L2:      MOVE.B  d3,$25000             ;Write new VSTART value to sprite
         MOVE.B  d3,d6                 ;Must now calculate new VSTOP
         ADD.B   #6,d6                 ;VSTOP always VSTART+6 for spaceship
         MOVE.B  d6,$25002             ;Write new VSTOP to sprite
         BRA     VLOOP                 ;Loop forever
```

Creating Additional Sprites

To use additional sprites, you must create a data structure for each one and arrange the display as shown in the previous section, naming the pointers SPR1PTH and SPR1PTL for sprite DMA channel 1, SPR2PTH and SPR2PTL for sprite DMA channel 2, and so on.

NOTE

When you enable sprite DMA for one sprite, you enable DMA for all the sprites and place them all in automatic mode. Thus, you do not need to repeat this step when using additional sprite DMA channels.

Once the sprite DMA channels are enabled, all eight sprite pointers *must* be initialized to either a real sprite or a safe null sprite. An uninitialized sprite could cause spurious sprite video to appear.

Remember that some sprites can become unusable when additional DMA cycles are allocated to displaying the screen, for example when an extra wide display or horizontal scrolling is enabled (see Figure 6-9: DMA Time Slot Allocation).

Also, recall that each pair of sprites takes its color from different color registers, as shown in Table 4-3.

Table 4-3: Color Registers for Sprite Pairs

Sprite Numbers	Color Registers
0 and 1	17 - 19
2 and 3	21 - 23
4 and 5	25 - 27
6 and 7	29 - 31

NOTE

Some sprites become unusable when additional DMA cycles are allocated to displaying the screen, e.g. when enabling an extra wide display or horizontal scrolling. (See Figure 6-11: DMA Time Slot Allocation.)

SPRITE PRIORITY

When you have more than one sprite on the screen, you may need to take into consideration their relative video priority, that is, which sprite appears in front of or behind another. Each sprite has a fixed video priority with respect to all the others. The lowest numbered sprite has the highest priority and appears in front of all other sprites; the highest numbered sprite has the lowest priority. This is illustrated in Figure 4-8.

NOTE

See Chapter 7, "System Control Hardware", for more information on sprite priorities.

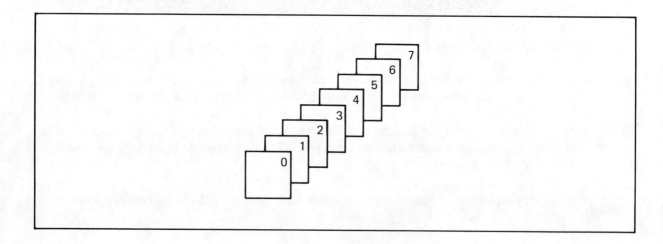

Figure 4-8: Sprite Priority

Reusing Sprite DMA Channels

Each of the eight sprite DMA channels can produce more than one independently controllable image. There may be times when you want more than eight objects, or you may be left with fewer than eight objects because you have attached some of the sprites to produce more colors or larger objects or overlapped some to produce more complex images. You can reuse each sprite DMA channel several times within the same display field, as shown in Figure 4-9.

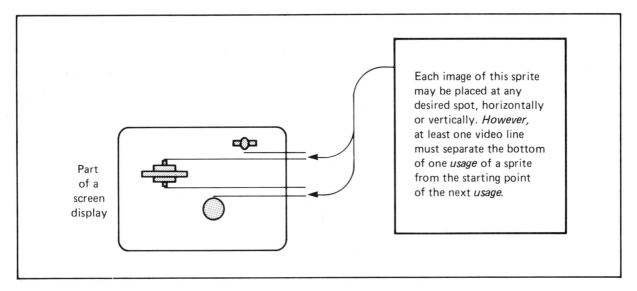

Each image of this sprite may be placed at any desired spot, horizontally or vertically. *However,* at least one video line must separate the bottom of one *usage* of a sprite from the starting point of the next *usage.*

Part of a screen display

Figure 4-9: Typical Example of Sprite Reuse

In single-sprite usage, two all-zero words are placed at the end of the data structure to stop the DMA channel from retrieving any more data for that particular sprite during that display field. To reuse a DMA channel, you replace this pair of zero words with another complete sprite data structure, which describes the reuse of the DMA channel at a position lower on the screen than the first use. You place the two all-zero words at the end of the data structure that contains the information for all usages of the DMA channel. For example, Figure 4-10 shows the data structure that describes the picture above.

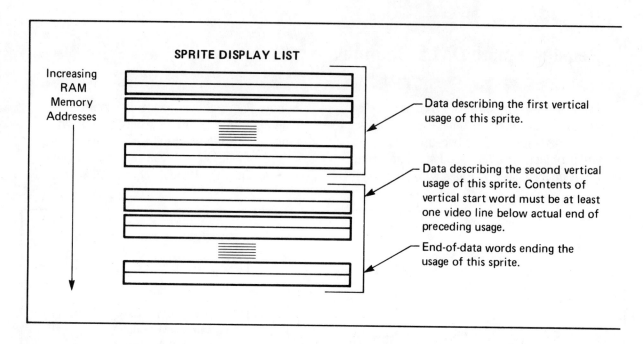

Figure 4-10: Typical Data Structure for Sprite Re-use

The only restrictions on the reuse of sprites during a single display field is that the bottom line of one usage of a sprite must be separated from the top line of the next usage by at least one horizontal scan line. This restriction is necessary because only two DMA cycles per horizontal scan line are allotted to each of the eight channels. The sprite channel needs the time during the blank line to fetch the control word describing the next usage of the sprite.

The following example displays the spaceship sprite and then redisplays it as a different object. Only the sprite data list is affected, so only the data list is shown here. However, the sprite looks best with the color registers set as shown in the example.

```
        LEA     CUSTOM,a0
        MOVE.W  #$0F00,COLOR17(a0)      ;Color 17 = red
        MOVE.W  #$0FF0,COLOR18(a0)      ;Color 18 = yellow
        MOVE.W  #$0FFF,COLOR19(a0)      ;Color 19 = white
SPRITE:
        DC.W    $6D60,$7200
        DC.W    $0990,$07E0
        DC.W    $13C8,$0FF0
        DC.W    $23C4,$1FF8
        DC.W    $13C8,$0FF0
        DC.W    $0990,$07E0
        DC.W    $8080,$8D00             ;VSTART, HSTART, VSTOP for new sprite
        DC.W    $1818,$0000
        DC.W    $7E7E,$0000
        DC.W    $7FFE,$0000
        DC.W    $FFFF,$2000
        DC.W    $FFFF,$2000
        DC.W    $FFFF,$3000
        DC.W    $FFFF,$3000
        DC.W    $7FFE,$1800
        DC.W    $7FFE,$0C00
        DC.W    $3FFC,$0000
        DC.W    $0FF0,$0000
        DC.W    $03C0,$0000
        DC.W    $0180,$0000
        DC.W    $0000,$0000             ;End of sprite data
```

Overlapped Sprites

For more complex or larger moving objects, you can overlap sprites. Overlapping simply means that the sprites have the same or relatively close screen positions. A relatively close screen position can result in an object that is wider than 16 pixels.

The built-in sprite video priority ensures that one sprite appears to be behind the other when sprites are overlapped. The priority circuitry gives the lowest-numbered sprite the highest priority and the highest numbered sprite the lowest priority. Therefore, when designing displays with overlapped sprites, make sure the "foreground" sprite has a lower number than the "background" sprite. In Figure 4-11, for example, the cage should be generated by a lower-numbered sprite DMA channel than the monkey.

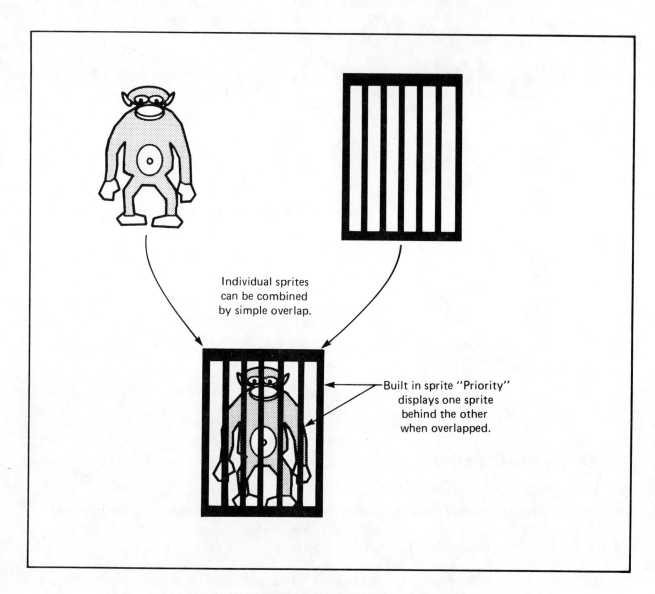

Individual sprites
can be combined
by simple overlap.

Built in sprite "Priority"
displays one sprite
behind the other
when overlapped.

Figure 4-11: Overlapping Sprites (Not Attached)

You can create a wider sprite display by placing two sprites next to each other. For instance, Figure 4-12 shows the spaceship sprite and how it can be made twice as large by using two sprites placed next to each other.

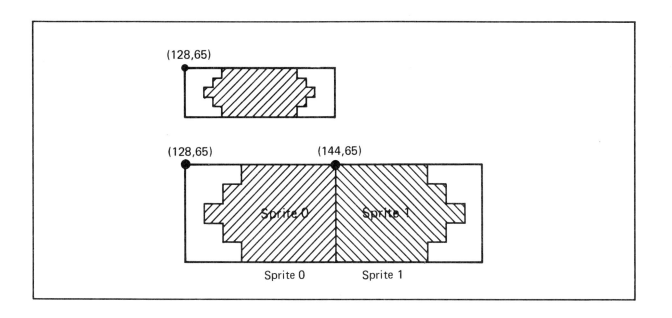

Figure 4-12: Placing Sprites Next to Each Other

Attached Sprites

You can create sprites that have fifteen possible color choices (plus transparent) instead of three (plus transparent), by "attaching" two sprites. To create attached sprites, you must:

- Use two channels per sprite, creating two sprites of the same size and located at the same position.

- Set a bit called ATTACH in the second sprite control word.

The fifteen colors are selected from the full range of color registers available to sprites — registers 17 through 31. The extra color choices are possible because each pixel contains four bits instead of only two as in the normal, unattached sprite. Each sprite in the attached pair contributes two bits to the binary color selector number. For example, if you are using sprite DMA channels 0 and 1, the high- and low-order color descriptor words for line 1 in both data structures are combined into line 1 of the attached object.

Sprites can be attached in the following combinations:

Sprite 1 to sprite 0
Sprite 3 to sprite 2
Sprite 5 to sprite 4
Sprite 7 to sprite 6

Any or all of these attachments can be active during the same display field. As an example, assume that you wish to have more colors in the spaceship sprite and you are using sprite DMA channels 0 and 1. There are five colors plus transparent in this sprite.

```
0000154444510000
0001564444651000
0015676446765100
0001564444651000
0000154444510000
```

The first line in this sprite requires the four data words shown in Table 4-4 to form the correct binary color selector numbers.

Table 4-4: Data Words for First Line of Spaceship Sprite

Pixel Number

	15	14	13	12	11	10	9	8	7	6	5	4	3	2	1	0
Line 1	0	0	0	0	0	0	0	0	0	0	0	0	0	0	0	0
Line 2	0	0	0	0	0	1	1	1	1	1	1	0	0	0	0	0
Line 3	0	0	0	0	0	0	0	0	0	0	0	0	0	0	0	0
Line 4	0	0	0	0	1	1	0	0	0	0	1	1	0	0	0	0

The highest numbered sprite (number 1, in this example) contributes the highest order bits (leftmost) in the binary number. The high-order data word in each sprite contributes the leftmost digit. Therefore, the lines above are written to the sprite data structures as follows:

Line 1   Sprite 1 high-order word for sprite line 1
Line 2   Sprite 1 low-order word for sprite line 1
Line 3   Sprite 0 high-order word for sprite line 1
Line 4   Sprite 0 low-order word for sprite line 1

See Figure 4-7 for the order these words are stored in memory. Remember that this data is contained in *two* sprite structures.

The binary numbers 0 through 15 select registers 17 through 31 as shown in Table 4-5.

Table 4-5: Color Registers in Attached Sprites

Decimal Number	Binary Number	Color Register Number
0	0000	16 *
1	0001	17
2	0010	18
3	0011	19
4	0100	20
5	0101	21
6	0110	22
7	0111	23
8	1000	24
9	1001	25
10	1010	26
11	1011	27
12	1100	28
13	1101	29
14	1110	30
15	1111	31

* Unused; yields transparent pixel.

Attachment is in effect only when the ATTACH bit, bit 7 in sprite control word 2, is set to 1 in the data structure for the odd-numbered sprite. So, in this example, you set bit 7 in sprite control word 2 in the data structure for sprite 1.

When the sprites are moved, the Copper list must keep them both at exactly the same position relative to each other. If they are not kept together on the screen, their pixels will change color. Each sprite will revert to three colors plus transparent, but the colors may be different than if they were ordinary, unattached sprites. The color selection for the lower numbered sprite will be from color registers 17-19. The color selection for the higher numbered sprite will be from color registers 20, 24, and 28.

The following data structure is for the six-color spaceship made with two attached sprites.

```
SPRITE0:
        DC.W    $6D60,$7200     ;VSTART = 65, HSTART = 128
        DC.W    $0C30,$0000     ;First color descriptor word
        DC.W    $1818,$0420
        DC.W    $342C,$0E70
        DC.W    $1818,$0420
        DC.W    $0C30,$0000
        DC.W    $0000,$0000     ;End of sprite 0
SPRITE1:
        DC.W    $6D60,$7280     ;Same as sprite 0 except attach bit on
        DC.W    $07E0,$0000     ;First descriptor word for sprite 1
        DC.W    $0FF0,$0000
        DC.W    $1FF8,$0000
        DC.W    $0FF0,$0000
        DC.W    $07E0,$0000
        DC.W    $0000,$0000     ;End of sprite 1
```

Manual Mode

It is almost always best to load sprites using the automatic DMA channels. Sometimes, however, it is useful to load these registers directly from one of the microprocessors. Sprites may be activated "manually" whenever they are not being used by a DMA channel. The same sprite that is showing a DMA-controlled icon near the top of the screen can also be reloaded manually to show a vertical colored bar near the bottom of the screen. Sprites can be activated manually even when the sprite DMA is turned off.

You display sprites manually by writing to the sprite data registers SPRxDATB and SPRxDATA, in that order. You write to SPRxDATA last because that address "arms" the sprite to be output at the next horizontal comparison. The data written will then be displayed on every line, at the horizontal position given in the "H" portion of the position registers SPRxPOS and SPRxCTL. If the data is unchanged, the result will be a vertical bar. If the data is reloaded for every line, a complex sprite can be produced.

The sprite can be terminated ("disarmed") by writing to the SPRxCTL register. If you write to the SPRxPOS register, you can manually move the sprite horizontally at any time, even during normal sprite usage.

Sprite Hardware Details

Sprites are produced by the circuitry shown in Figure 4-13. This figure shows in block form how a pair of data words becomes a set of pixels displayed on the screen.

The circuitry elements for sprite display are explained below.

- Sprite data registers. The registers SPRxDATA and SPRxDATB hold the bit patterns that describe one horizontal line of a sprite for each of the eight sprites. A line is 16 pixels wide, and each line is defined by two words to provide selection of three colors and transparent.

- Parallel-to-serial converters. Each of the 16 bits of the sprite data bit pattern is individually sent to the color select circuitry at the time that the pixel associated with that bit is being displayed on-screen.

  Immediately after the data is transferred from the sprite data registers, each parallel-to-serial converter begins shifting the bits out of the converter, most significant (leftmost) bit first. The shift occurs once during each low-resolution pixel time and continues until all 16 bits have been transferred to the display circuitry. The shifting and data output does not begin again until the next time this converter is loaded from the data registers.

  Because the video image is produced by an electron beam that is being swept from left to right on the screen, the bit-image of the data corresponds exactly to the image that actually appears on the screen (most significant data on the left).

- Sprite serial video data. Sprite data goes to the priority circuit to establish the priority between sprites and playfields.

- Sprite position registers. These registers, called SPRxPOS, contain the horizontal position value (X value) and vertical position value (Y value) for each of the eight sprites.

- Sprite control registers. These registers, called SPRxCTL, contain the stopping position for each of the eight sprites and whether or not a sprite is attached.

- Beam counter. The beam counter tells the system the current location of the video beam that is producing the picture.

- Comparator. This device compares the value of the beam counter to the Y value in the position register SPRxPOS. If the beam has reached the position at which the leftmost upper pixel of the sprite is to appear, the comparator issues a load signal to the serial-to-parallel converter and the sprite display begins.

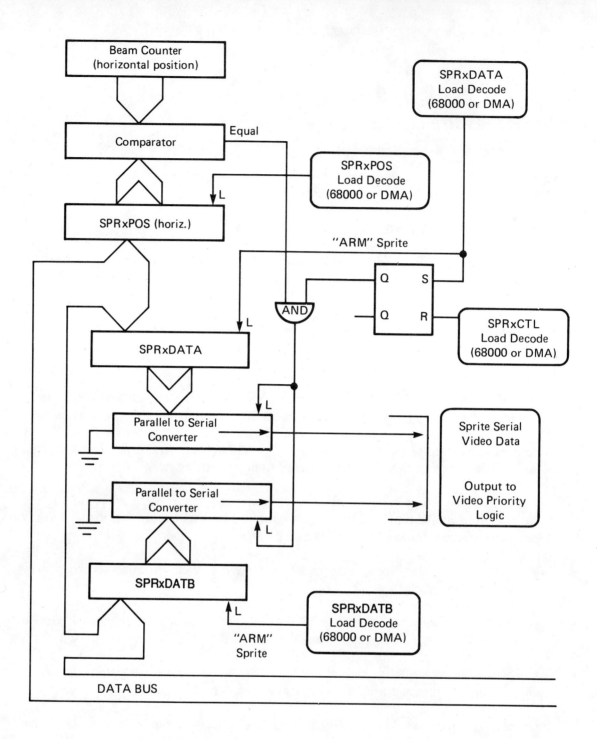

Figure 4-13: Sprite Control Circuitry

Figure 4-13 shows the following:

- Writing to the sprite *control* registers *disables* the horizontal comparator circuitry. This prevents the system from sending any output from the data registers to the serial converter or to the screen.

- Writing to the sprite A *data* register *enables* the horizontal comparator. This enables output to the screen when the horizontal position of the video beam equals the horizontal value in the position register.

- If the comparator is enabled, the sprite data will be sent to the display, with the leftmost pixel of the sprite data placed at the position defined in the horizontal part of SPRxPOS.

- As long as the comparator remains enabled, the current contents of the sprite data register will be output at the selected horizontal position on a video line.

- The data in the sprite data registers does not change. It is either rewritten by the user or modified under DMA control.

The components described above produce the automatic DMA display as follows: When the sprites are in DMA mode, the 18-bit sprite pointer register (composed of SPRxPTH and SPRxPTL) is used to read the first two words from the sprite data structure. These words contain the starting and stopping position of the sprite. Next, the pointers write these words into SPRxPOS and SPRxCTL. After this write, the value in the pointers points to the address of the first data word (low word of data for line 1 of the sprite.)

Writing into the SPRxCTL register disabled the sprite. Now the sprite DMA channel will wait until the vertical beam counter value is the same as the data in the VSTART (Y value) part of SPRxPOS. When these values match, the system enables the sprite data access.

The sprite DMA channel examines the contents of VSTOP (from SPRxCTL, which is the location of the line after the last line of the sprite) and VSTART (from SPRxPOS) to see how many lines of sprite data are to be fetched. Two words are fetched per line of sprite height, and these words are written into the sprite data registers. The first word is stored in SPRxDATA and the second word in SPRxDATB.

The fetch and store for each horizontal scan line occurs during a horizontal blanking interval, far to the left of the start of the screen display. This arms the sprite horizontal comparators and allows them to start the output of the sprite data to the screen when the horizontal beam count value matches the value stored in the HSTART (X value) part of SPRxPOS.

If the count of VSTOP - VSTART equals zero, no sprite output occurs. The next data word pair will be fetched, but it will not be stored into the sprite data registers. It will instead become the next pair of data words for SPRxPOS and SPRxCTL.

When a sprite is used only once within a single display field, the final pair of data words, which follow the sprite color descriptor words, is loaded automatically as the next contents of the SPRxPOS and SPRxCTL registers. To stop the sprite after that first data set, the pair of words should contain all zeros.

Thus, if you have formed a sprite pattern in memory, this same pattern will be produced as pixels automatically under DMA control one line at a time.

Summary of Sprite Registers

There are eight complete sets of registers used to describe the sprites. Each set consists of five registers. Only the registers for sprite 0 are described here. All of the others are the same, except for the name of the register, which includes the appropriate number.

POINTERS

Pointers are registers that are used by the system to point to the *current* data being used. During a screen display, the registers are incremented to point to the data being used as the screen display progresses. Therefore, pointer registers must be freshly written during the start of the vertical blanking period.

SPR0PTH and SPR0PTL

This pair of registers contains the 32-bit word address of Sprite 0 DMA data.

Pointer register names for the other sprites are:

SPR1PTH	SPR1PTL
SPR2PTH	SPR2PTL
SPR3PTH	SPR3PTL
SPR4PTH	SPR4PTL
SPR5PTH	SPR5PTL
SPR6PTH	SPR6PTL
SPR7PTH	SPR7PTL

CONTROL REGISTERS

SPR0POS

This is the sprite 0 position register. The word written into this register controls the position on the screen at which the upper left-hand corner of the sprite is to be placed. The most significant bit of the first data word will be placed in this position on the screen.

The sprites have a placement resolution on a full screen of 320 by 200 NTSC (320 by 256 PAL). The sprite resolution is independent of the bit-plane resolution.

Bit positions:

- Bits 15-8 specify the vertical start position, bits V7 - V0.

- Bits 7-0 specify the horizontal start position, bits H8 - H1.

NOTE

This register is normally only written by the sprite DMA channel itself. See the details above regarding the organization of the sprite data. This register is usually updated directly by DMA.

SPR0CTL

This register is normally used only by the sprite DMA channel. It contains control information that is used to control the sprite data-fetch process. Bit positions:

- Bits 15-8 specify vertical stop position for a sprite image, bits V7 - V0.

- Bit 7 is the attach bit. This bit is valid only for odd-numbered sprites. It indicates that sprites 0, 1 (or 2,3 or 4,5 or 6,7) will, for color interpretation, be considered as paired, and as such will be called four bits deep. The odd-numbered (higher number) sprite contains bits with the higher binary significance.

  During attach mode, the attached sprites are normally moved horizontally and vertically together under processor control. This allows a greater selection of colors within the boundaries of the sprite itself. The sprites, although attached, remain capable of independent motion, however, and they will assume this larger color set only when their edges overlay one another.

- Bits 6-3 are reserved for future use (make zero).

- Bit 2 is bit V8 of vertical start.

- Bit 1 is bit V8 of vertical stop.

- Bit 0 is bit H0 of horizontal start.

Position and control registers for the other sprites are:

SPR1POS	SPR1CTL
SPR2POS	SPR2CTL
SPR3POS	SPR3CTL
SPR4POS	SPR4CTL
SPR5POS	SPR5CTL
SPR6POS	SPR6CTL
SPR7POS	SPR7CTL

DATA REGISTERS

The following registers, although defined in the address space of the main processor, are normally used only by the display processor. They are the holding registers for the data obtained by DMA cycles.

SPR0DATA, SPR0DATB	data registers for Sprite 0
SPR1DATA, SPR1DATB	data registers for Sprite 1
SPR2DATA, SPR2DATB	data registers for Sprite 2
SPR3DATA, SPR3DATB	data registers for Sprite 3
SPR4DATA, SPR4DATB	data registers for Sprite 4
SPR5DATA, SPR5DATB	data registers for Sprite 5
SPR6DATA, SPR6DATB	data registers for Sprite 6
SPR7DATA, SPR7DATB	data registers for Sprite 7

Summary of Sprite Color Registers

Sprite data words are used to select the color of the sprite pixels from the system color register set as indicated in the following tables.

If the bit combinations from single sprites are as shown in Table 4-6, then the colors will be taken from the registers shown.

Table 4-6: Color Registers for Single Sprites

Single Sprites		Color
Sprite	Value	Register
0 or 1	00	Not used *
	01	17
	10	18
	11	19
2 or 3	00	Not used *
	01	21
	10	22
	11	23
4 or 5	00	Not used *
	01	25
	10	26
	11	27
6 or 7	00	Not used *
	01	29
	10	30
	11	31

* Selects transparent mode.

If the bit combinations from attached sprites are as shown in Table 4-7, then the colors will be taken from the registers shown.

Table 4-7: Color Registers for Attached Sprites

Value	Attached Sprites Color Register
0000	Selects transparent mode
0001	17
0010	18
0011	19
0100	20
0101	21
0110	22
0111	23
1000	24
1001	25
1010	26
1011	27
1100	28
1101	29
1110	30
1111	31

INTERACTIONS AMONG SPRITES AND OTHER OBJECTS

Playfields share the display with sprites. Chapter 7, "System Control Hardware," shows how playfields can be given different video display priorities relative to the sprites and how playfields can collide with (overlap) the sprites or each other.

Chapter 5

AUDIO HARDWARE

Introduction

This chapter shows you how to directly access the audio hardware to produce sounds. The major topics in this chapter are:

- A brief overview of how a computer produces sound.

- How to produce simple steady and changing sounds and more complex ones.

- How to use the audio channels for special effects, wiring them for stereo sound if desired, or using one channel to modulate another.

- How to produce quality sound within the system limitations.

A section at the end of the chapter gives you values to use for creating musical notes on the equal-tempered musical scale.

This chapter is not a tutorial on computer sound synthesis; a thorough description of creating sound on a computer would require a far longer document. The purpose here is to point the way and show you how to use the Amiga's features. Computer sound production is fun but complex, and it usually requires a great deal of trial and error on the part of the user—you use the instructions to create some sound and play it back, readjust the parameters and play it again, and so on.

The following works are recommended for more information on creating music with computers:

- Wayne A. Bateman, *Introduction to Computer Music* (New York: John Wiley and Sons, 1980).

- Hal Chamberlain, *Musical Applications of Microprocessors* (Rochelle Park, New Jersey: Hayden, 1980).

INTRODUCING SOUND GENERATION

Sound travels through air to your ear drums as a repeated cycle of air pressure variations, or sound waves. Sounds can be represented as graphs that model how the air pressure varies over time. The attributes of a sound, as you hear it, are related to the shape of the graph. If the waveform is regular and repetitive, it will sound like a tone with steady pitch (highness or lowness), such as a single musical note. Each repetition of a waveform is called a cycle of the sound. If the waveform is irregular, the sound will have little or no pitch, like a loud clash or rushing water. How often the waveform repeats (its frequency) has an effect upon its pitch; sounds with higher frequencies are higher in pitch. Humans can hear sounds that have a frequency of between 20 and 20,000 cycles per second. The amplitude of the waveform (highest point on the graph), is related to the perceived loudness of the sound. Finally, the general shape of the waveform determines its tone quality, or timbre. Figure 5-1 shows a particular kind of waveform, called a sine wave, that represents one cycle of a simple tone.

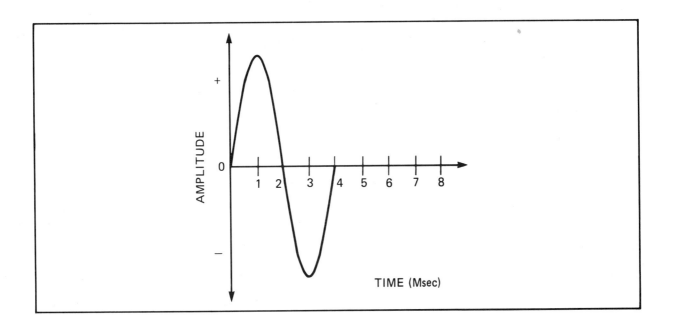

Figure 5-1: Sine Waveform

In electronic sound recording and output devices, the attributes of sounds are represented by the parameters of amplitude and frequency. Frequency is the number of cycles per second, and the most common unit of frequency is the Hertz (Hz), which is 1 cycle per second. Large values, or high frequencies, are measured in kilohertz (KHz) or megahertz (MHz).

Frequency is strongly related to the perceived pitch of a sound. When frequency increases, pitch rises. This relationship is exponential. An increase from 100 Hz to 200 Hz results in a large rise in pitch, but an increase from 1,000 Hz to 1,100 Hz is hardly noticeable. Musical pitch is represented in octaves. A tone that is one octave higher than another has a frequency twice as high as that of the first tone, and its perceived pitch is twice as high.

The second parameter that defines a waveform is its amplitude. In an electronic circuit, amplitude relates to the voltage or current in the circuit. When a signal is going to a speaker, the amplitude is expressed in watts. Perceived sound intensity is measured in decibels (db). Human hearing has a range of about 120 db; 1 db is the faintest audible sound. Roughly every 10 db corresponds to a doubling of sound, and 1 db is the smallest change in amplitude that is noticeable in a moderately loud sound. Volume, which is the amplitude of the sound signal which is output, corresponds logarithmically to decibel level.

The frequency and amplitude parameters of a sine wave are completely independent. When sound is heard, however, there is interaction between loudness and pitch. Lower-frequency sounds decrease in loudness much faster than high-frequency sounds.

The third attribute of a sound, timbre, depends on the presence or absence of overtones, or harmonics. Any complex waveform is actually a mixture of sine waves of different amplitudes, frequencies, and phåses (the starting point of the waveform on the time axis). These component sine waves are called harmonics. A square waveform, for example, has an infinite number of harmonics.

In summary, all steady sounds can be described by their frequency, overall amplitude, and relative harmonic amplitudes. The audible equivalents of these parameters are pitch, loudness, and timbre, respectively. Changing sound is a steady sound whose parameters change over time.

In electronic production of sound, an analog device, such as a tape recorder, records sound waveforms and their cycle frequencies as a continuously variable representation of air pressure. The tape recorder then plays back the sound by sending the waveforms to an amplifier where they are changed into analog voltage waveforms. The amplifier sends the voltage waveforms to a loudspeaker, which translates them into air pressure vibrations that the listener perceives as sound.

A computer cannot store analog waveform information. In computer production of sound, a waveform has to be represented as a finite string of numbers. This transformation is made by dividing the time axis of the graph of a single waveform into equal segments, each of which represents a short enough time so the waveform does not change a great deal. Each of the resulting points is called a sample. These samples are stored in memory, and you can play them back at a frequency that you determine. The computer feeds the samples to a digital-to-analog converter (DAC), which changes them into an analog voltage waveform. To produce the sound, the analog waveforms are sent first to an amplifier, then to a loudspeaker.

Figure 5-2 shows an example of a sine wave, a square wave, and a triangle wave, along with a table of samples for each.

NOTE

The illustrations are not to scale and there are fewer dots in the wave forms than there are samples in the table. The amplitude axis values 127 and -128 represent the high and low limits on relative amplitude.

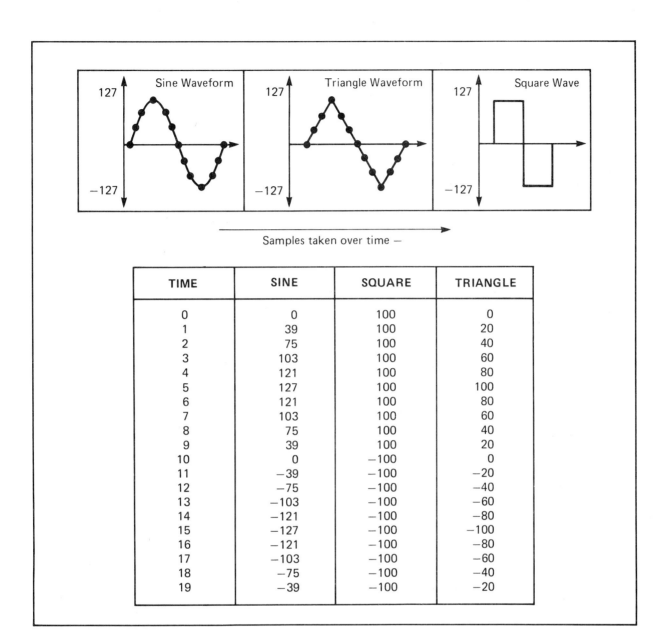

TIME	SINE	SQUARE	TRIANGLE
0	0	100	0
1	39	100	20
2	75	100	40
3	103	100	60
4	121	100	80
5	127	100	100
6	121	100	80
7	103	100	60
8	75	100	40
9	39	100	20
10	0	−100	0
11	−39	−100	−20
12	−75	−100	−40
13	−103	−100	−60
14	−121	−100	−80
15	−127	−100	−100
16	−121	−100	−80
17	−103	−100	−60
18	−75	−100	−40
19	−39	−100	−20

Figure 5-2: Digitized Amplitude Values

THE AMIGA SOUND HARDWARE

The Amiga has four hardware sound channels. You can independently program each of the channels to produce complex sound effects. You can also attach channels so that one channel modulates the sound of another or combine two channels for stereo effects.

Each audio channel includes an eight-bit digital-to-analog converter driven by a direct memory access (DMA) channel. The audio DMA can retrieve two data samples during each horizontal video scan line. For simple, steady tones, the DMA can automatically play a waveform repeatedly; you can also program all kinds of complex sound effects.

There are two methods of basic sound production on the Amiga — automatic (DMA) sound generation and direct (non-DMA) sound generation. When you use automatic sound generation, the system retrieves data automatically by direct memory access.

Forming and Playing a Sound

This section shows you how to create a simple, steady sound and play it. Many basic concepts that apply to all sound generation on the Amiga are introduced in this section.

To produce a steady tone, follow these basic steps:

1. Decide which channel to use.

2. Define the waveform and create the sample table in memory.

3. Set registers telling the system where to find the data and the length of the data.

4. Select the volume at which the tone is to be played.

5. Select the sampling period, or output rate of the data.

6. Select an audio channel and start up the DMA.

DECIDING WHICH CHANNEL TO USE

The Amiga has four audio channels. Channels 0 and 3 are connected to the left-side stereo output jack. Channels 1 and 2 are connected to the right-side output jack. Select a channel on the side from which the output is to appear.

CREATING THE WAVEFORM DATA

The waveform used as an example in this section is a simple sine wave, which produces a pure tone. To conserve memory, you normally define only one full cycle of a waveform in memory. For a steady, unchanging sound, the values at the waveform's beginning and ending points and the trend or slope of the data at the beginning and end should be closely related. This ensures that a continuous repetition of the waveform sounds like a continuous stream of sound.

Sound data is organized as a set of eight-bit data items; each item is a sample from the waveform. Each data word retrieved for the audio channel consists of two samples. Sample values can range from -128 to +127.

As an example, the data set shown below produces a close approximation to a sine wave.

NOTE

The data is stored in byte address order with the first digitized amplitude value at the lowest byte address, the second at the next byte address, and so on. Also, note that the first byte of data must start at a word-address boundary. This is because the audio DMA retrieves one word (16 bits) at a time and uses the sample it reads as two bytes of data.

To use audio channel 0, write the address of "audiodata" into AUD0LC, where the audio data is organized as shown below. For simplicity, "AUDxLC" in the table below stands for the combination of the two actual location registers (AUDxLCH and AUDxLCL). For the audio DMA channels to be able to retrieve the data, the data address to which AUD0LC points must be somewhere in chip RAM.

Table 5-1: Sample Audio Data Set for Channel 0

audiodata --->	AUD0LC *	100	98
	AUD0LC + 2 **	92	83
	AUD0LC + 4	71	56
	AUD0LC + 6	38	20
	AUD0LC + 8	0	-20
	AUD0LC + 10	-38	-56
	AUD0LC + 12	-71	-83
	AUD0LC + 14	-92	-83
	AUD0LC + 16	-100	-98
	AUD0LC + 18	-92	-83
	AUD0LC + 20	-71	-56
	AUD0LC + 22	-38	-20
	AUD0LC + 24	0	20
	AUD0LC + 26	38	56
	AUD0LC + 28	71	83
	AUD0LC + 30	92	98

Notes

* Audio data is located on a word-address boundary.

** AUD0LC stands for AUD0LCL and AUD0LCH.

TELLING THE SYSTEM ABOUT THE DATA

In order to retrieve the sound data for the audio channel, the system needs to know where the data is located and how long (in words) the data is.

The location registers AUDxLCH and AUDxLCL contain the high three bits and the low fifteen bits, respectively, of the starting address of the audio data. Since these two register addresses are contiguous, writing a long word into AUDxLCH moves the audio data address into both locations. The ''x'' in the register names stands for the number of the audio channel where the output will occur. The channels are numbered 0, 1, 2, and 3.

These registers are *location* registers, as distinguished from *pointer* registers. You need to specify the contents of these registers only once; no resetting is necessary when you wish the audio channel to keep on repeating the same waveform. Each time the system retrieves the last audio word from the data area, it uses the contents of these location registers to again find the start of the data. Assuming the first word of data starts at location ''audiodata'' and you are using channel 0, here is how to set the location registers:

```
WHERE0DATA:
        LEA     CUSTOM,a0       ; Base chip address...
        LEA     AUDIODATA,a1
        MOVE.L  a1,AUD0LCH(a0)  ;Put address (32 bits)
                                ;  into location register.
```

The length of the data is the number of samples in your waveform divided by 2, or the number of words in the data set. Using the sample data set above, the length of the data is 16 words. You write this length into the audio data length register for this channel. The length register is called AUDxLEN, where ''x'' refers to the channel number. You set the length register AUD0LEN to 16 as shown below.

```
SETAUD0LENGTH:
        LEA     CUSTOM,a0       ; Base chip address
        MOVE.W  #16,AUD0LEN(a0) ; Store the length...
```

SELECTING THE VOLUME

The volume you set here is the overall volume of all the sound coming from the audio channel. The relative loudness of sounds, which will concern you when you combine notes, is determined by the amplitude of the wave form. There is a six-bit volume register for each audio channel. To control the volume of sound that will be output through the selected audio channel, you write the desired value into the register AUDxVOL, where ''x'' is replaced by the channel number. You can specify values from 64 to 0. These volume values correspond to decibel levels. At the end of this chapter is a table showing the decibel value for each of the 65 volume levels.

For a typical output at volume 64, with maximum data values of -128 to 127, the voltage output is between +.4 volts and -.4 volts. Some volume levels and the corresponding decibel values are shown in Table 5-2.

Table 5-2: Volume Values

Volume	Decibel Value	
64	0	(maximum volume)
48	-2.5	
32	-6.0	
16	-12.0	(12 db down from the volume at maximum level)

For any volume setting from 64 to 0, you write the value into bits 5-0 of AUD0VOL. For example:

```
SETAUD0VOLUME:
        LEA     CUSTOM,a0
        MOVE.W  #48,AUD0VOL(a0)
```

The decibels are shown as negative values from a maximum of 0 because this is the way a recording device, such as a tape recorder, shows the recording level. Usually, the recorder has a dial showing 0 as the optimum recording level. Anything less than the optimum value is shown as a minus quantity.

SELECTING THE DATA OUTPUT RATE

The pitch of the sound produced by the waveform depends upon its frequency. To tell the system what frequency to use, you need to specify the sampling period. The sampling period specifies the number of system clock ticks, or timing intervals, that should elapse between each sample (byte of audio data) fed to the digital-to-analog converter in the audio channel. There is a period register for each audio channel. The value of the period register is used for count-down purposes; each time the register counts down to 0, another sample is retrieved from the waveform data set for output. In units, the period value represents clock ticks per sample. The minimum period value you should use is 124 ticks per sample NTSC (123 PAL) and the maximum is 65535. These limits apply to both PAL and NTSC machines. For high-quality sound, there are other constraints on the sampling period (see the section called ''Producing High-quality Sound'').

NOTE

A low period value corresponds to a higher frequency sound and a high period value corresponds to a lower frequency sound.

Limitations on Selection of Sampling Period

The sampling period is limited by the number of DMA cycles allocated to an audio channel. Each audio channel is allocated one DMA slot per horizontal scan line of the screen display. An audio channel can retrieve two data samples during each horizontal scan line. The following calculation gives the maximum sampling rate in samples per second.

$$2 \; samples/line * 262.5 \; lines/frame * 59.94 \; frames/second = 31,469 \; samples/second$$

The figure of 31,469 is a theoretical maximum. In order to save buffers, the hardware is designed to handle 28,867 samples/second. The system timing interval is 279.365 nanoseconds, or .279365 microseconds. The maximum sampling rate of 28,867 samples per second is 34.642 microseconds per sample (1/28,867 = .000034642). The formula for calculating the sampling period is:

$$Period \; value = \frac{sample \; interval}{clock \; interval} = \frac{clock \; constant}{samples \; per \; second}$$

Thus, the minimum period value is derived by dividing 34.642 microseconds per sample by the number of microseconds per interval:

$$Minumum \; period = \frac{34.642 \; microseconds/sample}{0.279365 \; microseconds/interval} = 124 \; timing \; intervals/sample$$

or:

$$Minumum \; period = \frac{3,579,545 \; ticks/second}{28,867 \; samples/second} = 124 \; ticks/sample$$

Therefore, a value of at least 124 must be written into the period register to assure that the audio system DMA will be able to retrieve the next data sample. If the period value is below 124, by the time the cycle count has reached 0, the audio DMA will not have had enough time to retrieve the next data sample and the previous sample will be reused.

28,867 samples/second is also the maximum sampling rate for PAL systems. Thus, for PAL systems, a value of at least 123 ticks/sample must be written into the period register.

Clock Values			
	NTSC	PAL	units
Clock Constant	3579545	3546895	ticks per second
Clock Interval	0.279365	0.281937	microseconds per interval

NOTE

The Clock Interval is derived from the clock constant, where:

$$clock\ interval = \frac{1}{clock\ constant}$$

then scale the result to microseconds. In all of these calculations "ticks" and "timing intervals" refer to the same thing.

Specifying the Period Value

After you have selected the desired interval between data samples, you can calculate the value to place in the period register by using the period formula:

$$Period\ value = \frac{desired\ interval}{clock\ interval} = \frac{clock\ constant}{samples\ per\ second}$$

As an example, say you wanted to produce a 1 KHz sine wave, using a table of eight data samples (four data words) (see Figure 5-3).

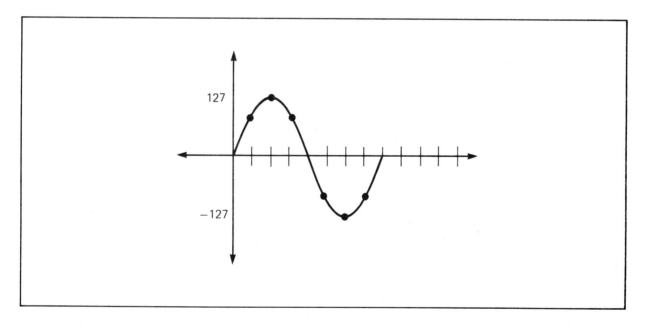

Figure 5-3: Example Sine Wave

```
Sampled Values:           0
                         90
                        127
                         90
                          0
                        -90
                       -127
                        -90
```

To output the series of eight samples at 1 KHz (1,000 cycles per second), each full cycle is output in 1/1000th of a second. Therefore, each individual value must be retrieved in 1/8th of that time. This translates to 1,000 microseconds per waveform or 125 microseconds per sample. To correctly produce this waveform, the period value should be:

$$Period\ value = \frac{125\ microseconds/sample}{0.279365\ microseconds/interval} = 447\ timing\ intervals/sample$$

To set the period register, you must write the period value into the register AUDxPER, where "x" is the number of the channel you are using. For example, the following instruction shows how to write a period value of 447 into the period register for channel 0.

```
SETAUD0PERIOD:
        LEA     CUSTOM,a0
        MOVE.W  #447,AUD0PER(a0)
```

To produce high-quality sound, avoiding aliasing distortion, you should observe the limitations on period values that are discussed in the section below called "Producing Quality Sound."

For the relationship between period and musical pitch, see the section at the end of the chapter, which contains a listing of the equal-tempered musical scale.

PLAYING THE WAVEFORM

After you have defined the audio data location, length, volume and period, you can play the waveform by starting the DMA for that audio channel. This starts the output of sound. Once started, the DMA continues until you specifically stop it. Thus, the waveform is played over and over again, producing the steady tone. The system uses the value in the location registers each time it replays the waveform.

For any audio DMA to occur (or any other DMA, for that matter), the DMAEN bit in DMACON must be set. When both DMAEN and AUDxEN are set, the DMA will start for channel x. All these bits and their meanings are shown in table 5-3.

Table 5-3: DMA and Audio Channel Enable Bits

DMACON Register

Bit	Name	Function
15	SET/CLR	When this bit is written as a 1, it sets any bit in DMACONW for which the corresponding bit position is also a 1, leaving all other bits alone.
9	DMAEN	Only while this bit is a 1 can *any* direct memory access occur.
3	AUD3EN	Audio channel 3 enable.
2	AUD2EN	Audio channel 2 enable.
1	AUD1EN	Audio channel 1 enable.
0	AUD0EN	Audio channel 0 enable.

For example, if you are using channel 0, then you write a 1 into bit 9 to enable DMA and a 1 into bit 0 to enable the audio channel, as shown below.

```
BEGINCHAN0:
        LEA     CUSTOM,a0
        MOVE.W  #(DMAF_SETCLR!DMAF_AUD0!DMAF_MASTER),DMACON(a0)
```

STOPPING THE AUDIO DMA

You can stop the channel by writing a 0 into the AUDxEN bit at any time. However, you cannot resume the output at the same point in the waveform by just writing a 1 in the bit again. Enabling an audio channel almost always starts the data output again from the top of the list of data pointed to by the location registers for that channel. If the channel is disabled for a very short time (less than two sampling periods) it may stay on and thus continue from where it left off.

The following example shows how to stop audio DMA for one channel.

```
STOPAUDCHAN0:
        LEA     CUSTOM,a0
        MOVE.W  #(DMAF_AUD0),DMACON(a0)
```

SUMMARY

These are the steps necessary to produce a steady tone:

1. Define the waveform.

2. Create the data set containing the pairs of data samples (data words). Normally, a data set contains the definition of one waveform.

3. Set the location registers:

    AUDxLCH (high three bits)

    AUDxLCL (low fifteen bits)

4. Set the length register, AUDxLEN, to the number of data words to be retrieved before starting at the address currently in AUDxLC.

5. Set the volume register, AUDxVOL.

6. Set the period register, AUDxPER

7. Start the audio DMA by writing a 1 into bit 9, DMAEN, along with a 1 in the SET/CLR bit and a 1 in the position of the AUDxEN bit of the channel or channels you want to start.

EXAMPLE

In this example, which gathers together all of the program segments from the preceding sections, a sine wave is played through channel 0. The example assumes exclusive access to the Audio hardware, and will not work directly in a multitasking environment.

```
MAIN:
        LEA     CUSTOM,a0       ; Custom chip base address
        LEA     SINEDATA(pc),a1 ;Address of data to
                                ;  audio location register 0
WHERE0DATA:
        MOVE.L  a1,AUD0LCH(a0)  ;The 68000 writes
                                ;  this as though it were
                                ;  a 32-bit register at the
                                ;  low-bits location
                                ;  (common to all locations
                                ;  and pointer registers
                                ;  in the system).
SETAUD0LENGTH:
        MOVE.W  #4,AUD0LEN(a0)  ;Set length in words
```

```
SETAUDOVOLUME:
        MOVE.W   #64,AUDOVOL(a0)  ;Use maximum volume
SETAUDOPERIOD:
        MOVE.W   #447,AUDOPER(a0)
BEGINCHANO:
        MOVE.W   #(DMAF_SETCLR!DMAF_AUDO!DMAF_MASTER),DMACON(a0)

        RTS                       ; Return to main code...

        DS.W     0       ;Be sure word-aligned
SINEDATA:
        DC.B     0, 90, 127, 90, 0, -90, -127, -90

        END
```

Producing Complex Sounds

In addition to simple tones, you can create more complex sounds, such as different musical notes joined into a one-voice melody, different notes played at the same time, or modulated sounds.

JOINING TONES

Tones are joined by writing the location and length registers, starting the audio output, and rewriting the registers in preparation for the next audio waveform that you wish to connect to the first one. This is made easy by the timing of the audio interrupts and the existence of back-up registers. The location and length registers are read by the DMA channel before audio output begins. The DMA channel then stores the values in back-up registers. Once the original registers have been read by the DMA channel, you can change their values without disturbing the operation you started with the original register contents. Thus, you can write the contents of these registers, start an audio output, and then rewrite the registers in preparation for the next waveform you want to connect to this one.

Interrupts occur immediately after the audio DMA channel has read the location and length registers and stored their values in the back-up registers. Once the interrupt has occurred, you can rewrite the registers with the location and length for the next waveform segment. This combination of back-up registers and interrupt timing lets you keep one step ahead of the audio DMA channel, allowing your sound output to be continuous and smooth.

If you do not rewrite the registers, the current waveform will be repeated. Each time the length counter reaches zero, both the location and length registers are reloaded with the same values to continue the audio output.

Example

This example details the system audio DMA action in a step-by-step fashion.

Suppose you wanted to join together a sine and a triangle waveform, end-to-end, for a special audio effect, alternating between them. The following sequence shows the action of your program as well as its interaction with the audio DMA system. The example assumes that the period, volume, and length of the data set remains the same for the sine wave and the triangle wave.

Interrupt Program

If (wave = triangle)
       write AUD0LCL with address of sine wave data.

Else if (wave = sine)
       write AUD0LCL with address of triangle wave data.

Main Program

1. Set up volume, period, and length.

2. Write AUD0LCL with address of sine wave data.

3. Start DMA.

4. Continue with something else.

System Response

As soon as DMA starts,

a.   Copy to ''back-up'' length register from AUD0LEN.

b.   Copy to ''back-up'' location register from AUD0LCL (will be used as a pointer showing current data word to fetch).

c.   Create an interrupt for the 68000 saying that it has completed retrieving working copies of length and location registers.

d.   Start retrieving audio data each allocated DMA time slot.

PLAYING MULTIPLE TONES AT THE SAME TIME

You can play multiple tones either by using several channels independently or by summing the samples in several data sets, playing the summed data sets through a single channel.

Since all four audio channels are independently programmable, each channel has its own data set; thus a different tone or musical note can be played on each channel.

MODULATING SOUND

To provide more complex audio effects, you can use one audio channel to modulate another. This increases the range and type of effects that can be produced. You can modulate a channel's frequency or amplitude, or do both types of modulation on a channel at the same time.

Amplitude modulation affects the volume of the waveform. It is often used to produce vibrato or tremolo effects. Frequency modulation affects the period of the waveform. Although the basic waveform itself remains the same, the pitch is increased or decreased by frequency modulation.

The system uses one channel to modulate another when you attach two channels. The attach bits in the ADKCON register control how the data from an audio channel is interpreted (see the table below). Normally, each channel produces sound when it is enabled. If the ''attach'' bit for an audio channel is set, that channel ceases to produce sound and its data is used to modulate the sound of the next higher-numbered channel. When a channel is used as a modulator, the words in its data set are no longer treated as two individual bytes. Instead, they are used as ''modulator'' words. The data words from the *modulator* channel are written into the corresponding registers of the *modulated* channel each time the period register of the modulator channel times out.

To modulate only the amplitude of the audio output, you must attach a channel as a volume modulator. Define the modulator channel's data set as a series of words, each containing volume information in the following format:

Bits	Function
15 - 7	Not used
6 - 0	Volume information, V6 - V0

To modulate only the frequency, you must attach a channel as a period modulator. Define the modulator channel's data set as a series of words, each containing period information in the following format:

Bits	Function
15 - 0	Period information, P15 - P0

If you want to modulate both period and volume on the same channel, you need to attach the channel as both a period and volume modulator. For instance, if channel 0 is used to modulate both the period and frequency of channel 1, you set two attach bits — bit 0 to modulate the volume and bit 4 to modulate the period. When period and volume are both modulated, words in the modulator channel's data set are defined alternately as volume and period information.

The sample set of data in Table 5-4 shows the differences in interpretation of data when a channel is used directly for audio, when it is attached as volume modulator, when it is attached as a period modulator, and when it is attached as a modulator of both volume and period.

Table 5-4: Data Interpretation in Attach Mode

Data Words	Independent (not Modulating)	Modulating Both Period and Volume	Modulating Period Only	Modulating Volume Only
Word 1	I data I data I	I volume for other channel I	I period I	I volume I
Word 2	I data I data I	I period for other channel I	I period I	I volume I
Word 3	I data I data I	I volume for other channel I	I period I	I volume I
Word 4	I data I data I	I period for other channel I	I period I	I volume I

The lengths of the data sets of the modulator and the modulated channels are completely independent.

Channels are attached by the system in a predetermined order, as shown in Table 5-5. To attach a channel as a modulator, you set its attach bit to 1. If you set either the volume or period attach bits for a channel, that channel's audio output will be disabled; the channel will be attached to the next higher channel, as shown in Table 5-5. Because an attached channel always modulates the next higher numbered channel, you cannot attach channel 3. Writing a 1 into channel 3's modulate bits only disables its audio output.

Table 5-5: Channel Attachment for Modulation

ADKCON Register

Bit	Name	Function
7	ATPER3	Use audio channel 3 to modulate nothing (disables audio output of channel 3)
6	ATPER2	Use audio channel 2 to modulate *period* of channel 3
5	ATPER1	Use audio channel 1 to modulate *period* of channel 2
4	ATPER0	Use audio channel 0 to modulate *period* of channel 1
3	ATVOL3	Use audio channel 3 to modulate nothing (disables audio output of channel 3)
2	ATVOL2	Use audio channel 2 to modulate *volume* of channel 3
1	ATVOL1	Use audio channel 1 to modulate *volume* of channel 2
0	ATVOL0	Use audio channel 0 to modulate *volume* of channel 1

Producing High-quality Sound

When trying to create high-quality sound, you need to consider the following factors:

- Waveform transitions.

- Sampling rate.

- Efficiency.

- Noise reduction.

- Avoidance of aliasing distortion.

- Limitations of the low pass filter.

MAKING WAVEFORM TRANSITIONS

To avoid unpleasant sounds when you change from one waveform to another, you need to make the transitions smooth. You can avoid "clicks" by making sure the waveforms start and end at approximately the same value. You can avoid "pops" by starting a waveform only at a zero-crossing point. You can avoid "thumps" by arranging the average amplitude of each wave to be about the same value. The average amplitude is the sum of the bytes in the waveform divided by the number of bytes in the waveform.

SAMPLING RATE

If you need high precision in your frequency output, you may find that the frequency you wish to produce is somewhere between two available sampling rates, but not close enough to either rate for your requirements. In those cases, you may have to adjust the length of the audio data table in addition to altering the sampling rate.

For higher frequencies, you may also need to use audio data tables that contain more than one full cycle of the audio waveform to reproduce the desired frequency more accurately, as illustrated in Figure 5-4.

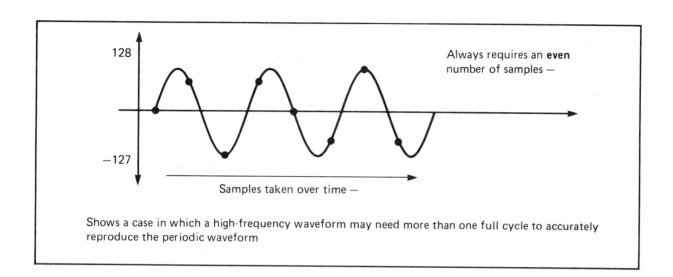

128

−127

Always requires an **even**
number of samples —

Samples taken over time —

Shows a case in which a high-frequency waveform may need more than one full cycle to accurately
reproduce the periodic waveform

Figure 5-4: Waveform with Multiple Cycles

EFFICIENCY

A certain amount of overhead is involved in the handling of audio DMA. If you are trying to produce a smooth continuous audio synthesis, you should try to avoid as much of the system control overhead as possible. Basically, the larger the audio buffer you provide to the system, the less often it will need to interrupt to reset the pointers to the top of the next buffer and, coincidentally, the lower the amount of system interaction that will be required. If there is only one waveform buffer, the hardware automatically resets the pointers, so no software overhead is used for resetting them.

The "Joining Tones" section illustrated how you could join "ends" of tones together by responding to interrupts and changing the values of the location registers to splice tones together. If your system is heavily loaded, it is possible that the response to the interrupt might not happen in time to assure a smooth audio transition. Therefore, it is advisable to utilize the longest possible audio table where a smooth output is required. This takes advantage of the audio DMA capability as well as minimizing the number of interrupts to which the 68000 must respond.

NOISE REDUCTION

To reduce noise levels and produce an accurate sound, try to use the full range of -128 to 127 when you represent a waveform. This reduces how much noise (quantization error) will be added to the signal by using more bits of precision. Quantization noise is caused by the introduction of round-off error. If you are trying to reproduce a signal, such as a sine wave, you can represent the amplitude of each sample with only so many digits of accuracy. The difference between the real number and your approximation is round-off error, or noise.

By doubling the amplitude, you create half as much noise because the size of the steps of the wave form stays the same and is therefore a smaller fraction of the amplitude.

In other words, if you try to represent a waveform using, for example, a range of only +3 to -3, the size of the error in the output would be considerably larger than if you use a range of +127 to -128 to represent the same signal. Proportionally, the digital value used to represent the waveform amplitude will have a lower error. As you increase the number of possible sample levels, you decrease the relative size of each step and, therefore, decrease the size of the error.

To produce quiet sounds, continue to define the waveform using the full range, but adjust the volume. This maintains the same level of accuracy (signal-to-noise ratio) for quiet sounds as for loud sounds.

ALIASING DISTORTION

When you use sampling to produce a waveform, a side effect is caused when the sampling rate "beats" or combines with the frequency you wish to produce. This produces two additional frequencies, one at the sampling rate plus the desired frequency and the other at the sampling rate minus the desired frequency. This phenomenon is called aliasing distortion.

Aliasing distortion is eliminated when the sampling rate exceeds the output frequency by at least 7 KHz. This puts the beat frequency outside the range of the low-pass filter, cutting off the undesirable frequencies. Figure 5-5 shows a frequency domain plot of the anti-aliasing low-pass filter used in the system.

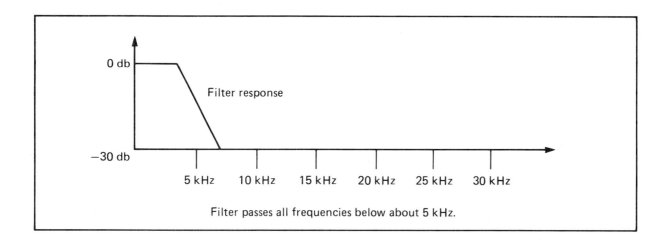

Figure 5-5: Frequency Domain Plot of Low-Pass Filter

Figure 5-6 shows that it is permissible to use a 12 KHz sampling rate to produce a 4 KHz waveform. Both of the beat frequencies are outside the range of the filter, as shown in these calculations:

$$12 + 4 = 16 \ KHz$$

$$12 - 4 = 8 \ KHz$$

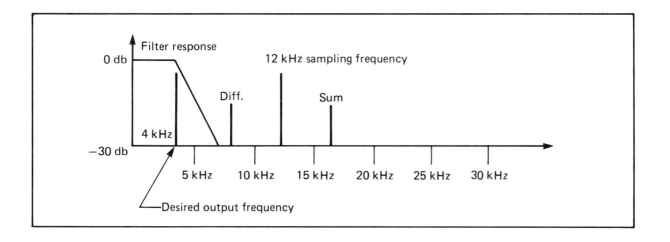

Figure 5-6: Noise-free Output (No Aliasing Distortion)

You can see in Figure 5-7 that is unacceptable to use a 10 KHz sampling rate to produce a 4 KHz waveform. One of the beat frequencies (10 - 4) is within the range of the filter, allowing some of that undesirable frequency to show up in the audio output.

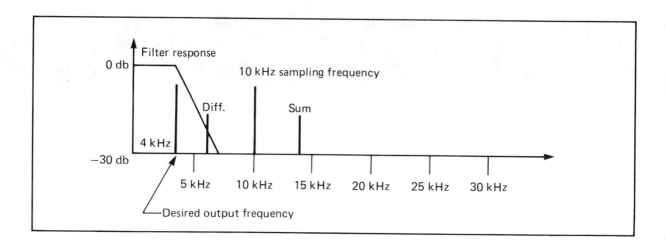

Figure 5-7: Some Aliasing Distortion

All of this gives rise to the following equation, showing that the sampling frequency must exceed the output frequency by at least 7 KHz, so that the beat frequency will be above the cutoff range of the anti-aliasing filter:

Minimum sampling rate = highest frequency component + 7 KHz

The frequency component of the equation is stated as "highest frequency component" because you may be producing a complex waveform with multiple frequency elements, rather than a pure sine wave.

LOW-PASS FILTER

The system includes a low-pass filter that eliminates aliasing distortion as described above. This filter becomes active around 4 KHz and gradually begins to attenuate (cut off) the signal. Generally, you cannot clearly hear frequencies higher than 7 KHz. Therefore, you get the most complete frequency response in the frequency range of 0 - 7 KHz. If you are making frequencies from 0 to 7 KHz, you should select a sampling rate no less than 14 KHz, which corresponds to a sampling period in the range 124 to 256.

At a sampling period around 320, you begin to lose the higher frequency values between 0 KHz and 7 KHz, as shown in Table 5-6.

Table 5-6: Sampling Rate and Frequency Relationship

	Sampling Period	Sampling Rate (KHz)	Maximum Output Frequency (KHz)
Maximum sampling rate	124	29	7
Minimum sampling rate for 7 KHz output	256	14	7
Sampling rate too low for 7 KHz output	320	11	4

In A2000s with 2 layer motherboards and later A500 models there is a control bit that allows the audio output to bypass the low pass filter. This control bit is the same output bit of the 8520 CIA that controls the brightness of the red ''power'' LED. Bypassing the filter allows for improved sound in some applications, but an external filter with an appropriate cutoff frequency may be required.

Using Direct (Non-DMA) Audio Output

It is possible to create sound by writing audio data one word at a time to the audio output addresses, instead of setting up a list of audio data in memory. This method of controlling the output is more processor-intensive and is therefore not recommended.

To use direct audio output, do not enable the DMA for the audio channel you wish to use; this changes the timing of the interrupts. The normal interrupt occurs after a data address has been read; in direct audio output, the interrupt occurs after one data word has been output.

Unlike in the DMA-controlled automatic data output, in direct audio output, if you do not write a new set of data to the output addresses before two sampling intervals have elapsed, the audio output will cease changing. The last value remains as an output of the digital-to-analog converter.

The volume and period registers are set as usual.

The Equal-tempered Musical Scale

Table 5-7 gives a close approximation of the equal-tempered scale over one octave when the sample size is 16 bytes. The "Period" column gives the period count you enter into the period register. The length register AUDxLEN should be set to 8 (16 bytes = 8 words). The sample should represent one cycle of the waveform.

Table 5-7: Equal-tempered Octave for a 16 Byte Sample

NTSC Period	PAL Period	Note	Ideal Frequency	Actual NTSC Frequency	Actual PAL Frequency
254	252	A	880.0	880.8	879.7
240	238	A#	932.3	932.2	931.4
226	224	B	987.8	989.9	989.6
214	212	C	1046.5	1045.4	1045.7
202	200	C#	1108.7	1107.5	1108.4
190	189	D	1174.7	1177.5	1172.9
180	178	D#	1244.5	1242.9	1245.4
170	168	E	1318.5	1316.0	1319.5
160	159	F	1396.9	1398.3	1394.2
151	150	F#	1480.0	1481.6	1477.9
143	141	G	1568.0	1564.5	1572.2
135	133	G#	1661.2	1657.2	1666.8

The table above shows the period values to use with a 16 byte sample to make tones in the second octave above middle C. To generate the tones in the lower octaves, there are two methods you can use, doubling the period value or doubling the sample size.

When you double the period, the time between each sample is doubled so the sample takes twice as long to play. This means the frequency of the tone generated is cut in half which gives you the next lowest octave. Thus, if you play a C with a period value of 214, then playing the same sample with a period value of 428 will play a C in the next lower octave.

Likewise, when you double the sample size, it will take twice as long to play back the whole sample and the frequency of the tone generated will be in the next lowest octave. Thus, if you have an 8 byte sample and a 16 byte sample of the same waveform played at the same speed, the 16 byte sample will be an octave lower.

A sample for an equal-tempered scale typically represents one full cycle of a note. To avoid aliasing distortion with these samples you should use period values in the range 124-256 only. Periods from 124-256 correspond to playback rates in the range 14-28K samples per second which makes the most effective use of the Amiga's 7 kHz cut-off filter to prevent noise. To stay within this range you will need a different sample for each octave.

If you cannot use a different sample for each octave, then you will have to adjust the period value over its full range 124-65536. This is easier for the programmer but can produce undesirable high-frequency noise in the resulting tone. Read the section called "Aliasing Distortion" for more about this.

The values in Table 5-7 were generated using the formula shown below. To calculate the tone generated with a given sample size and period use:

$$Frequency = \frac{Clock\ Constant}{Sample\ Bytes*Period} = \frac{3579545}{16*Period} = 880.8Hz$$

The clock constant in an NTSC system is 3579545 ticks per second. In a PAL system, the clock constant is 3546895 ticks per second. Sample bytes is the number of bytes in one cycle of the waveform sample. (The clock constant is derived from dividing the system clock value by 2. The value will vary when using an external system clock, such as a genlock.)

Using the formula above you can generate the values needed for the even-tempered scale for any arbitrary sample. Table 5-8 gives a close approximation of a five octave even tempered-scale using five samples. The values were derived using the formula above. Notice that in each octave period values are the same but the sample size is halved. The samples listed represent a simple triangular wave form.

Table 5-8: Five Octave Even-tempered Scale

NTSC Period	PAL Period	Note	Ideal Frequency	Actual NTSC Frequency	Actual PAL Frequency
254	252	A	55.00	55.05	54.98
240	238	A#	58.27	58.26	58.21
226	224	B	61.73	61.87	61.85
214	212	C	65.40	65.34	65.35
202	200	C#	69.29	69.22	69.27
190	189	D	73.41	73.59	73.30
180	178	D#	77.78	77.68	77.83
170	168	E	82.40	82.25	82.47
160	159	F	87.30	87.39	87.13
151	150	F#	92.49	92.60	92.36
143	141	G	98.00	97.78	98.26
135	133	G#	103.82	103.57	104.17

Sample size = 256 bytes, AUDxLEN = 128

NTSC Period	PAL Period	Note	Ideal Frequency	Actual NTSC Frequency	Actual PAL Frequency
254	252	A	110.00	110.10	109.96
240	238	A#	116.54	116.52	116.43
226	224	B	123.47	123.74	123.70
214	212	C	130.81	130.68	130.71
202	200	C#	138.59	138.44	138.55
190	189	D	146.83	147.18	146.61
180	178	D#	155.56	155.36	155.67
170	168	E	164.81	164.50	164.94
160	159	F	174.61	174.78	174.27
151	150	F#	184.99	185.20	184.73
143	141	G	196.00	195.56	196.52
135	133	G#	207.65	207.15	208.35

Sample size = 128 bytes, AUDxLEN = 64

NTSC Period	PAL Period	Note	Ideal Frequency	Actual NTSC Frequency	Actual PAL Frequency
254	252	A	220.00	220.20	219.92
240	238	A#	233.08	233.04	232.86
226	224	B	246.94	247.48	247.41
214	212	C	261.63	261.36	261.42
202	200	C#	277.18	276.88	277.10
190	189	D	293.66	294.37	293.23
180	178	D#	311.13	310.72	311.35
170	168	E	329.63	329.00	329.88
160	159	F	349.23	349.56	348.55
151	150	F#	369.99	370.40	369.47
143	141	G	392.00	391.12	393.05
135	133	G#	415.30	414.30	416.70

Sample size = 64 bytes, AUDxLEN = 32

NTSC Period	PAL Period	Note	Ideal Frequency	Actual NTSC Frequency	Actual PAL Frequency
254	252	A	440.0	440.4	439.8
240	238	A#	466.16	466.09	465.72
226	224	B	493.88	494.96	494.82
214	212	C	523.25	522.71	522.83
202	200	C#	554.37	553.77	554.20
190	189	D	587.33	588.74	586.46
180	178	D#	622.25	621.45	622.70
170	168	E	659.26	658.00	659.76
160	159	F	698.46	699.13	697.11
151	150	F#	739.99	740.80	738.94
143	141	G	783.99	782.24	786.10
135	133	G#	830.61	828.60	833.39

Sample size = 32 bytes, AUDxLEN = 16

NTSC Period	PAL Period	Note	Ideal Frequency	Actual NTSC Frequency	Actual PAL Frequency
254	252	A	880.0	880.8	879.7
240	238	A#	932.3	932.2	931.4
226	224	B	987.8	989.9	989.6
214	212	C	1046.5	1045.4	1045.7
202	200	C#	1108.7	1107.5	1108.4
190	189	D	1174.7	1177.5	1172.9
180	178	D#	1244.5	1242.9	1245.4
170	168	E	1318.5	1316.0	1319.5
160	159	F	1396.9	1398.3	1394.2
151	150	F#	1480.0	1481.6	1477.9
143	141	G	1568.0	1564.5	1572.2
135	133	G#	661.2	1657.2	1666.8

Sample size = 16 bytes, AUDxLEN = 8

256 Byte Sample

0	2	4	6	8	10	12	14	16	18	20	22	24	26	28	30
32	34	36	38	40	42	44	46	48	50	52	54	56	58	60	62
64	66	68	70	72	74	76	78	80	82	84	86	88	90	92	94
96	98	100	102	104	106	108	110	112	114	116	118	120	122	124	126
128	126	124	122	120	118	116	114	112	110	108	106	104	102	100	98
96	94	92	90	88	86	84	82	80	78	76	74	72	70	68	66
64	62	60	58	56	54	52	50	48	46	44	42	40	38	36	34
32	30	28	26	24	22	20	18	16	14	12	10	8	6	4	2
0	-2	-4	-6	-8	-10	-12	-14	-16	-18	-20	-22	-24	-26	-28	-30
-32	-34	-36	-38	-40	-42	-44	-46	-48	-50	-52	-54	-56	-58	-60	-62
-64	-66	-68	-70	-72	-74	-76	-78	-80	-82	-84	-86	-88	-90	-92	-94
-96	-98	-100	-102	-104	-106	-108	-110	-112	-114	-116	-118	-120	-122	-124	-126
-127	-126	-124	-122	-120	-118	-116	-114	-112	-110	-108	-106	-104	-102	-100	-98
-96	-94	-92	-90	-88	-86	-84	-82	-80	-78	-76	-74	-72	-70	-68	-66
-64	-62	-60	-58	-56	-54	-52	-50	-48	-46	-44	-42	-40	-38	-36	-34
-32	-30	-28	-26	-24	-22	-20	-18	-16	-14	-12	-10	-8	-6	-4	-2

128 Byte Sample

0	4	8	12	16	20	24	28	32	36	40	44	48	52	56	60
64	68	72	76	80	84	88	92	96	100	104	108	112	116	120	124
128	124	120	116	112	108	104	100	96	92	88	84	80	76	72	68
64	60	56	52	48	44	40	36	32	28	24	20	16	12	8	4
0	4	8	12	16	20	24	28	32	36	40	44	48	52	56	60
64	68	72	76	80	84	88	92	96	100	104	108	112	116	120	124
-127	-124	-120	-116	-112	-108	-104	-100	-96	-92	-88	-84	-80	-76	-72	-68
-64	-60	-56	-52	-48	-44	-40	-36	-32	-28	-24	-20	-16	-12	-8	-4

64 Byte Sample

0	8	16	24	32	40	48	56	64	72	80	88	96	104	112	120
128	120	112	104	96	88	80	72	64	56	48	40	32	24	16	8
0	-8	-16	-24	-32	-40	-48	-56	-64	-72	-80	-88	-96	-104	-112	-120
-127	-120	-112	-104	-96	-88	-80	-72	-64	-56	-48	-40	-32	-24	-16	-8

32 Byte Sample

0	16	32	48	64	80	96	112	128	112	96	80	64	48	32	16
0	-16	-32	-48	-64	-80	-96	-112	-127	-112	-96	-80	-64	-48	-32	-16

16 Byte Sample

0	32	64	96	128	96	64	32	0	-32	-64	-96	-127	-96	-64	-32

Decibel Values for Volume Ranges

Table 5-9 provides the corresponding decibel values for the volume ranges of the Amiga system.

Table 5-9: Decibel Values and Volume Ranges

Volume	Decibel Value	Volume	Decibel Value
64	0.0	32	-6.0
63	-0.1	31	-6.3
62	-0.3	30	-6.6
61	-0.4	29	-6.9
60	-0.6	28	-7.2
59	-0.7	27	-7.5
58	-0.9	26	-7.8
57	-1.0	25	-8.2
56	-1.2	24	-8.5
55	-1.3	23	-8.9
54	-1.5	22	-9.3
53	-1.6	21	-9.7
52	-1.8	20	-10.1
51	-2.0	19	-10.5
50	-2.1	18	-11.0
49	-2.3	17	-11.5
48	-2.5	16	-12.0
47	-2.7	15	-12.6
46	-2.9	14	-13.2
45	-3.1	13	-13.8
44	-3.3	12	-14.5
43	-3.5	11	-15.3
42	-3.7	10	-16.1
41	-3.9	9	-17.0
40	-4.1	8	-18.1
39	-4.3	7	-19.2
38	-4.5	6	-20.6
37	-4.8	5	-22.1
36	-5.0	4	-24.1
35	-5.2	3	-26.6
34	-5.5	2	-30.1
33	-5.8	1	-36.1
		0	Minus infinity

The Audio State Machine

For an explanation of the various states, refer to Figure 5-8. There is one audio state machine for each channel. The machine has eight states and is clocked at the clock constant rate (3.58 MHz NTSC). Three of the states are basically unused and just transfer back to the idle (000) state. One of the paths out of the idle state is designed for interrupt-driven operation (processor provides the data), and the other path is designed for DMA-driven operation (the "Agnus" special chip provides the data).

In interrupt-driven operation, transfer to the main loop (states 010 and 011) occurs immediately after data is written by the processor. In the 010 state the upper byte is output, and in the 011 state the lower byte is output. Transitions such as 010→011→010 occur whenever the period counter counts down to one. The period counter is reloaded at these transitions. As long as the interrupt is cleared by the processor in time, the machine remains in the main loop. Otherwise, it enters the idle state. Interrupts are generated on every word transition (011→010).

In DMA-driven operation, transition to the 001 state occurs and DMA requests are sent to Agnus as soon as DMA is turned on. Because of pipelining in Agnus, the first data word must be thrown away. State 101 is entered as soon as this word arrives; a request for the next data word has already gone out. When the data arrives, state 010 is entered and the main loop continues until the DMA is turned off. The length counter counts down once with each word that comes in. When it finishes, a DMA restart request goes to Agnus along with the regular DMA request. This tells Agnus to reset the pointer to the beginning of the table of data. Also, the length counter is reloaded and an interrupt request goes out soon after the length counter finishes (counts to one). The request goes out just as the last word of the waveform starts its output.

DMA requests and restart requests are transferred to Agnus once each horizontal line, and the data comes back about 14 clock cycles later (the duration of a clock cycle is 280 ns).

In attach mode, things run a little differently. In attach volume, requests occur as they do in normal operation (on the 011→010 transition). In attach period, a set of requests occurs on the 010→011 transition. When both attach period and attach volume are high, requests occur on both transitions.

If the sampling rate is set much higher than the normal maximum sampling rate (approximately 29 KHz), the two samples in the buffer register will be repeated. If the filter on the Amiga is bypassed and the volume is set to the maximum ($40), this feature can be used to make modulated carriers up to 1.79 MHz. The modulation is placed in the memory map, with plus values in the even bytes and minus values in the odd bytes.

The symbols used in the state diagram are explained in the following list. Upper-case names indicate external signals; lower-case names indicate local signals.

AUDxON	DMA on ''x'' indicates channel number (signal from DMACON).
AUDxIP	Audio interrupt pending (input to channel from interrupt circuitry).
AUDxIR	Audio interrupt request (output from channel to interrupt circuitry)
intreq1	Interrupt request that combines with intreq2 to form AUDxIR..
intreq2	Prepare for interrupt request. Request comes out after the next 011→010 transition in normal operation.
AUDxDAT	Audio data load signal. Loads 16 bits of data to audio channel.
AUDxDR	Audio DMA request to Agnus for one word of data.
AUDxDSR	Audio DMA request to Agnus to reset pointer to start of block.
dmasen	Restart request enable.
percntrld	Reload period counter from back-up latch typically written by processor with AUDxPER (can also be written by attach mode).
percount	Count period counter down one latch.
perfin	Period counter finished (value = 1).
lencntrld	Reload length counter from back-up latch.
lencount	Count length counter down one notch.
lenfin	Length counter finished (value = 1).
volcntrld	Reload volume counter from back-up latch.
pbufld1	Load output buffer from holding latch written to by AUDxDAT.
pbufld2	Like pbufld1, but only during 010→011 with attach period.
AUDxAV	Attach volume. Send data to volume latch of next channel instead of to D→A converter.
AUDxAP	Attach period. Send data to period latch of next channel instead of to the D→A converter.
penhi	Enable the high 8 bits of data to go to the D→A converter.

napnav   /AUDxAV * /AUDxAP + AUDxAV—no attach stuff or else attach
                    volume. Condition for normal DMA and interrupt requests.

sq2,1,0   The name of the state flip-flops, MSB to LSB.

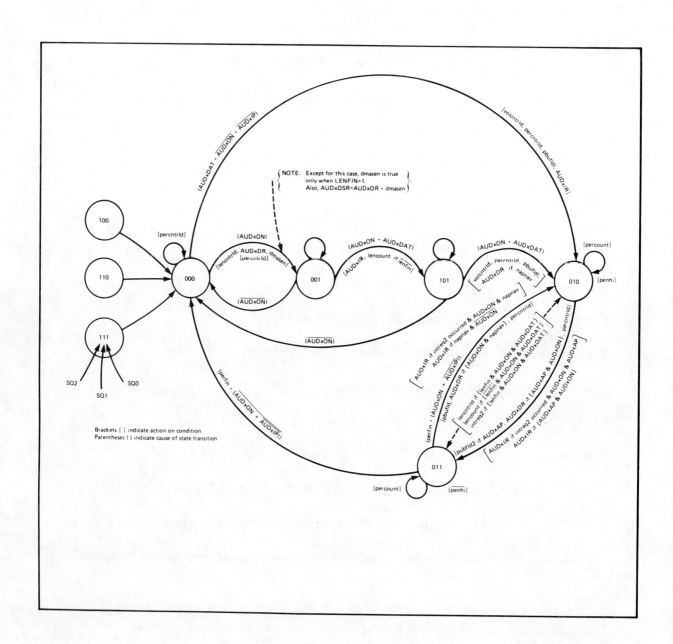

Figure 5-8: Audio State Diagram

Chapter 6

BLITTER HARDWARE

Introduction

The blitter is one of the two coprocessors in the Amiga. Part of the Agnus chip, it is used to copy rectangular blocks of memory around and to draw lines. When copying memory, it is approximately twice as fast as the 68000, able to move almost four megabytes per second. It can draw lines at almost a million pixels per second.

In block move mode, the blitter can perform any logical operation on up to three source areas, it can shift up to two of the source areas by one to fifteen bits, it can fill outlined shapes, and it can mask the first and last words of each raster row. In line mode, any pattern can be imposed on a line, or the line can be drawn such that only one pixel per horizontal line is set.

The blitter can only access CHIP memory — that portion of memory accessible by the display hardware. Attempting to use the blitter to read or write FAST or other non-CHIP memory may result in destruction of the contents of CHIP memory.

A "blit" is a single operation of the blitter — perhaps the drawing of a line or movement of a block of memory. A blit is performed by initializing the blitter registers with appropriate values and then starting the blitter by writing the BLTSIZE register. As the blitter is an asynchronous coprocessor, the 68000 continues to run as the blit is executing.

Memory Layout

The blitter is a word blitter, not a bit blitter. All data fetched, modified, and written are in full 16-bit words. Through careful programming, the blitter can do many "bit" type operations.

The blitter is particularly well suited to graphics operations. As an example, a 320 by 200 screen set up to display 16 colors is organized as four bitplanes of 8,000 bytes each. Each bitplane consists of 200 rows of 40 bytes or 20 16-bit words. (From here on, a "word" will mean a 16-bit word.)

DMA Channels

The blitter has four DMA channels — three source channels, labeled A, B, and C, and one destination channel, called D. Each of these channels has separate address pointer, modulo and data registers and an enable bit. Two have shift registers, and one has a first and last word mask register. All four share a single blit size register.

The address pointer registers are each composed of two words, named BLTxPTH and BLTxPTL. (Here and later, in referring to a register, any "x" in the name should be replaced by the channel label, A, B, C, or D.) The two words of each register are adjacent in the 68000 address space, with the high address word first, so they can both be written with one 32-bit write from the processor. The pointer registers should be written with an address in bytes. Because the blitter works only on words, the least significant bit of the address is ignored. Because only CHIP memory is accessible, some of the most significant bits will be ignored as well. On machines with 512 KB of CHIP memory, the most significant 13 bits are ignored. Future machines will have more CHIP memory and fewer bits will be ignored. A valid, even, CHIP memory address should always be written to these registers.

NOTE

Be sure to write zeros to all unused bits in the custom chip registers. These bits may be used by later versions of the custom chips. Writing non-zero values to these bits may cause unexpected results on future machines.

Each of the DMA channels can be independently enabled or disabled. The enable bits are bits SRCA, SRCB, SRCC, and DEST in control register zero (BLTCON0).

When disabled, no memory cycles will be executed for that channel and, for a source channel, the constant value stored in the data register of that channel will be used for each blitter cycle. For this purpose, each of the three source channels have preloadable data registers, called BLTxDAT.

Images in memory are usually stored in a linear fashion; each word of data on a line is located at an address that is one greater than the word on its left. i.e. Each line is a "plus one" continuation of the previous line. (See Figure 6-1.)

20	21	22	23	24	24	26
27	28	29	30	31	32	33
34	35	36	37	38	39	40
41	42	43	44	45	46	47
48	49	50	51	52	53	54
55	56	57	58	59	60	61

Figure 6-1: How Images are Stored in Memory

The map in Figure 6-1 represents a single bit-plane (one bit of color) of an image at word addresses 20 through 61. Each of these addresses accesses one word (16 pixels) of a single bit-plane. If this image required sixteen colors, four bit-planes like this would be required in memory, and four copy (move) operations would be required to completely move the image.

The blitter is very efficient at copying such blocks because it needs to be told only the starting address (20), the destination address, and the size of the block (height = 6, width = 7). It will then automatically move the data, one word at a time, whenever the data bus is available. When the transfer is complete, the blitter will signal the processor with a flag and an interrupt.

NOTE

This copy (move) operation operates on memory and may or may not change the memory currently being used for display.

All data copy blits are performed as rectangles of words, with a given width and height. All four DMA channels use a single blit size register, called BLTSIZE, used for both the width and height. The width can take a value of from 1 to 64 words (16 to 1024 bits). The height can run from 1 to 1024 rows. The width is stored in the least significant six bits of the BLTSIZE register. If a value of zero is stored, a width count of 64 words is used. This is the only parameter in the blitter that is given in words. The height is stored in the upper ten bits of the BLTSIZE register, with zero representing a height of 1024 rows. Thus, the largest blit possible with the current Amiga blitter is 1024 by 1024 pixels. However, shifting and masking operations may require an extra word be fetched for each raster scan line, making the maximum practical horizontal width 1008 pixels.

NOTE

To emphasize the above paragraph: Blit width is in *words* with a zero representing 64 words. Blit height is in *lines* with a zero representing 1024 lines.

The blitter also has facilities, called modulos, for accessing images smaller than the entire bit-plane. Each of the four DMA channels has a 16-bit modulo register called BLTxMOD. As each word is fetched (or written) for an enabled channel, the address pointer register is incremented by two (bytes, or one word.) After each row of the blit is completed, the signed 16-bit modulo value for that DMA channel is added to the address pointer. (A row is defined by the width stored in BLTSIZE.)

NOTE

The modulo values are in bytes, not words. Since the blitter can only operate on words, the least significant bit is ignored. The value is sign-extended to the full width of the address pointer registers. Negative modulos can be useful in a variety of ways, such as repeating a row by setting the modulo to the negative of the width of the bit-plane.

As an example, suppose we want to operate on a section of a full 320 by 200 pixel bitmap that started at row 13, byte 12 (where both are numbered from zero) and the section is 10 bytes wide. We would initialize the pointer register to the address of the bitplane plus 40 bytes per row times 13 rows, plus 12 bytes to get to the correct horizontal position. We would set the width to 5 words (10 bytes). At the end of each row, we would want to skip over 30 bytes to get to the beginning of the next row, so we would use a modulo value of 30. In general, the width (in words) times two plus the modulo value (in bytes) should equal the full width, in bytes, of the bit-plane containing the image.

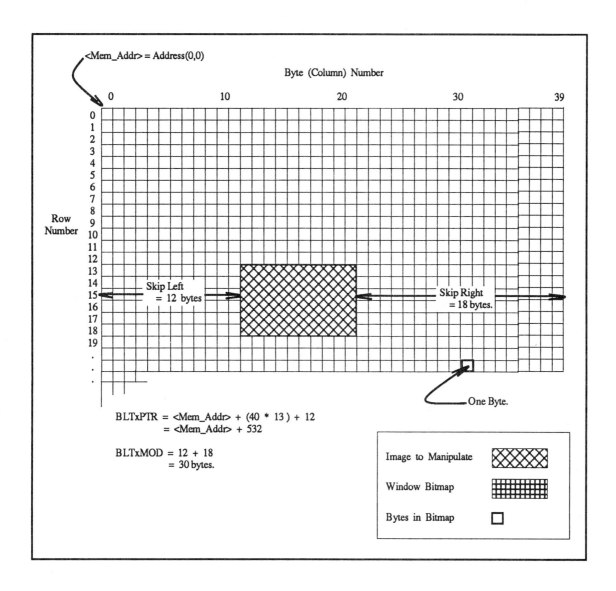

Figure 6-2: BLTxPTR and BLTxMOD calculations

NOTE

The blitter can be used to process linear rather than rectangular regions by setting the horizontal or vertical count in BLTSIZE to 1.

Because each DMA channel has its own modulo register, data can be moved among bitplanes of different widths. This is most useful when moving small images into larger screen bitplanes.

Function Generator

The blitter can combine the data from the three source DMA channels in up to 256 different ways to generate the values stored by the destination DMA channel. These sources might be one bit-plane from each of three separate graphics images. While each of these sources is a rectangular region composed of many points, the same logic operation will be performed on each point throughout the rectangular region. Thus, for purposes of defining the blitter logic operation it is only necessary to consider what happens for all of the possible combinations of one bit from each of the three sources.

There are eight possible combinations of values of the three bits, for each of which we need to specify the corresponding destination bit as a zero or one. This can be visualized with a standard truth table, as shown below. We have listed the three source channels, and the possible values for a single bit from each one.

A	B	C	D	BLTCON0 position	Minterm
0	0	0	?	0	$\overline{A}\,\overline{B}\,\overline{C}$
0	0	1	?	1	$\overline{A}\,\overline{B}\,C$
0	1	0	?	2	$\overline{A}\,B\,\overline{C}$
0	1	1	?	3	$\overline{A}\,B\,C$
1	0	0	?	4	$A\,\overline{B}\,\overline{C}$
1	0	1	?	5	$A\,\overline{B}\,C$
1	1	0	?	6	$A\,B\,\overline{C}$
1	1	1	?	7	$A\,B\,C$

This information is collected in a standard format, the LF control byte in the BLTCON0 register. This byte programs the blitter to perform one of the 256 possible logic operations on three sources for a given blit.

To calculate the LF control byte in BLTCON0, fill in the truth table with desired values for D, and read the function value from the bottom of the table up.

For example, if we wanted to set all bits in the destination where the corresponding A source bit is 1 or the corresponding B source bit is 1, we would fill in the last four entries of the truth table with 1 (because the A bit is set) and the third, fourth, seven, and eight entries with 1 (because the B bit is set), and all others (the first and second) with 0, because neither A nor B is set. Then, we read the truth table from the bottom up, reading 11111100, or $FC.[1]

---

[1] "$" indicates hex notation.

For another example, an LF control byte of $80 (= 1000 0000 binary) turns on bits only for those points of the D destination rectangle where the corresponding bits of A, B, and C sources were all on (ABC = 1, bit 7 of LF on). All other points in the rectangle, which correspond to other combinations for A, B, and C, will be 0. This is because bits 6 through 0 of the LF control byte, which specify the D output for these situations, are set to 0.

DESIGNING THE LF CONTROL BYTE WITH MINTERMS

One approach to designing the LF control byte uses logic equations. Each of the rows in the truth table corresponds to a "minterm", which is a particular assignment of values to the A, B, and C bits. For instance, the first minterm is usually written $\overline{A}\overline{B}\overline{C}$, or "not A and not B and not C". The last is written as ABC.

NOTE

>   Two terms that are adjacent are and'ed, and two terms that are separated by "+" are or'ed. "And" has a higher precedence, so AB + BC is equal to (AB) + (BC).

Any function can be written as a sum of minterms. If we wanted to calculate the function where D is one when the A bit is set and the C bit is clear, or when the B bit is set, we can write that as $A\overline{C}+B$, or "A and not C or B". Since "1 and A" is "A":

$$D = A\overline{C} + B$$

$$D = A(1)\overline{C} + (1)B(1)$$

Since either A or $\overline{A}$ is true ($1 = A + \overline{A}$), and similarly for B, and C; we can expand the above equation further:

$$D = A(1)\overline{C} + (1)B(1)$$

$$D = A(B + \overline{B})\overline{C} + (A + \overline{A})B(C + \overline{C})$$

$$D = AB\overline{C} + A\overline{B}\overline{C} + AB(C + \overline{C}) + \overline{A}B(C + \overline{C})$$

$$D = AB\overline{C} + A\overline{B}\overline{C} + ABC + AB\overline{C} + \overline{A}BC + \overline{A}B\overline{C}$$

After eliminating duplicates, we end up with the five minterms:

$$A\overline{C}+B = AB\overline{C} + A\overline{B}\overline{C} + ABC + \overline{A}BC + \overline{A}B\overline{C}$$

These correspond to BLTCON0 bit positions of 6, 4, 7, 3, and 2, according to our truth table, which we would then set, and clear the rest.

The wide range of logic operations allow some sophisticated graphics techniques. For instance, you can move the image of a car across some pre-existing building images with a few blits. Producing this effect requires predrawn images of the car, the buildings (or background), and a car "mask" that contains bits set wherever the car image is not transparent. This mask can be visualized as the shadow of the car from a light source at the same position as the viewer.

NOTE

The mask for the car need only be a single bitplane regardless of the depth of the background bitplane. This mask can be used in turn on each of the background bitplanes.

To animate the car, first save the background image where the car will be placed. Next copy the car to its first location with another blit. Your image is now ready for display. To create the next image, restore the old background, save the next portion of the background where the car will be, and redraw the car, using three separate blits. (This technique works best with beam-synchronized blits or double buffering.)

To temporarily save the background, copy a rectangle of the background (from the A channel, for instance) to some backup buffer (using the D channel). In this case, the function we would use is "A", the standard copy function. From Table 6-1, we note that the corresponding LF code has a value of $F0.

To draw the car, we might use the A DMA channel to fetch the car mask, the B DMA channel to fetch the actual car data, the C DMA channel to fetch the background, and the D DMA channel to write out the new image.

NOTE

We must fetch the destination background before we write it, as only a portion of a destination word might need to be modified, and there is no way to do a write to only a portion of a word.

When blitting the car to the background we would want to use a function that, whenever the car mask (fetched with DMA channel A) had a bit set, we would pass through the car data from B, and whenever A did not have a bit set, we would pass through the original background from C. The corresponding function, commonly referred to as the cookie-cut function, is AB+$\overline{A}$C, which works out to an LF code value of $CA.

To restore the background and prepare for the next frame, we would copy the information saved in the first step back, with the standard copy function ($F0).

If you shift the data and the mask to a new location and repeat the above three steps over and over, the car will appear to move across the background (the buildings).

NOTE

This may not be the most effective method of animation, depending on the application, but the cookie-cut function will appear often.

Table 6-1 lists some of the most common functions and their values, for easy reference.

Table 6-1: Table of Common Minterm Values

Selected Equation	BLTCON0 LF Code	Selected Equation	BLTCON0 LF Code
$D = A$	$F0	$D = AB$	$C0
$D = \overline{A}$	$0F	$D = A\overline{B}$	$30
$D = B$	$CC	$D = \overline{A}B$	$0C
$D = \overline{B}$	$33	$D = \overline{AB}$	$03
$D = C$	$AA	$D = BC$	$88
$D = \overline{C}$	$55	$D = B\overline{C}$	$44
$D = AC$	$A0	$D = \overline{B}C$	$22
$D = A\overline{C}$	$50	$D = \overline{AC}$	$11
$D = \overline{A}C$	$0A	$D = A + \overline{B}$	$F3
$D = \overline{AC}$	$05	$D = \overline{A} + \overline{B}$	$3F
$D = A + B$	$FC	$D = A + \overline{C}$	$F5
$D = \overline{A} + B$	$CF	$D = \overline{A} + \overline{C}$	$5F
$D = A + C$	$FA	$D = B + \overline{C}$	$DD
$D = \overline{A} + C$	$AF	$D = \overline{B} + \overline{C}$	$77
$D = B + C$	$EE	$D = AB + \overline{A}C$	$CA
$D = \overline{B} + C$	$BB		

DESIGNING THE LF CONTROL BYTE WITH VENN DIAGRAMS

Another way to arrive at a particular function is through the use of Venn diagrams:

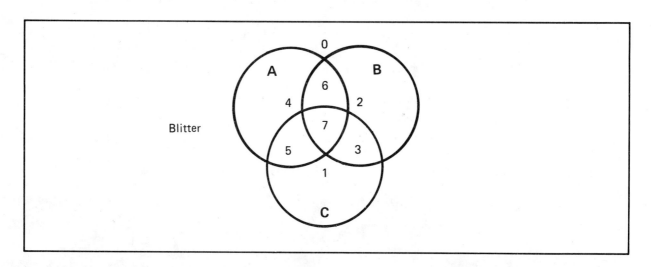

Figure 6-3: Blitter Minterm Venn Diagram

1. To select a function D=A (that is, destination = A source only), select only the minterms that are totally enclosed by the A-circle in the Figure above. This is the set of minterms 7, 6, 5, and 4. When written as a set of 1s for the selected minterms and 0s for those not selected, the value becomes:

Minterm Number	7 6 5 4 3 2 1 0
Selected Minterms	1 1 1 1 0 0 0 0

    F 0   equals $F0

2. To select a function that is a combination of two sources, look for the minterms by both of the circles (their intersection). For example, the combination AB (A "and" B) is represented by the area common to both the A and B circles, or minterms 7 and 6.

Minterm Numbers	7 6 5 4 3 2 1 0
Selected Minterms	1 1 0 0 0 0 0 0

    C 0   equals $C0

3. To use a function that is the inverse, or "not", of one of the sources, such as $\overline{A}$, take all of the minterms not enclosed by the circle represented by A on the above Figure. In this case, we have minterms 0, 1, 2, and 3.

Minterm Numbers	7 6 5 4 3 2 1 0	
Selected Minterms	0 0 0 0 1 1 1 1	
	0 F	equals $0F

4. To combine minterms, or "or" them, "or" the values together. For example, the equation AB+BC becomes

Minterm Numbers	7 6 5 4 3 2 1 0	
AB	1 1 0 0 0 0 0 0	
BC	1 0 0 0 1 0 0 0	
AB+BC	1 1 0 0 1 0 0 0	
	C 8	equals $C8

Shifts and Masks

Up to now we have dealt with the blitter only in moving words of memory around and combining them with logic operations. This is sufficient for moving graphic images around, so long as the images stay in the same position relative to the beginning of a word. If our car image has its left-most pixel on the second pixel from the left, we can easily draw it on the screen in any position where the leftmost pixel also starts two pixels from the beginning of some word. But often we want to draw that car shifted left or right by a few pixels. To this end, both the A and B DMA channels have a barrel shifter that can shift an image between 0 and 15 bits.

This shifting operation is completely free; it requires no more time to execute a blit with shifts than a blit without shifts, as opposed to shifting with the 68000. The shift is normally towards the right. This shifter allows movement of images on pixel boundaries, even though the pixels are addressed 16 at a time by each word address of the bit-plane image.

So if the incoming data is shifted to the right, what is shifted in from the left? For the first word of the blit, zeros are shifted in; for each subsequent word of the same blit, the data shifted out from the previous word is shifted in.

The shift value for the A channel is set with bits 15 through 12 of BLTCON0; the B shift value is set with bits 15 through 12 of BLTCON1. For most operations, the same value will be used for both shifts. For shifts of greater than fifteen bits, load the address register pointer of the destination with a higher address; a shift of 100 bits would require the destination pointer to be advanced 100/16 or 6 words (12 bytes), and a right shift of the remaining 4 bits to be used.

As an example, let us say we are doing a blit that is three words wide, two words high, and we are using a shift of 4 bits. For simplicity, let us assume we are doing a straight copy from A to D. The first word that will be written to D is the first word fetched from A, shifted right four bits with zeros shifted in from the left. The second word will be the second word fetched from the A, shifted right, with the least significant (rightmost) four bits of the first word shifted in. Next, we will write the first word of the second row fetched from A, shifted four bits, with the least significant four bits of the last word from the first row shifted in. This would continue until the blit is finished.

On shifted blits, therefore, we only get zeros shifted in for the first word of the first row. On all other rows the blitter will shift in the bits that it shifted out of the previous row. For most graphics applications, this is undesirable. For this reason, the blitter has the ability to mask the first and last word of each row coming through the A DMA channel. Thus, it is possible to extract rectangular data from a source whose right and left edges are between word boundaries. These two registers are called BLTAFWM and BLTALWM, for blitter A channel first and last word masks. When not in use, both should be initialized to all ones ($FFFF).

NOTE

Text fonts on the Amiga are stored in a packed bit map. Individual characters from the font are extracted using the blitter, masking out unwanted bits. The character may then be positioned to any pixel alignment by shifting it the appropriate amount.

These masks are "anded" with the source data, before any shifts are applied. Only when there is a 1 bit in the first-word mask will that bit of source A actually appear in the logic operation. The first word of each row is anded with BLTAFWM, and the last word is "anded" with BLTALWM. If the width of the row is a single word, both masks are applied simultaneously.

The masks are also useful for extracting a certain range of "columns" from some bitplane. Let us say we have, for example, a predrawn rectangle containing text and graphics that is 23 pixels wide. The leftmost edge is the leftmost bit in its bitmap, and the bitmap is two words wide. We wish to render this rectangle starting at pixel position 5 into our 320 by 200 screen bitmap, without disturbing anything that lies outside of the rectangle.

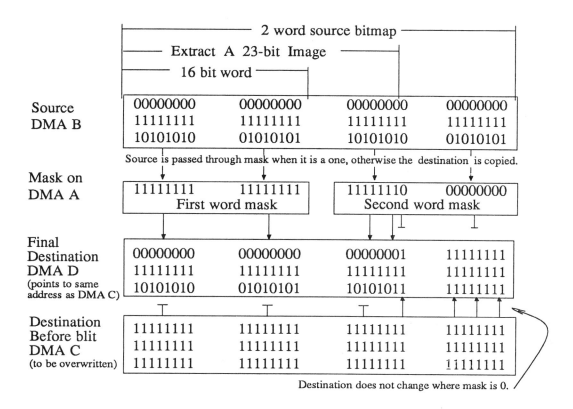

Figure 6-4: Extracting a Range of Columns

To do this, we point the B DMA channel at the bitmap containing the source image, and the D DMA channel at the screen bitmap. We use a shift value of 5. We also point the C DMA channel at the screen bitmap. We use a blit width of 2 words. What we need is a simple copy operation, except we wish to leave the first five bits of the first word, and the last four bits (2 times 16, less 23, less 5) of the last word alone. The A DMA channel comes to the rescue. We preload the A data register with $FFFF (all ones), and use a first word mask with the most significant five bits set to zero ($07FF) and a last word mask with the least significant four bits set to zero ($FFF0). We do not enable the A DMA channel, but only the B, C, and D channels, since we want to use the A channel as a simple row mask. We then wish to pass the B (source) data along wherever the A channel is 1 (for a minterm of AB) and pass along the original destination data (from the C channel) wherever A is 0 (for a minterm of AC), yielding our classic cookie-cut function of AB+AC, or $CA.

NOTE

Even though the A channel is disabled, we use it in our logic function and preload the data register. Disabling a channel simply turns off the memory fetches for that channel; all other operations are still performed, only from a constant value stored in the channel's data register.

An alternative but more subtle way of accomplishing the same thing is to use an A shift of five, a first word mask of all ones, and a last word mask with the rightmost nine bits set to zero. All other registers remain the same.

NOTE

Be sure to load the blitter immediate data registers only after setting the shift count in BLTCON0/BLTCON1, as loading the data registers first will lead to unpredictable results. For instance, if the last person left BSHIFT to be "4", and I load BDATA with "1" and then change BSHIFT to "2", the resulting BDATA that is used is "1<<4", not "1<<2". The act of loading one of the data registers "draws" the data through the machine and shifts it.

Descending Mode

Our standard memory copy blit works fine if the source does not overlap the destination. If we want to move an image one row down (towards increasing addresses), however, we run into a problem — we overwrite the second row before we get a chance to copy it! The blitter has a special mode of operation — descending mode — that solves this problem nicely.

Descending mode is turned on by setting bit one of BLTCON1 (defined as BLITREVERSE). If you use descending mode the address pointers will be decremented by two (bytes) instead of incremented by two for each word fetched. In addition, the modulo values will be subtracted rather than added. Shifts are then towards the left, rather than the right, the first word mask masks the last word in a row (which is still the first word fetched), and the last word mask masks the first word in a row.

Thus, for a standard memory copy, the only difference in blitter setup (assuming no shifting or masking) is to initialize the address pointer registers to point to the last word in a block, rather than the first word. The modulo values, blit size, and all other parameters should be set the same.

NOTE

This differs from predecrement versus postincrement in the 68000, where an address register would be initialized to point to the word after the last, rather than the last word.

Descending mode is also necessary for area filling, which will be covered in a later section.

Copying Arbitrary Regions

One of the most common uses of the blitter is to move arbitrary rectangles of data from one bit-plane to another, or to different positions within a bitplane. These rectangles are usually on arbitrary bit coordinates, so shifting and masking are necessary. There are further complications. It may take several readings and some experimentation before everything in this section can be understood.

A source image that spans only two words may, when copied with certain shifts, span three words. Our 23 pixel wide rectangle above, for instance, when shifted 12 bits, will span three words. Alternatively, an image spanning three words may fit in two for certain shifts. Under all such circumstances, the blit size should be set to the larger of the two values, such that both source and destination will fit within the blit size. Proper masking should be applied to mask out unwanted data.

Some general guidelines for copying an arbitrary region are as follows.

1. Use the A DMA channel, disabled, preloaded with all ones and the appropriate mask and shift values, to mask the cookie cut function. Use the B channel to fetch the source data, the C channel to fetch the destination data, and the D channel to write the destination data. Use the cookie-cut function $CA.

2. If shifting, always use ascending mode if bit shifting to the right, and use descending mode if bit shifting to the left.

NOTE

These shifts are the shifts of the bit position of the leftmost edge within a word, rather than absolute shifts, as explained previously.

3. If the source and destination overlap, use ascending mode if the destination has a lower memory address (is higher on the display) and descending mode otherwise.

4. If the source spans more words than the destination, use the same shift value for the A channel as for the source B channel and set the first and last word masks as if they were masking the B source data.

5. If the destination spans more words than the source, use a shift value of zero for the A channel and set the first and last word masks as if they were masking the destination D data.

6. If the source and destination span the same number of words, use the A channel to mask either the source, as in 4, or the destination, as in 5.

NOTE

Conditions 2 and 3 can be contradictory if, for instance, you are trying to move an image one pixel down and to the right. In this case, we would want to use descending mode so our destination does not overwrite our source before we use the source, but we would want to use ascending mode for the right shift. In some situations, it is possible to get around general guideline 2 above with clever masking. But occasionally just masking the first or last word may not be sufficient; it may be necessary to mask more than 16 bits on one or the other end. In such a case, a mask can be built in memory for a single raster row, and the A DMA channel enabled to explicitly fetch this mask. By setting the A modulo value to the negative of the width of the mask, the mask will be repeatedly fetched for each row.

Area Fill Mode

In addition to copying data, the blitter can simultaneously perform a fill operation during the copy. The fill operation has only one restriction — the area to fill must be defined first by drawing untextured lines with only one bit set per horizontal row. A special line draw mode is available for this operation. Use a standard copy blit (or any other blit, as area fills take place after all shifts, masks and logical combination of sources). Descending mode must be used. Set either the inclusive-fill-enable bit (FILL_OR, or bit 3) or the exclusive-fill-enable bit (FILL_XOR, or bit 4) in BLTCON1. The inclusive fill mode fills between lines, leaving the lines intact. The exclusive fill mode fills between lines, leaving the lines bordering the right edge of filled regions but deleting the lines bordering the left edge. Exclusive fill yields filled shapes one pixel narrower than the same pattern filled with inclusive fill.

For instance, the pattern:

    00100100-00011000

filled with inclusive fill, yields:

    00111100-00011000

with exclusive fill, the result would be

    00011100-00001000

(Of course, fills are always done on full 16-bit words.)

There is another bit (FILL_CARRYIN or bit 3 in BLTCON1) that forces the area "outside" the lines be filled; for the above example, with inclusive fill, the output would be

11100111-11111111

with exclusive fill, the output would be

11100011-11110111

```
        Before                          After

   1    1   1    1              11111          11111
   1    1   1    1              11111          11111
     1  1     1  1               1111           1111
      1 1      1 1                111            111
       11       11                11             11
      1 1      1 1                111            111
     1  1     1  1               1111           1111
   1    1   1    1              11111          11111
```

Figure 6-5: Use of the FCI Bit - Bit Is a 0

If the FCI bit is a 1 instead of a 0, the area outside the lines is filled with 1s and the area inside the lines is left with 0s in between.

```
        Before                          After

   1    1   1    1            111    111111     11
   1    1   1    1            111    1111111    11
     1  1     1  1            1111   11111111   11
      1 1      1 1            11111 111111111 11
       11       11            1111111111111111111
      1 1      1 1            11111 111111111 11
     1  1     1  1            1111   11111111   11
   1    1   1    1            111    1111111    11
```

Figure 6-6: Use of the FCI Bit - Bit Is a 1

If you wish to produce very sharp, single-point vertices, exclusive-fill enable must be used. Figure 6-7 shows how a single-point vertex is produced using exclusive-fill enable.

```
        Before              After Exclusive Fill

   ┌─────────────────┐      ┌─────────────────┐
   │ 1   1     1   1 │      │ 1111       1111 │
   │   1 1     1 1   │      │  111        111 │
   │     1 1     1 1 │      │   11         11 │
   │       11     11 │      │    1          1 │
   │     1 1     1 1 │      │   11         11 │
   │   1 1     1 1   │      │  111        111 │
   │ 1   1     1   1 │      │ 1111       1111 │
   └─────────────────┘      └─────────────────┘
```

Figure 6-7: Single-Point Vertex Example

The blitter uses the fill carry-in bit as the starting fill state beginning at the rightmost edge of each line. For each "1" bit in the source area, the blitter flips the fill state, either filling or not filling the space with ones. This continues for each line until the left edge of the blit is reached, at which point the filling stops.

Blitter Done Flag

When the BLTSIZE register is written the blit is started. The processor does not stop while the blitter is working, though; they can both work concurrently, and this provides much of the speed evident in the Amiga. This does require some amount of care when using the blitter.

A blitter done flag, also called the blitter busy flag, is provided as DMAF_BLTDONE in DMACONR. This flag is set when a blit is in progress.

NOTE

If a blit has just been started but has been locked out of memory access because of, for instance, display fetches, this bit may not yet be set. The processor, on the other hand, may be running completely uninhibited out of FAST memory or its internal cache, so it will continue to have memory cycles.

The solution is to read a chip memory or hardware register address with the processor before testing the bit. This can easily be done with the sequence:

```
btst.b    #DMAB_BLTDONE-8,DMACONR(a1)
btst.b    #DMAB_BLTDONE-8,DMACONR(a1)
```

where a1 has been preloaded with the address of the hardware registers. The first "test" of the blitter done bit may not return the correct result, but the second will.

NOTE

Starting with the Fat Agnus the blitter busy bit has been "fixed" to be set as soon as you write to BLTSIZE to start the blit, rather than when the blitter gets its first DMA cycle. However, not all machines will use these newer chips, so it is best to rely on the above method of testing.

MULTITASKING AND THE BLITTER

When a blit is in progress, none of the blitter registers should be written. For details on arbitration of blitter access in the system, please refer to the ROM Kernel Manual. In particular, read the discussion about the OwnBlitter() and DisownBlitter() functions. Even after the blitter has been "owned", a blit may still be finishing up, so the blitter done flag should be checked before using it even the first time. Use of the ROM kernel function WaitBlit() is recommended.

You should also check the blitter done flag before using results of a blit. The blit may not be finished, so the data may not be ready yet. This can lead to difficult to find bugs, because a 68000 may be slow enough for a blit to finish without checking the done flag, while a 68020, perhaps running out of its cache, may be able to get at the data before the blitter has finished writing it.

Let us say that we have a subroutine that displays a text box on top of other imagery temporarily. This subroutine might allocate a chunk of memory to hold the original screen image while we are displaying our text box, then draw the text box. On exit, the subroutine might blit the original imagery back and then free the allocated memory. If the memory is freed before the blitter done flag is checked, some other process might allocate that memory and store new data into it before the blit is finished, trashing the blitter source and, thus, the screen imagery being restored.

Interrupt Flag

The blitter also has an interrupt flag that is set whenever a blit finishes. This flag, INTF_BLIT, can generate a 68000 interrupt if enabled. For more information on interrupts, see Chapter 7 "System Control Hardware."

Zero Flag

A blitter zero flag is provided that can be tested to determine if the logic operation selected has resulted in zero bits for all destination bits, even if those destination bits are not written due to the D DMA channel being disabled. This feature is often useful for collision detection, by performing a logical "and" on two source images to test for overlap. If the images do not overlap, the zero flag will stay true.

The Zero flag is only valid after the blitter has completed its operation and can be read from bit DMAF_BLTNZERO of the DMACONR register.

Pipeline Register

The blitter performs many operations in each cycle — shifting and masking source words, logical combination of sources, and area fill and zero detect on the output. To enable so many things to take place so quickly, the blitter is pipelined. This means that rather than performing all of the above operations in one blitter cycle, the operations are spread over two blitter cycles. (Here "cycle" is used very loosely for simplicity.) To clarify this, the blitter can be imagined as two chips connected in series. Every cycle, a new set of source operations come in, and the first chip performs its operations on the data. It then passes the half-processed data to the second chip to be finished during the next cycle, when the first chip will be busy at work on the next set of data. Each set of data takes two "cycles" to get through the two chips, overlapped so a set of data can be pumped through each cycle.

What all this means is that the first two sets of sources are fetched before the first destination is written. This allows you to shift a bitmap up to one word to the right using ascending mode, for instance, even though normally parts of the destination would be overwritten before they were fetched.

Table 6-2: Typical Blitter Cycle Sequence

USE Code in BLTCON0	Active Channels				Cycle Sequence
F	A	B	C	D	A0 B0 C0 - A1 B1 C1 D0 A2 B2 C2 D1 D2
E	A	B	C		A0 B0 C0 A1 B1 C1 A2 B2 C2
D	A	B		D	A0 B0 - A1 B1 D0 A2 B2 D1 - D2
C	A	B			A0 B0 - A1 B1 - A2 B2
B	A		C	D	A0 C0 - A1 C1 D0 A2 C2 D1 - D2
A	A		C		A0 C0 A1 C1 A2 C2
9	A			D	A0 - A1 D0 A2 D1 - D2
8	A				A0 - A1 - A2
7		B	C	D	B0 C0 - - B1 C1 D0 - B2 C2 D1 - D2
6		B	C		B0 C0 - B1 C1 - B2 C2
5		B		D	B0 - - B1 D0 - B2 D1 - D2
4		B			B0 - - B1 - - B2
3			C	D	C0 - - C1 D0 - C2 D1 - D2
2			C		C0 - C1 - C2
1				D	D0 - D1 - D2
0	none				- - - -

Notes for the above Table:

- No fill.

- No competing bus activity.

- Three-word blit.

- Typical operation involves fetching all sources twice before the first destination becomes available. This is due to internal pipelining. Care must be taken with overlapping source and destination regions.

NOTE

This Table is only meant to be an illustration of the typical order of blitter cycles on the bus. Bus cycles are dynamically allocated based on blitter operating mode; competing bus activity from processor, bit-planes, and other DMA channels; and other factors. Commodore Amiga does not guarantee the accuracy of or future adherence to this chart. We reserve the right to make product improvements or design changes in this area without notice.

Line Mode

In addition to all of the functions described above, the blitter can draw patterned lines. The line draw mode is selected by setting bit 0 (LINEMODE) of BLTCON1, which changes the meaning of some other bits in BLTCON0 and BLTCON1. In line draw mode, the blitter can draw lines up to 1024 pixels long, it can draw them in a variety of modes, with a variety of textures, and can even draw them in a special way for simple area fill.

Many of the blitter registers serve other purposes in line-drawing mode. Consult Appendix A for more detailed descriptions of the use of these registers and control bits in line-drawing mode.

In line mode, the blitter draws a line from one point to another, which can be viewed as a vector. The direction of the vector can lie in any of the following eight octants. (In the following diagram, the standard Amiga convention is used, with x increasing towards the right and y increasing down.) The number in parenthesis is the octant numbering; the other number represents the value that should be placed in bits 4 through 2 of BLTCON1.

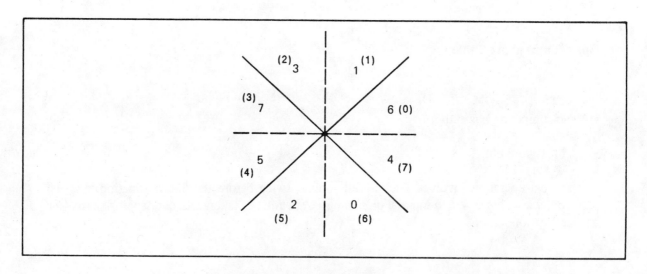

Figure 6-8: Octants for Line Drawing

Line drawing based on octants is a simplification that takes advantage of symmetries between x and $-x$, y and $-y$. The following Table lists the octant number and corresponding values:

Table 6-3: BLTCON1 Code Bits for Octant Line Drawing

BLTCON1 Code Bits	Octant #
4 3 2	
1 1 0	0
0 0 1	1
0 1 1	2
1 1 1	3
1 0 1	4
0 1 0	5
0 0 0	6
1 0 0	7

We initialize BLTCON1 bits 4 through 2 according to the above Table. Now, we introduce the variables dx and dy, and set them to the absolute values of the difference between the x coordinates and the y coordinates of the endpoints of the line, respectively.

```
dx = abs(x2 - x1) ;
dy = abs(y2 - y1) ;
```

Now, we rearrange them if necessary so dx is greater than dy.

```
if (dx < dy)
        {
        temp = dx ;
        dx = dy ;
        dy = temp ;
        }
```

Alternately, set dx and dy as follows:

```
dx = max(abs(x2 - x1), abs(y2 - y1)) ;
dy = min(abs(x2 - x1), abs(y2 - y1)) ;
```

These calculations have the effect of "normalizing" our line into octant 0; since we have already informed the blitter of the real octant to use, it has no difficulty drawing the line.

We initialize the A pointer register to $4 * dy - 2 * dx$. If this value is negative, we set the sign bit (SIGNFLAG in BLTCON1), otherwise we clear it. We set the A modulo register to $4 * (dy - dx)$ and the B modulo register to $4 * dy$.

The A data register should be preloaded with $8000. Both word masks should be set to $FFFF. The A shift value should be set to the x coordinate of the first point ($x1$) modulo 15.

The B data register should be initialized with the line texture pattern, if any, or $FFFF for a solid line. The B shift value should be set to the bit number at which to start the line texture (zero means the last significant bit.)

The C and D pointer registers should be initialized to the word containing the first pixel of the line; the C and D modulo registers should be set to the width of the bitplane in bytes.

The SRCA, SRCC, and DEST bits of BLTCON0 should be set to one, and the SRCB flag should be set to zero. The OVFLAG should be cleared. If only a single bit per horizontal row is desired, the ONEDOT bit of BLTCON1 should be set; otherwise it should be cleared.

The logic function remains. The C DMA channel represents the original source, the A channel the bit to set in the line, and the B channel the pattern to draw. Thus, to draw a line, the function AB+AC is the most common. To draw the line using exclusive-or mode, so it can be easily erased by drawing it again, the function ABC+AC can be used.

We set the blit height to the length of the line, which is $dx + 1$. The width must be set to two for all line drawing. (Of course, the BLTSIZE register should not be written until the very end, when all other registers have been filled.)

REGISTER SUMMARY FOR LINE MODE

Preliminary setup:

> The line goes from $(x1, y1)$ to $(x2, y2)$.

```
dx = max(abs(x2 - x1), abs(y2 - y1)) ;
dy = min(abs(x2 - x1), abs(y2 - y1)) ;
```

Register setup:

> BLTADAT = $8000
> BLTBDAT = line texture pattern ($FFFF for a solid line)
>
> BLTAFWM = $FFFF
> BLTALWM = $FFFF
>
> BLTAMOD = 4 * $(dy - dx)$
> BLTBMOD = 4 * dy
> BLTCMOD = width of the bitplane in bytes
> BLTDMOD = width of the bitplane in bytes
>
> BLTAPT = $(4 * dy) - (2 * dx)$
> BLTBPT = unused
> BLTCPT = word containing the first pixel of the line
> BLTDPT = word containing the first pixel of the line

BLTCON0 bits 15-12 = *x1* modulo 15
BLTCON0 bits SRCA, SRCC, and SRCD = 1
BLTCON0 bit SRCB = 0
if exclusive-or line mode:
    then BLTCON0 LF control byte = AB$\overline{\text{C}}$ $\pm$ $\overline{\text{A}}$C
    else BLTCON0 LF control byte = AB + $\overline{\text{A}}$C

BLTCON1 bit LINEMODE = 1
BLTCON1 bit OVFLAG = 0
BLTCON1 bits 4-2 = octant number from table
BLTCON1 bits 15-12 = start bit for line texture (0 = last significant bit)
if (((4 * *dy*) - (2 * *dx*)) < 0):
    then BLTCON1 bit SIGNFLAG = 1
    else BLTCON1 bit SIGNFLAG = 0
if one pixel/row:
    then BLTCON1 bit ONEDOT = 1
    else BLTCON1 bit ONEDOT = 0

BLTSIZE bits 15-6 = *dx* + 1
BLTSIZE bits 5-0 = 2

NOTE

You must set the BLTSIZE register last as it starts the blit.

Blitter Speed

The speed of the blitter depends entirely on which DMA channels are enabled. You might be using a DMA channel as a constant, but unless it is enabled, it does not count against you. The minimum blitter cycle is four ticks; the maximum is eight ticks. Use of the A register is always free. Use of the B register always adds two ticks to the blitter cycle. Use of either C or D is free, but use of both adds another two ticks. Thus, a copy cycle, using A and D, takes four clock ticks per cycle; a copy cycle using B and D takes six ticks per cycle, and a generalized bit copy using B, C, and D takes eight ticks per cycle. When in line mode, each pixel takes eight ticks.

The system clock speed for NTSC Amigas is 7.16 megahertz (PAL Amigas 7.09 megahertz). The clock for the blitter is the system clock. To calculate the total time for the blit in microseconds, excluding setup and DMA contention, you use the equation (for NTSC):

$$t = \frac{n * H * W}{7.16}$$

For PAL:

$$t = \frac{n * H * W}{7.09}$$

where t is the time in microseconds, n is the number of clocks per cycle, and H and W are the height and width (in words) of the blit, respectively.

For instance, to copy one bitplane of a 320 by 200 screen to another bitplane, we might choose to use the A and D channels. This would require four ticks per blitter cycle, for a total of

$$\frac{4 * 200 * 20}{7.16} = 2235 \text{ microseconds.}$$

These timings do not take into account blitter setup time, which is the time required to calculate and load the blitter registers and start the blit. They also ignore DMA contention.

Blitter Operations and System DMA

The operations of the blitter affect the performance of the rest of the system. The following sections explain how system performance is affected by blitter direct memory access priority, DMA time slot allocation, bus sharing between the 68000 and the display hardware, the operations of the blitter and Copper, and different playfield display sizes.

The blitter performs its various data-fetch, modify, and store operations through DMA sequences, and it shares memory access with other devices in the system. Each device that accesses memory has a priority level assigned to it, which indicates its importance relative to other devices.

Disk DMA, audio DMA, display DMA, and sprite DMA all have the highest priority level. Display DMA has priority over sprite DMA under certain circumstances. Each of these four devices is allocated a group of time slots during each horizontal scan of the video beam. If a device does not request one of its allocated time slots, the slot is open for other uses. These devices are given first priority because missed DMA cycles can cause lost data, noise in the sound output, or on-screen interruptions.

The Copper has the next priority because it has to perform its operations at the same time during each display frame to remain synchronized with the display beam sweeping across the screen.

The lowest priorities are assigned to the blitter and the 68000, in that order. The blitter is given the higher priority because it performs data copying, modifying, and line drawing operations operations much faster than the 68000.

During a horizontal scan line (about 63 microseconds), there are 227.5 "color clocks", or memory access cycles. A memory cycle is approximately 280 ns in duration. The total of 227.5 cycles per horizontal line includes both display time and non-display time. Of this total time, 226 cycles are available to be allocated to the various devices that need memory access.

The time-slot allocation per horizontal line is

    4 cycles for memory refresh
    3 cycles for disk DMA
    4 cycles for audio DMA (2 bytes per channel)
    16 cycles for sprite DMA (2 words per channel)
    80 cycles for bit-plane DMA (even- or odd-numbered slots
            according to the display size used)

Figure 6-9 shows one complete horizontal scan line and how the clock cycles are allocated.

DMA Time Slot Allocation/Horizontal line

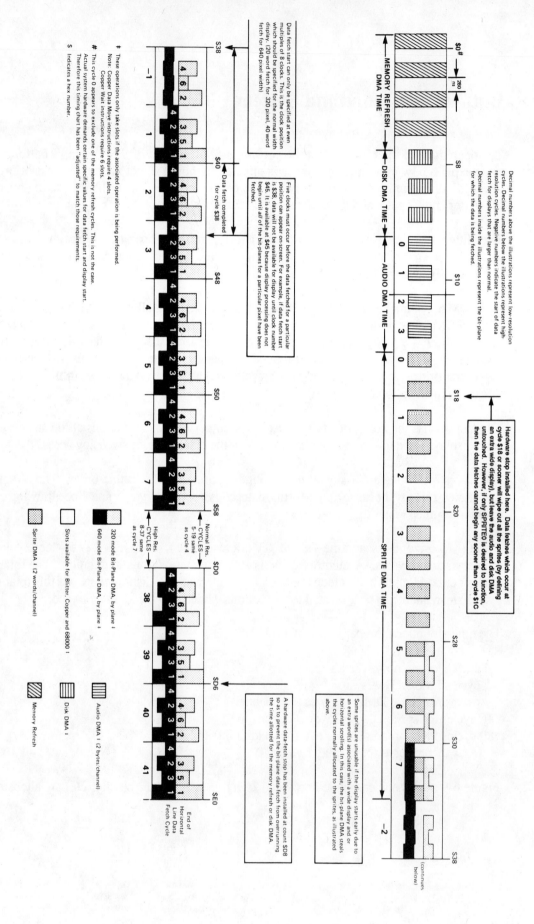

Figure 6-9: DMA Time Slot Allocation

‡ These operations only take slots if the associated operation is being performed.

Note: Copper Data Move instructions require 4 slots.
Copper Wait instructions require 6 slots.

This cycle 0 appears to exclude one of the memory refresh cycles. This is not the case.
Actual system hardware demands certain specific values for data fetch start and display start.
Therefore this timing chart has been "adjusted" to match those requirements.

$ Indicates a hex number.

Slots available for Blitter, Copper and 68000 ‡

Sprite DMA ‡ (2 words/channel)

320 mode Bit-Plane DMA, by plane ‡

640 mode Bit-Plane DMA, by plane ‡

Audio DMA ‡ (2 bytes/channel)

Disk DMA ‡

Memory Refresh

The 68000 uses only the even-numbered memory access cycles. The 68000 spends about half of a complete processor instruction time doing internal operations and the other half accessing memory. Therefore, the allocation of alternate memory cycles to the 68000 makes it appear to the 68000 that it has the memory all of the time, and it will run at full speed.

Some 68000 instructions do not match perfectly with the allocation of even cycles and cause cycles to be missed. If cycles are missed, the 68000 must wait until its next available memory slot before continuing. However, most instructions do not cause cycles to be missed, so the 68000 runs at full speed most of the time if there is no blitter DMA interference.

Figure 6-10 illustrates the normal cycle of the 68000.

NOTE

The 68000 test-and-set instruction (TAS) should never be used in the Amiga; the indivisible read-modify-write cycle that is used only in this instruction will not fit into a DMA memory access slot.

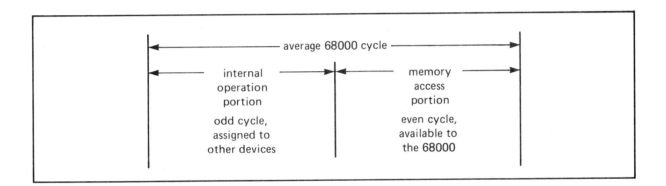

Figure 6-10: Normal 68000 Cycle

If the display contains four or fewer low-resolution bit-planes, the 68000 can be granted alternate memory cycles (if it is ready to ask for the cycle and is the highest priority item at the time). However, if there are more than four bit-planes, bit-plane DMA will begin to steal cycles from the 68000 during the display.

During the display time for a six-bit-plane display (low resolution, 320 pixels wide), 160 time slots will be taken by bit-plane DMA for each horizontal line. As you can see from Figure 6-11, bit-plane DMA steals 50 percent of the open slots that the processor might have used if there were only four bit-planes displayed.

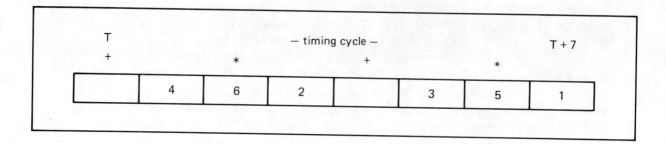

Figure 6-11: Time Slots Used by a Six Bit Plane Display

If you specify four high-resolution bit-planes (640 pixels wide), bit-plane DMA needs all of the available memory time slots during the display time just to fetch the 40 data words for each line of the four bit-planes (40 * 4 = 160 time slots). This effectively locks out the 68000 (as well as the blitter or Copper) from any memory access during the display, except during horizontal and vertical blanking.

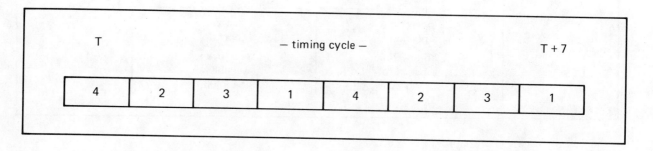

Figure 6-12: Time Slots Used by a High Resolution Display

Each horizontal line in a normal, full-sized display contains 320 pixels in low-resolution mode or 640 pixels in high-resolution mode. Thus, either 20 or 40 words will be fetched during the horizontal line display time. If you want to scroll a playfield, one extra data word per line must be fetched from the memory.

Display size is adjustable (see Chapter 3, "Playfield Hardware"), and bit-plane DMA takes precedence over sprite DMA. As shown in Figure 6-9, larger displays may block out one or more of the highest-numbered sprites, especially with scrolling.

As mentioned above, the blitter normally has a higher priority than the processor for DMA cycles. There are certain cases, however, when the blitter and the 68000 can share memory cycles. If given the chance, the blitter would steal every available memory cycle. Display, disk, and audio DMA take precedence over the blitter, so it cannot block them from bus access. Depending on the setting of the blitter DMA mode bit, commonly referred to as the "blitter-nasty" bit, the processor may be blocked from bus access. This bit is called DMAF_BLITHOG and is in register DMACON.

If DMAF_BLITHOG is a 1, the blitter will keep the bus for every available memory cycle. This could potentially be every cycle.

If DMAF_BLITHOG is a 0, the DMA manager will monitor the 68000 cycle requests. If the 68000 is unsatisfied for three consecutive memory cycles, the blitter will release the bus for one cycle.

Blitter Block Diagram

- Figure 6-13 shows the basic building blocks for a single bit of a 16-bit wide operation of the blitter. It does not cover the line-drawing hardware.

- The upper left corner shows how the first— and last— word masks are applied to the incoming A-source data. When the blit shrinks to one word wide, both masks are applied.

- The shifter (upper right and center left) drawing illustrates how 16 bits of data is taken from a specified position within a 32-bit register, based on the A shift or B shift values shown in BLTCON0 and BLTCON1.

- The minterm generator (center right) illustrates how the minterm select bits either allow or inhibit the use of a specific minterm.

- The drawing shows how the fill operation works on the data generated by the minterm combinations. Fill operations can be performed simultaneously with other complex logic operations.

- At the bottom, the drawing shows that data generated for the destination can be prevented from being written to a destination by using one of the blitter control bits.

- Not shown on this diagram is the logic for zero detection, which looks at every bit generated for the destination. If there are any 1-bits generated, this logic indicates that the area of the blit contained at least one 1-bit (zero detect is false.)

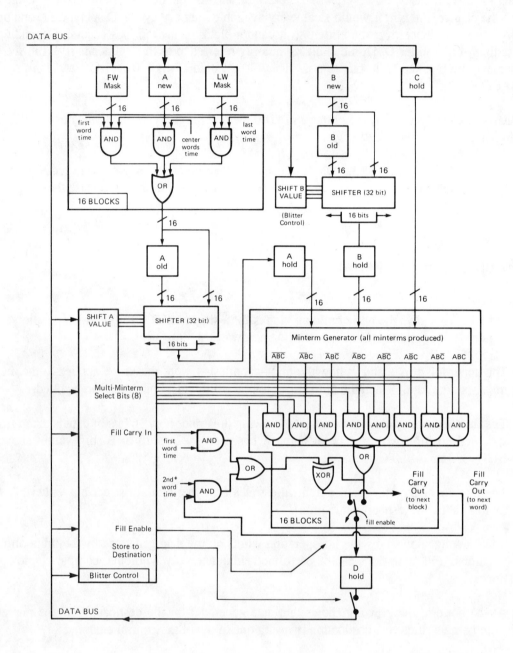

Figure 6-13: Blitter Block Diagram

Blitter Key Points

This is a list of some key points that should be remembered when programming the blitter.

- Write BLTSIZE last; writing this register starts the blit.

- Modulos and pointers are in bytes; width is in words and height is in pixels. The least significant bit of all pointers and modulos is ignored.

- The order of operations in the blitter is masking, shifting, logical combination of sources, area fill, and zero flag setting.

- In ascending mode, the blitter increments the pointers, adds the modulos, and shifts to the right.

- In descending mode, the blitter decrements the pointers, subtracts the modulos, and shifts to the left.

- Area fill only works correctly in descending mode.

- Check BLTDONE before writing blitter registers or using the results of a blit.

- Shifts are done on immediate data as soon as it is loaded.

EXAMPLE: ClearMem

```
;
;     Blitter example---memory clear
;
        include 'exec/types.i'
        include 'hardware/custom.i'
        include 'hardware/dmabits.i'
        include 'hardware/blit.i'
        include 'hardware/hw_examples.i"

        xref    _custom
;
;     Wait for previous blit to complete.
;
waitblit:
        btst.b  #DMAB_BLTDONE-8,DMACONR(a1)
waitblit2:
        btst.b  #DMAB_BLTDONE-8,DMACONR(a1)
        bne     waitblit2
        rts
;
;     This routine uses a side effect in the blitter.  When each
```

```
;       of the blits is finished, the pointer in the blitter is pointing
;       to the next word to be blitted.
;
;       When this routine returns, the last blit is started and might
;       not be finished, so be sure to call waitblit above before
;       assuming the data is clear.
;
;       a0 = pointer to first word to clear
;       d0 = number of bytes to clear (must be even)
;
        xdef    clearmem
clearmem:
        lea     _custom,a1      ; Get pointer to chip registers
        bsr     waitblit        ; Make sure previous blit is done
        move.l  a0,BLTDPT(a1)   ; Set up the D pointer to the region to clear
        clr.w   BLTDMOD(a1)     ; Clear the D modulo (don't skip no bytes)
        asr.l   #1,d0           ; Get number of words from number of bytes
        clr.w   BLTCON1(a1)     ; No special modes
        move.w  #DEST,BLTCON0(a1)       ; only enable destination
;
;   First we deal with the smaller blits
;
        moveq   #$3f,d1         ; Mask out mod 64 words
        and.w   d0,d1
        beq     dorest          ; none?  good, do one blit
        sub.l   d1,d0           ; otherwise remove remainder
        or.l    #$40,d1         ; set the height to 1, width to n
        move.w  d1,BLTSIZE(a1)  ; trigger the blit
;
;   Here we do the rest of the words, as chunks of 128k
;
dorest:
        move.w  #$ffc0,d1       ; look at some more upper bits
        and.w   d0,d1           ; extract 10 more bits
        beq     dorest2         ; any to do?
        sub.l   d1,d0           ; pull of the ones we're doing here
        bsr     waitblit        ; wait for prev blit to complete
        move.w  d0,BLTSIZE(a1)  ; do another blit
dorest2:
        swap    d0              ; more?
        beq     done            ; nope.
        clr.w   d1              ; do a 1024x64 word blit (128K)
keepon:
        bsr     waitblit        ; finish up this blit
        move.w  d1,BLTSIZE(a1)  ; and again, blit
        subq.w  #1,d0           ; still more?
        bne     keepon          ; keep on going.
done:
        rts                     ; finished.  Blit still in progress.
        end
```

EXAMPLE: SimpleLine

```
;
;    This example uses the line draw mode of the blitter
;    to draw a line.  The line is drawn with no pattern
;    and a simple 'or' blit into a single bitplane.
;
;    Input:  d0=x1 d1=y1 d2=x2 d3=y2 d4=width a0=aptr
;
        include 'exec/types.i'
        include 'hardware/custom.i'
        include 'hardware/blit.i'
        include 'hardware/dmabits.i'

        include 'hardware/hw_examples.i'
;
        xref    _custom
;
        xdef    simpleline
;
;    Our entry point.
;
simpleline:
        lea     _custom,a1      ; snarf up the custom address register
        sub.w   d0,d2           ; calculate dx
        bmi     xneg            ; if negative, octant is one of [3,4,5,6]
        sub.w   d1,d3           ; calculate dy  ''   is one of [1,2,7,8]
        bmi     yneg            ; if negative, octant is one of [7,8]
        cmp.w   d3,d2           ; cmp |dx|,|dy|  ''   is one of [1,2]
        bmi     ygtx            ; if y>x, octant is 2
        moveq.l #OCTANT1+LINEMODE,d5    ; otherwise octant is 1
        bra     lineagain       ; go to the common section
ygtx:
        exg     d2,d3           ; X must be greater than Y
        moveq.l #OCTANT2+LINEMODE,d5    ; we are in octant 2
        bra     lineagain       ; and common again.
yneg:
        neg.w   d3              ; calculate abs(dy)
        cmp.w   d3,d2           ; cmp |dx|,|dy|, octant is [7,8]
        bmi     ynygtx          ; if y>x, octant is 7
        moveq.l #OCTANT8+LINEMODE,d5    ; otherwise octant is 8
        bra     lineagain
ynygtx:
        exg     d2,d3           ; X must be greater than Y
        moveq.l #OCTANT7+LINEMODE,d5    ; we are in octant 7
        bra     lineagain
xneg:
        neg.w   d2              ; dx was negative! octant is [3,4,5,6]
        sub.w   d1,d3           ; we calculate dy
        bmi     xyneg           ; if negative, octant is one of [5,6]
        cmp.w   d3,d2           ; otherwise it's one of [3,4]
        bmi     xnygtx          ; if y>x, octant is 3
        moveq.l #OCTANT4+LINEMODE,d5    ; otherwise it's 4
        bra     lineagain
xnygtx:
        exg     d2,d3           ; X must be greater than Y
        moveq.l #OCTANT3+LINEMODE,d5    ; we are in octant 3
        bra     lineagain
```

```
xyneg:
        neg.w    d3              ; y was negative, in one of [5,6]
        cmp.w    d3,d2           ; is y>x?
        bmi      xynygtx         ; if so, octant is 6
        moveq.l  #OCTANT5+LINEMODE,d5    ; otherwise, octant is 5
        bra      lineagain
xynygtx:
        exg      d2,d3           ; X must be greater than Y
        moveq.l  #OCTANT6+LINEMODE,d5    ; we are in octant 6
lineagain:
        mulu.w   d4,d1           ; Calculate y1 * width
        ror.l    #4,d0           ; move upper four bits into hi word
        add.w    d0,d0           ; multiply by 2
        add.l    d1,a0           ; ptr += (x1 >> 3)
        add.w    d0,a0           ; ptr += y1 * width
        swap     d0              ; get the four bits of x1
        or.w     #$BFA,d0        ; or with USEA, USEC, USED, F=A+C
        lsl.w    #2,d3           ; Y = 4 * Y
        add.w    d2,d2           ; X = 2 * X
        move.w   d2,d1           ; set up size word
        lsl.w    #5,d1           ; shift five left
        add.w    #$42,d1         ; and add 1 to height, 2 to width
        btst     #DMAB_BLTDONE-8,DMACONR(a1)    ; safety check
waitblit:
        btst     #DMAB_BLTDONE-8,DMACONR(a1)    ; wait for blitter
        bne      waitblit
        move.w   d3,BLTBMOD(a1)  ; B mod = 4 * Y
        sub.w    d2,d3
        ext.l    d3
        move.l   d3,BLTAPT(a1)   ; A ptr = 4 * Y - 2 * X
        bpl      lineover        ; if negative,
        or.w     #SIGNFLAG,d5    ; set sign bit in con1
lineover:
        move.w   d0,BLTCON0(a1)  ; write control registers
        move.w   d5,BLTCON1(a1)
        move.w   d4,BLTCMOD(a1)  ; C mod = bitplane width
        move.w   d4,BLTDMOD(a1)  ; D mod = bitplane width
        sub.w    d2,d3
        move.w   d3,BLTAMOD(a1)  ; A mod = 4 * Y - 4 * X
        move.w   #$8000,BLTADAT(a1)    ; A data = 0x8000
        moveq.l  #-1,d5          ; Set masks to all ones
        move.l   d5,BLTAFWM(a1)  ; we can hit both masks at once
        move.l   a0,BLTCPT(a1)   ; Pointer to first pixel to set
        move.l   a0,BLTDPT(a1)
        move.w   d1,BLTSIZE(a1)  ; Start blit
        rts                      ; and return, blit still in progress.
        end
```

EXAMPLE: RotateBits

```
;
;       Here we rotate bits.  This code takes a single raster row of a
;       bitplane, and 'rotates' it into an array of 16-bit words, setting
;       the specified bit of each word in the array according to the
;       corresponding bit in the raster row.  We use the line mode in
;       conjunction with patterns to do this magic.
;
;       Input:  d0 contains the number of words in the raster row.  d1
;       contains the number of the bit to set (0..15).  a0 contains a
;       pointer to the raster data, and a1 contains a pointer to the
;       array we are filling; the array must be at least (d0)*16 words
;       (or (d0)*32 bytes) long.
;
        include 'exec/types.i'
        include 'hardware/custom.i'
        include 'hardware/blit.i'
        include 'hardware/dmabits.i'

        include 'hardware/hw_examples.i'

        xref    _custom
;
        xdef    rotatebits
;
;   Our entry point.
;
rotatebits:
        lea     _custom,a2      ; We need to access the custom registers
        tst     d0              ; if no words, just return
        beq     gone
        lea     DMACONR(a2),a3  ; get the address of dmaconr
        moveq.l #DMAB_BLTDONE-8,d2       ; get the bit number BLTDONE
        btst    d2,(a3)         ; check to see if we're done
wait1:
        btst    d2,(a3)         ; check again.
        bne     wait1           ; not done?  Keep waiting
        moveq.l #-30,d3         ; Line mode:  aptr = 4Y-2X, Y=0; X=15
        move.l  d3,BLTAPT(a2)
        move.w  #-60,BLTAMOD(a2)          ; amod = 4Y-4X
        clr.w   BLTBMOD(a2)     ; bmod = 4Y
        move.w  #2,BLTCMOD(a2)  ; cmod = width of bitmap (2)
        move.w  #2,BLTDMOD(a2)  ; ditto
        ror.w   #4,d1           ; grab the four bits of the bit number
        and.w   #$f000,d1       ; mask them out
        or.w    #$bca,d1        ; USEA, USEC, USED, F=AB+~AC
        move.w  d1,BLTCON0(a2)  ; stuff it
        move.w  #$f049,BLTCON1(a2)        ; BSH=15, SGN, LINE
        move.w  #$8000,BLTADAT(a2)        ; Initialize A dat for line
        move.w  #$ffff,BLTAFWM(a2)        ; Initialize masks
        move.w  #$ffff,BLTALWM(a2)
        move.l  a1,BLTCPT(a2)   ; Initialize pointer
        move.l  a1,BLTDPT(a2)
        lea     BLTBDAT(a2),a4  ; For quick access, we grab these two
        lea     BLTSIZE(a2),a5  ; addresses
        move.w  #$402,d1        ; Stuff bltsize; width=2, height=16
        move.w  (a0)+,d3        ; Get next word
```

```
                bra       inloop            ; Go into the loop
again:
                move.w    (a0)+,d3          ; Grab another word
                btst      d2,(a3)           ; Check blit done
wait2:
                btst      d2,(a3)           ; Check again
                bne       wait2             ; oops, not ready, loop around
inloop:
                move.w    d3,(a4)           ; stuff new word to make vertical
                move.w    d1,(a5)           ; start the blit
                subq.w    #1,d0             ; is that the last word?
                bne       again             ; keep going if not
gone:
                rts
                end
```

Chapter 7

SYSTEM CONTROL HARDWARE

Introduction

This chapter covers the control hardware of the Amiga system, including the following topics:

- How playfield priorities may be specified relative to the sprites

- How collisions between objects are sensed

- How system direct memory access (DMA) is controlled

- How interrupts are controlled and sensed

- How reset and early powerup are controlled

Video Priorities

You can control the priorities of various objects on the screen to give the illusion of three dimensions. The section below shows how playfield priority may be changed relative to sprites.

FIXED SPRITE PRIORITIES

You cannot change the relative priorities of the sprites. They will always appear on the screen with the lower-numbered sprites appearing in front of (having higher screen priority than) the higher-numbered sprites. This is shown in Figure 7-1. Each box represents the image of the sprite number shown in that box.

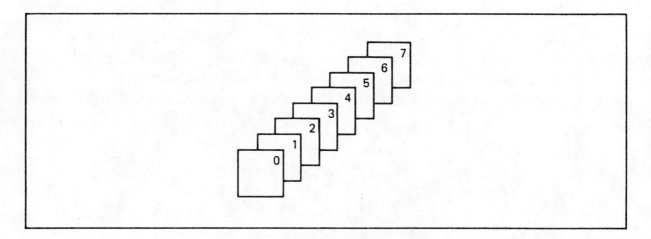

Figure 7-1: Inter-Sprite Fixed Priorities

HOW SPRITES ARE GROUPED

For playfield priority and collision purposes only, sprites are treated as four groups of two sprites each. The groups of sprites are:

> Sprites 0 and 1
> Sprites 2 and 3
> Sprites 4 and 5
> Sprites 6 and 7

UNDERSTANDING VIDEO PRIORITIES

The concept of video priorities is easy to understand if you imagine that four fingers of one of your hands represent the four pairs of sprites and two fingers of your other hand represent the two playfields. Just as you cannot change the sequence of the four fingers on the one hand, neither can you change the relative priority of the sprites. However, just as you can intertwine the two fingers of one hand in many different ways relative to the four fingers of the other hand, so can you position the playfields in front of or behind the sprites. This is illustrated in Figure 7-2.

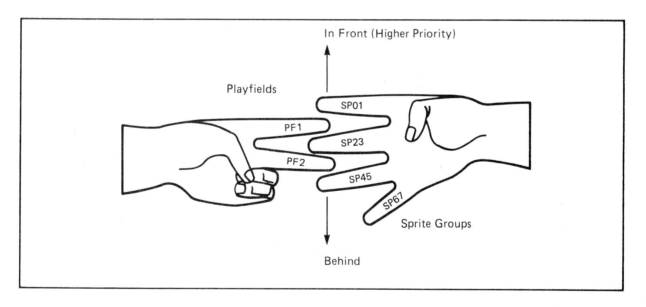

Figure 7-2: Analogy for Video Priority

Five possible positions can be chosen for each of the two "playfield fingers." For example, you can place playfield 1 on top of sprites 0 and 1 (0), between sprites 0 and 1 and sprites 2 and 3 (1), between sprites 2 and 3 and sprites 4 and 5 (2), between sprites 4 and 5 and sprites 6 and 7 (3), or beneath sprites 6 and 7 (4). You have the same possibilities for playfield 2.

The numbers 0 through 4 shown in parentheses in the preceding paragraph are the actual values you use to select the playfield priority positions. See "Setting the Priority Control Register" below.

You can also control the priority of playfield 2 relative to playfield 1. This gives you additional choices for the way you can design the screen priorities.

SETTING THE PRIORITY CONTROL REGISTER

This register lets you define how objects will pass in front of each other or hide behind each other. Normally, playfield 1 appears in front of playfield 2. The PF2PRI bit reverses this relationship, making playfield 2 more important. You control the video priorities by using the bits in BPLCON2 (for "bit-plane control register number 2") as shown in Table 7-1.

Table 7-1: Bits in BPLCON2

Bit Number	Name	Function
15-7		Not used (keep at 0)
6	PF2PRI	Playfield 2 priority
5-3	PF2P2 - PF2P0	Playfield 2 placement with respect to the sprites
2-0	PF1P2 - PF1P0	Playfield 1 placement with respect to the sprites

The binary values that you give to bits PF1P2-PF1P0 determine where playfield 1 occurs in the priority chain as shown in Table 7-2. This matches the description given in the previous section.

NOTE

PF2P2 - PF2P0, bits 5-3, are the priority bits for normal (non-dual) playfields.

Table 7-2: Priority of Playfields Based on Values of Bits PF1P2-PF1P0

Value	Placement (from most important to least important)				
000	PF1	SP01	SP23	SP45	SP67
001	SP01	PF1	SP23	SP45	SP67
010	SP01	SP23	PF1	SP45	SP67
011	SP01	SP23	SP45	PF1	SP67
100	SP01	SP23	SP45	SP67	PF1

In this table, PF1 stands for playfield 1, and SP01 stands for the group of sprites numbered 0 and 1. SP23 stands for sprites 2 and 3 as a group; SP45 stands for sprites 4 and 5 as a group; and SP67 stands for sprites 6 and 7 as a group.

Bits PF2P2-PF2P0 let you position playfield 2 among the sprite priorities in exactly the same way. However, it is the PF2PRI bit that determines which of the two playfields appears in front of the other on the screen. Here is a sample of possible BPLCON2 register contents that would create something a little unusual:

BITS	15-7	PF2PRI	PF2P2-0	PF1P2-0
VALUE	0s	1	010	000

This will result in a sprite/playfield priority placement of:

PF1 SP01 SP23 PF2 SP45 SP67

In other words, where objects pass across each other, playfield 1 is in front of sprite 0 or 1; and sprites 0 through 3 are in front of playfield 2. However, playfield 2 is in front of playfield 1 in any area where they overlap and where playfield 2 is not blocked by sprites 0 through 3.

Figure 7-3 shows one use of sprite/playfield priority. The single sprite object shown on the diagram is sprite 0. The sprite can "fly" across playfield 2, but when it crosses playfield 1 the sprite disappears behind that playfield. The result is an unusual video effect that causes the object to disappear when it crosses an invisible boundary on the screen.

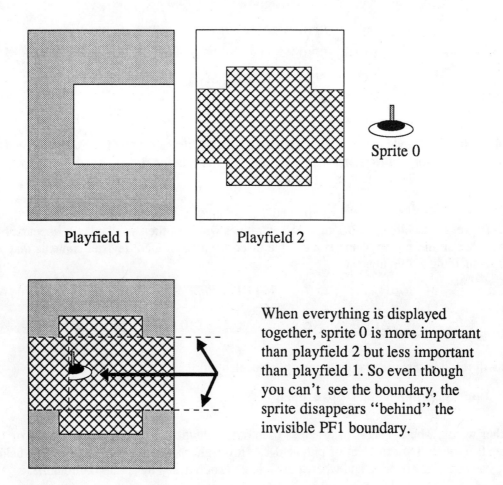

Playfield 1   Playfield 2

Sprite 0

When everything is displayed together, sprite 0 is more important than playfield 2 but less important than playfield 1. So even though you can't see the boundary, the sprite disappears "behind" the invisible PF1 boundary.

Figure 7-3: Sprite/Playfield Priority

Collision Detection

You can use the hardware to detect collisions between one sprite group and another sprite group, any sprite group and either of the playfields, the two playfields, or any combination of these items.

The first kind of collision is typically used in a game operation to determine if a missile has collided with a moving player. The second kind of collision is typically used to keep a moving object within specified on-screen boundaries. The third kind of collision detection allows you to define sections of playfield as individual objects, which you may move using the blitter. This is called playfield animation. If one playfield is defined as the backdrop or playing area and the other playfield is used to define objects (in addition to the sprites), you can sense collisions between the playfield-objects and the sprites or between the playfield-objects and the other playfield.

HOW COLLISIONS ARE DETERMINED

The video output is formed when the input data from all of the bit-planes and the sprites is combined into a common data stream for the display. For each of the pixel positions on the screen, the color of the highest priority object is displayed. Collisions are detected when two or more objects attempt to overlap in the same pixel position. This will set a bit in the collision data register.

HOW TO INTERPRET THE COLLISION DATA

The collision data register, CLXDAT, is *read-only*, and its contents are automatically cleared to 0 after it is read. Its bits are as shown in Table 7-3.

Table 7-3: CLXDAT Bits

Bit Number	Collisions Registered
15	not used
14	Sprite 4 (or 5) to sprite 6 (or 7)
13	Sprite 2 (or 3) to sprite 6 (or 7)
12	Sprite 2 (or 3) to sprite 4 (or 5)
11	Sprite 0 (or 1) to sprite 6 (or 7)
10	Sprite 0 (or 1) to sprite 4 (or 5)
9	Sprite 0 (or 1) to sprite 2 (or 3)
8	Even bit-planes to sprite 6 (or 7)
7	Even bit-planes to sprite 4 (or 5)
6	Even bit-planes to sprite 2 (or 3)
5	Even bit-planes to sprite 0 (or 1)
4	Odd bit-planes to sprite 6 (or 7)
3	Odd bit-planes to sprite 4 (or 5)
2	Odd bit-planes to sprite 2 (or 3)
1	Odd bit-planes to sprite 0 (or 1)
0	Even bit-planes to odd bit-planes

NOTE

The numbers in parentheses in Table 7-3 refer to collisions that will register only if you want them to show up. The collision control register described below lets you either ignore or include the odd-numbered sprites in the collision detection.

Notice that in this table, collision detection does *not* change when you select either single- or dual-playfield mode. Collision detection depends only on the actual bits present in the odd-numbered or even-numbered bit-planes. The collision control register specifies how to handle the bit-planes during collision detect.

HOW COLLISION DETECTION IS CONTROLLED

The collision control register, CLXCON, contains the bits that define certain characteristics of collision detection. Its bits are shown in Table 7-4.

Table 7-4: CLXCON Bits

Bit Number	Name	Function
15	ENSP7	Enable sprite 7 (OR with sprite 6)
14	ENSP5	Enable sprite 5 (OR with sprite 4)
13	ENSP3	Enable sprite 3 (OR with sprite 2)
12	ENSP1	Enable sprite 1 (OR with sprite 0)
11	ENBP6	Enable bit-plane 6 (match required for collision)
10	ENBP5	Enable bit-plane 5 (match required for collision)
9	ENBP4	Enable bit-plane 4 (match required for collision)
8	ENBP3	Enable bit-plane 3 (match required for collision)
7	ENBP2	Enable bit-plane 2 (match required for collision)
6	ENBP1	Enable bit-plane 1 (match required for collision)
5	MVBP6	Match value for bit-plane 6 collision
4	MVBP5	Match value for bit-plane 5 collision
3	MVBP4	Match value for bit-plane 4 collision
2	MVBP3	Match value for bit-plane 3 collision
1	MVBP2	Match value for bit-plane 2 collision
0	MVBP1	Match value for bit-plane 1 collision

Bits 15-12 let you specify that collisions with a sprite pair are to include the odd-numbered sprite of a pair of sprites. The even-numbered sprites always are included in the collision detection. Bits 11-6 let you specify whether to include or exclude specific bit-planes from the collision detection. Bits 5-0 let you specify the polarity (true-false condition) of bits that will cause a collision. For example, you may wish to register collisions only when the object collides with "something green" or "something blue." This feature, along with the collision enable bits, allows you to specify the exact bits, and their polarity, for the collision to be registered.

NOTE

This register is *write-only*. If all bit-planes are excluded (disabled), then a bit-plane collision will *always* be detected.

Beam Position Detection

Sometimes you might want to synchronize the 68000 processor to the video beam that is creating the screen display. In some cases, you may also wish to update a part of the display memory *after* the system has already accessed the data from the memory for the display area.

The address for accessing the beam counter is provided so that you can determine the value of the video beam counter and perform certain operations based on the beam position.

NOTE

The Copper is already capable of watching the display position for you and doing certain register-based operations automatically. Refer to "Copper Interrupts" below and Chapter 2, "Coprocessor Hardware," for further information.

In addition, when you are using a light pen with this system, this same address is used to read the light pen position rather than the beam position. This is described fully in Chapter 8, "Interface Hardware."

USING THE BEAM POSITION COUNTER

There are four addresses that access the beam position counter. Their usage is described in Table 7-5.

Table 7-5: Contents of the Beam Position Counter

VPOSR	*Read-only*	Read the high bit of the vertical position (V8) and the frame-type bit.
	Bit 15	LOF (Long-frame bit). Used to initialize interlaced displays.
	Bits 14-1	Unused
	Bit 0	High bit of the vertical position (V8). Allows PAL line counts (313) to appear in PAL versions of the Amiga.
VHPOSR	*Read-only*	Read vertical and horizontal position of the counter that is producing the beam on the screen (also reads the light pen).
	Bits 15-8	Low bits of the vertical position, bits V7-V0
	Bits 7-0	The horizontal position, bits H8-H1. Horizontal resolution is 1/160th of the screen width.
VPOSW	*Write only*	Bits same as VPOSR above.
VHPOSW	*Write only*	Bits same as VHPOSR above. Used for counter synchronization with chip test patterns.

As usual, the address pairs VPOSR,VHPOSR and VPOSW,VHPOSW can be read from and written to as long words, with the most significant addresses being VPOSR and VPOSW.

Interrupts

This system supports the full range of 68000 processor interrupts. The various kinds of interrupts generated by the hardware are brought into the peripherals chip and are translated into six of the seven available interrupts of the 68000.

NONMASKABLE INTERRUPT

Interrupt level 7 is the nonmaskable interrupt and is not generated anywhere in the current system. The raw interrupt lines of the 68000, IPL2 through IPL0, are brought out to the expansion connector and can be used to generate this level 7 interrupt for debugging purposes.

MASKABLE INTERRUPTS

Interrupt levels 1 through 6 are generated. Control registers within the peripherals chip allow you to mask certain of these sources and prevent them from generating a 68000 interrupt.

USER INTERFACE TO THE INTERRUPT SYSTEM

The system software has been designed to correctly handle all system hardware interrupts at levels 1 through 6. A separate set of input lines, designated INT2* and INT6* [1] have been routed to the expansion connector for use by external hardware for interrupts. These are known as the external low- and external high-level interrupts.

These interrupt lines are connected to the peripherals chip and create interrupt levels 2 and 6, respectively. It is recommended that you take advantage of the interrupt handlers built into the operating system by using these external interrupt lines rather than generating interrupts directly on the processor interrupt lines.

INTERRUPT CONTROL REGISTERS

There are two interrupt registers, interrupt enable (mask) and interrupt request (status). Each register has both a read and a write address.

The names of the interrupt addresses are

INTENA
Interrupt enable (mask) - *write only*. Sets or clears specific bits of INTENA.

INTENAR
Interrupt enable (mask) read - *read only*. Reads contents of INTENA.

---

[1] A * indicates an active low signal.

INTREQ

Interrupt request (status) - *write only*. Used by the processor to force a certain kind of interrupt to be processed (software interrupt). Also used to clear interrupt request flags once the interrupt process is completed.

INTREQR

Interrupt request (status) read - *read only*. Contains the bits that define which items are requesting interrupt service.

The bit positions in the interrupt request register correspond directly to those same positions in the interrupt enable register. The only difference between the read-only and the write-only addresses shown above is that bit 15 has no meaning in the read-only addresses.

SETTING AND CLEARING BITS

Below are the meanings of the bits in the interrupt control registers and how you use them.

Set and Clear

The interrupt registers, as well as the DMA control register, use a special way of selecting which of the bits are to be set or cleared. Bit 15 of these registers is called the SET/CLR bit.

When you wish to *set* a bit (make it a 1), you must place a 1 in the position you want to set *and a 1 into position 15*.

When you wish to *clear* a bit (make it a 0), you must place a 1 in the position you wish to clear *and a 0 into position 15*.

Positions 14-0 are bit-selectors. You write a 1 to any one or more bits to *select* that bit. At the same time you write a 1 or 0 to bit 15 to either *set* or *clear* the bits you have selected. Positions 14-0 that have 0 value will *not* be affected when you do the write. If you want to set some bits and clear others, you will have to write this register twice (once for setting some bits, once for clearing others).

Master Interrupt Enable

Bit 14 of the interrupt registers (INTEN) is for interrupt enable. This is the master interrupt enable bit. If this bit is a 0, it disables *all* other interrupts. You may wish to clear this bit to temporarily disable all interrupts to do some critical processing task.

NOTE

This bit is used for enable/disable only. It creates no interrupt request.

External Interrupts

Bits 13 and 3 of the interrupt registers are reserved for external interrupts.

Bit 13, EXTER, becomes a 1 when the system line called INT6* becomes a logic 0. Bit 13 generates a level 6 interrupt.

Bit 3, PORTS, becomes a 1 when the system line called INT2* becomes a logic 0. Bit 3 causes a level 2 interrupt.

Vertical Blanking Interrupt

Bit 5, VERTB, causes an interrupt at line 0 (start of vertical blank) of the video display frame. The system is often required to perform many different tasks during the vertical blanking interval. Among these tasks are the updating of various pointer registers, rewriting lists of Copper tasks when necessary, and other system-control operations.

The minimum time of vertical blanking is 20 horizontal scan lines for an NTSC system and 25 horizontal scan lines for a PAL system. The range starts at line 0 and ends at line 20 for NTSC or line 25 for PAL. After the minimum vertical blanking range, you can control where the display actually starts by using the DIWSTRT (display window start) register to extend the effective vertical blanking time. See Chapter 3, "Playfield Hardware," for more information on DIWSTRT.

If you find that you still require additional time during vertical blanking, you can use the Copper to create a level 3 interrupt. This Copper interrupt would be timed to occur just after the last line of display on the screen (after the display window stop which you have defined by using the DIWSTOP register).

Copper Interrupt

Bit 4, COPER, is used by the Copper to issue a level 3 interrupt. The Copper can change the content of *any* of the bits of this register, as it can write any value into most of the machine registers. However, this bit has been reserved for specifically identifying the Copper as the interrupt source.

Generally, you use this bit when you want to sense that the display beam has reached a specific position on the screen, and you wish to change something in memory based on this occurrence.

Audio Interrupts

Bits 10 - 7, AUD3 - 0, are assigned to the audio channels. They are called AUD3, AUD2, AUD1, and AUD0 and are assigned to channels 3, 2, 1, and 0, respectively.

This level 4 interrupt signals "audio block done." When the audio DMA is operating in automatic mode, this interrupt occurs when the last word in an audio data stream has been accessed. In manual mode, it occurs when the audio data register is ready to accept another word of data.

See Chapter 5, "Audio Hardware," for more information about interrupt generation and timing.

Blitter Interrupt

Bit 6, BLIT, signals "blitter finished." If this bit is a 1, it indicates that the blitter has completed the requested data transfer. The blitter is now ready to accept another task. This bit generates a level 3 interrupt.

Disk Interrupt

Bits 12 and 1 of the interrupt registers are assigned to disk interrupts.

Bit 12, DSKSYN, indicates that the sync register matches disk data. This bit generates a level 5 interrupt.

Bit 1, DSKBLK, indicates "disk block finished." It is used to indicate that the specified disk DMA task that you have requested has been completed. This bit generates a level 1 interrupt.

More information about disk data transfer and interrupts may be found in Chapter 8, "Interface Hardware."

Serial Port Interrupts

The following serial interrupts are associated with the specified bits of the interrupt registers.

Bit 11, RBF (for receive buffer full), specifies that the input buffer of the UART has data that is ready to read. This bit generates a level 5 interrupt.

Bit 0, TBE (for "transmit buffer empty"), specifies that the output buffer of the UART needs more data and data can now be written into this buffer. This bit generates a level 1 interrupt.

Hardware priority	Exec	Software priority Description	Label
1	1	software interrupt	SOFTINT
	2	disk block complete	DSKBLK
	3	transmitter buffer empty	TBE
2	4	external INT2 & CIAA	PORTS
3	5	graphics coprocessor	COPER
	6	vertical blank interval	VERTB
	7	blitter finished	BLIT
4	8	audio channel 2	AUD2
	9	audio channel 0	AUD0
	10	audio channel 3	AUD3
	11	audio channel 1	AUD1
5	12	receiver buffer full	RBF
	13	disk sync pattern found	DSKSYNC
6	14	external INT6 & CIAB	EXTER
	15	special (master enable)	INTEN
7	--	non-maskable interrupt	NMI

Figure 7-4: Interrupt Priorities

DMA Control

Many different direct memory access (DMA) functions occur during system operation. There is a read address as well as a write address to the DMA register so you can tell which DMA channels are enabled.

The address names for the DMA register are as follows:

DMACONR - Direct Memory Access Control - *read-only*.

DMACON - Direct Memory Access Control - *write-only*.

The contents of this register are shown in Table 7-5 (bit on if enabled).

Processor Access to Chip Memory

The Amiga chips access chip memory directly, rather than utilizing traditional bus arbitration mechanisms. Therefore, processor supplied features for multiprocessor support, such as the 68000 TAS (test and set) instruction, cannot serve their intended purpose and are not supported by the Amiga architecture.

Table 7-6: Contents of DMA Register

Bit Number	Name	Function
15	SET/CLR	The set/reset control bit. See description of bit 15 under "Interrupts" above.
14	BBUSY	Blitter busy status - *read-only*
13	BZERO	Blitter zero status - *read-only*. Remains 1 if, during a blitter operation, the blitter output was always zero.
12, 11		Unassigned
10	BLTPRI	Blitter priority. Also known as "blitter-nasty." When this is a 1, the blitter has full (instead of partial) priority over the 68000.
9	DMAEN	DMA enable. This is a master DMA enable bit. It enables the DMA for all of the channels at bits 8-0.
8	BPLEN	Bit-plane DMA enable
7	COPEN	Coprocessor DMA enable
6	BLTEN	Blitter DMA enable
5	SPREN	Sprite DMA enable
4	DSKEN	Disk DMA enable
3-0	AUDxEN	Audio DMA enable for channels 3-0 (x = 3 - 0).

For more information on using the DMA, see the following chapters:

Copper	Chapter 2	"Coprocessor Hardware"
Bit-planes	Chapter 3	"Playfield Hardware"
Sprites	Chapter 4	"Sprite Hardware"
Audio	Chapter 5	"Audio Hardware"
Blitter	Chapter 6	"Blitter Hardware"
Disk	Chapter 8	"Interface Hardware"

Reset and Early Startup Operation

When the Amiga is turned on or externally reset, the memory map is in a special state. An additional copy of the system ROM responds starting at memory location $00000000. The system RAM that would normally be located at this address is not available. On some Amiga models, portions of the RAM still respond. On other models, no RAM responds. Software must assume that memory is not available. The OVL bit in one of the 8520 Chips disables the overlay (See Appendix F for the bit location).

The Amiga System ROM contains an ID code as the first word. The value of the ID code may change in the future. The second word of the ROM contains a JMP instruction ($4ef9). The next two words are used as the initial program counter by the 68000 processor.

The 68000 "RESET" instruction works much like external reset or power on. All memory and AUTOCONFIG™ cards disappear, and the ROM image appears at location $00000000. The difference is that the CPU continues execution with the next instruction. Since RAM may not be available, special care is needed to write reboot code that will reliably reboot all Amiga models. Here is a source code listing of the *only* supported reboot code:

```
;------ The *only* supported reboot code
        CNOP    0,4     ;IMPORTANT: Must be longword aligned
MagicResetCode:
        lea.l   2,a0    ;Point to JMP instruction at start of ROM
        RESET           ;all RAM goes away now!
        jmp     (a0)    ;Rely on prefetch to execute this instruction
```

The RESET instruction must be executed when the CPU is at the Supervisor privilege level. If running under Exec, the following code must be used:

```
_ColdReboot:
        move.l  4,a6                    ;Get a pointer to ExecBase
        lea.l   MagicResetCode(pc),a5   ;Location of code to trap to
        jsr     _LVOSupervisor(a6)      ;start code (must use JSR)
```

Chapter 8

INTERFACE HARDWARE

Introduction

This chapter covers the interface hardware through which the Amiga talks to the outside world, including the following features:

- Two multiple purpose mouse/joystick/light pen control ports

- Disk controller (for floppy disk drives & other MFM and GCR devices)

- Keyboard

- Centronics compatible parallel I/O interface (for printers)

- RS232-C compatible serial interface (for external modems or other serial devices)

- Video output connectors (RGB, monochrome, NTSC, RF modulator, video slot)

Controller Port Interface

Each Amiga has two nine-pin connectors that can be used for input or output with many different kinds of controllers. The figure shows one of the two connectors and the corresponding face-on view of the typical controller plug.

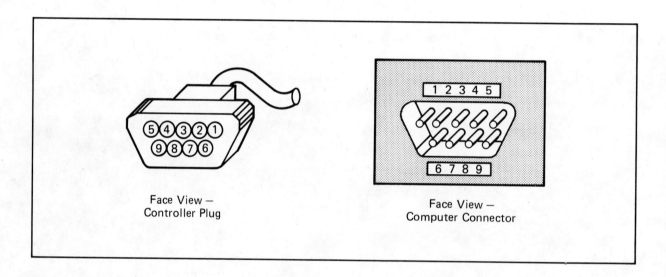

Figure 8-1: Controller Plug and Computer Connector

Table 8-1: Typical Controller Connections

Pin	Joystick	Mouse, Trackball, Driving Controller	Proportional Controller (Pair)	X-Y Proportional Joystick	Light Pen
1	Forward	V-pulse	---	Button 3 ‡	---
2	Back	H-pulse	---	---	---
3	Left	VQ-pulse	Left button	Button 1	---
4	Right	HQ-pulse	Right button	Button 2	---
5 †	---	Middle button ‡	Right POT	POT X	Pen pressed to screen
6 †	Button 1	Left button	---	---	Beam trigger
7	---	+5V	+5V	+5V	+5V
8	GND	GND	GND	GND	GND
9 †	Button 2 ‡	Right button	Left POT	POT Y	Button 2 ‡
† These pins may also be configured as outputs ‡ These buttons are optional					

REGISTERS USED WITH THE CONTROLLER PORT

JOY0DAT	($DFF00A)	Counter for digital (mouse) input (port 1)
JOY1DAT	($DFF00C)	Counter for digital (mouse) input (port 2)
CIAAPRA	($BFE001)	Input and output for pin 6 (port 1 and 2 fire buttons)
POT0DAT	($DFF012)	Counter for proportional input (port 1)
POT1DAT	($DFF014)	Counter for proportional input (port 2)
POTGO	($DFF034)	Write proportional pin values and start counters
POTGOR	($DFF016)	Read proportional pin values
BPLCON0	($DFF100)	Bit 3 enables the light pen latch
VPOSR	($DFF004)	Read light pen position (high order bits)
VHPOSR	($DFF006)	Read light pen position (low order bits)

READING MOUSE/TRACKBALL CONTROLLERS

Pulses entering the mouse inputs are converted to separate horizontal and vertical counts. The 8 bit wide horizontal and vertical counter registers can track mouse movement without processor intervention.

The mouse uses quadrature inputs. For each direction, a mechanical wheel inside the mouse will produce two pulse trains, one 90 degrees out of phase with the other (see Figure 8-2 for details). The phase relationship determines direction.

The counters increment when the mouse is moved to the right or "down" (toward you).
The counters decrement when the mouse is moved to the left or "up" (away from you).

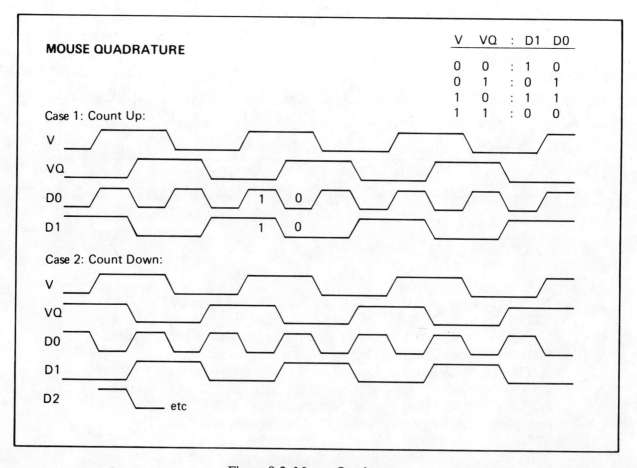

Figure 8-2: Mouse Quadrature

Reading the Counters

The mouse/trackball counter contents can be accessed by reading register addresses named JOY0DAT and JOY1DAT. These contains counts for ports 1 and 2 respectively.

The contents of each of these 16-bit registers are as follows:

> Bits 15-8   Mouse/trackball vertical count
> Bits 7-0   Mouse/trackball horizontal count

Counter Limitations

These counters will ''wrap around'' in either the positive or negative direction. If you wish to use the mouse to control something that is happening on the screen, you must read the counters at least once each vertical blanking period and save the previous contents of the registers. Then you can subtract from the previous readings to determine direction of movement and speed.

The mouse produces about 200 count pulses per inch of movement in either a horizontal or vertical direction. Vertical blanking happens once each 1/60th of a second. If you read the mouse once each vertical blanking period, you will most likely find a count difference (from the previous count) of less than 127. Only if a user moves the mouse at a speed of more than 38 inches per second will the counter values wrap. Fast-action games may need to read the mouse register twice per frame to prevent counter overrun.

If you subtract the current count from the previous count, the absolute value of the difference will represent the speed. The sign of the difference (positive or negative) lets you determine which direction the mouse is traveling.

The easiest way to calculate mouse velocity is with 8-bit signed arithmetic. The new value of a counter minus the previous value will represent the number of mouse counts since the last check. The example shown in Table 8-2 presents an alternate method. It treats both counts as unsigned values, ranging from 0 to 255. A count of 100 pulses is measured in each case.

Table 8-2: Determining the Direction of the Mouse

Previous Count	Current Count	Direction
200	100	Up (Left)
100	200	Down (Right)
200	45	Down *
45	200	Up **

Notes for Table 8-1:

* Because 200-45 = 155, which is more than 127, the true count must be 255 - (200-45) = 100; the direction is down.

** 45-200 = -155. Because the absolute value of -155 exceeds 127, the true count must be 255 + (-155) = 100; the direction is up.

Mouse Buttons

There are two buttons on the standard Amiga mouse. However, the control circuitry and software support up to three buttons.

- The left button on the Amiga mouse is connected to, CIAAPRA ($BFE001). The button for port 1 is connected to bit 6, port 2 is connected to bit 7. See the 8520 Appendix for more information. A logic state of 1 means "switch open." A logic state of 0 means "switch closed."

- Button 2 (right button on Amiga mouse) is connected to pin 9 of the controller ports, one of the proportional pins. See "DIGITAL INPUT/OUTPUT ON THE CONTROLLER PORT" for details.

- Button 3, when used, is connected to pin 5, the other proportional controller input.

READING DIGITAL JOYSTICK CONTROLLERS

Digital joysticks contain four directional switches. Each switch can be individually activated by the control stick. When the stick is pressed diagonally, two adjacent switches are activated. The total number of possible directions from a digital joystick is 8. All digital joysticks have at least one fire button.

Digital joystick switches are of the normally open type. When the switches are pressed, the input line is shorted to ground. An open switch reads as "1", a closed switch as "0".

Reading the joystick input data logic states is not so simple, however, because the data registers for the joysticks are the same as the counters that are used for the mouse or trackball controllers. The joystick registers are named JOY0DAT and JOY1DAT.

Table 8-2 shows how to interpret the data once you have read it from these registers. The true logic state of the switch data in these registers is "1 = switch closed."

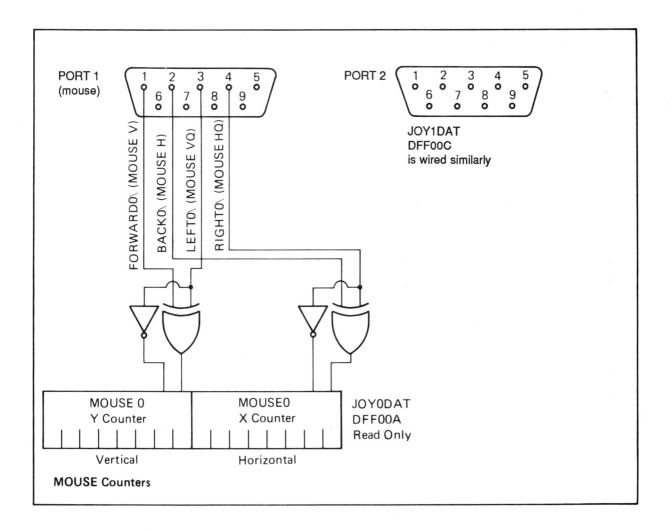

Table 8-3: Interpreting Data from JOY0DAT and JOY1DAT

Data Bit	Interpretation
1	True logic state of "right" switch.
9	True logic state of "left" switch.
1 (XOR) 0	You must calculate the exclusive-or of bits 1 and 0 to obtain the logic state of the "back" switch.
9 (XOR) 8	You must calculate the exclusive-or of bits 9 and 8 to obtain the logic state of the "forward" switch.

The fire buttons for ports 0 and 1 are connected to bits 6 and 7 of CIAAPRA ($BFE001). A 0 here indicates the switch is closed.

Some, but not all, joysticks have a second button. We encourage the use of this button *if* the function the button controls is duplicated via the keyboard or another mechanism. This button may be read in the same manner as the right mouse button.

READING PROPORTIONAL CONTROLLERS

Each of the game controller ports can handle two variable-resistance input devices, also known as proportional input devices. This section describes how the positions of the proportional input devices can be determined. There are two common types of proportional controllers: the "paddle" controller pair and the X-Y proportional joystick. A paddle controller pair consists of two individual enclosures, each containing a single resistor and fire-button and each connected to a common controller port input connector. Typical connections are shown in Figure 8-3.

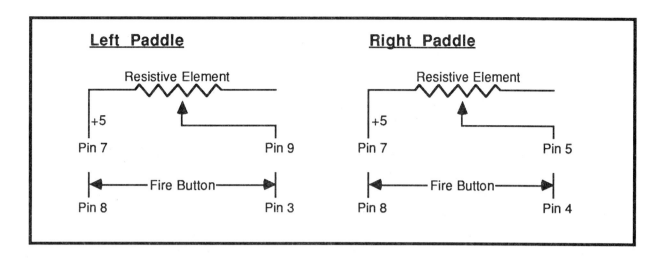

Figure 8-4: Typical Paddle Wiring Diagram

In an X-Y proportional joystick, the resistive elements are connected individually to the X and Y axes of a single controller stick.

Reading Proportional Controller Buttons

For the paddle controllers, the left and right joystick direction lines serve as the fire buttons for the left and right paddles.

Interpreting Proportional Controller Position

Interpreting the position of the proportional controller normally requires some preliminary work during the vertical blanking interval.

During vertical blanking, you write a value into an address called POTGO. For a standard X-Y joystick, this value is hex 0001. Writing to this register starts the operation of some special hardware that reads the potentiometer values and sets the values contained in the POT registers (described below) to zero.

The read circuitry stays in a reset state for the first seven or eight horizontal video scan lines. Following the reset interval, the circuit allows a charge to begin building up on a timing capacitor whose charge rate will be controlled by the position of the external controller resistance. For each horizontal scan line thereafter, the circuit compares the charge on the timing capacitor to a preset value. If the charge is below the preset, the POT counter is incremented. If the charge is above the preset, the counter value will be held until the next POTGO is issued.

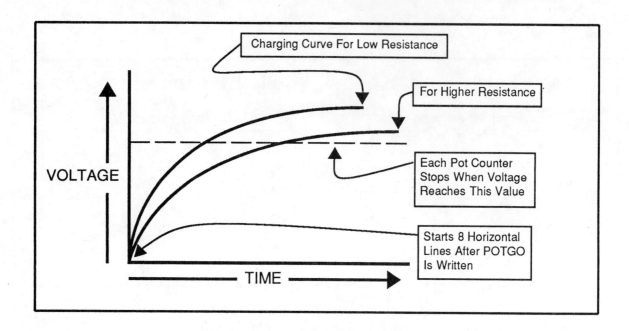

Figure 8-5: Effects of Resistance on Charging Rate

You normally issue POTGO at the beginning of a video screen, then read the values in the POT registers during the next vertical blanking period, just before issuing POTGO again.

Nothing in the system prevents the counters from overflowing (wrapping past a count of 255). However, the system is designed to insure that the counter cannot overflow within the span of a single screen. This allows you to know for certain whether an overflow is indicated by the controller.

Proportional Controller Registers

The following registers are used for the proportional controllers:

> POT0DAT - port 1 data (vertical/horizontal)
> POT1DAT - port 2 data (vertical/horizontal)

> Bit positions:

> Bits 15-8   POT0Y value or POT1Y value
> Bits 7-0   POT0X value or POT1X value

All counts are reset to zero when POTGO is written with bit zero high. Counts are normally read one frame after the scan circuitry is enabled.

Potentiometer Specifications

The resistance of the potentiometers should be a linear taper. Based on the design of the integrating analog-to-digital converter used, the maximum resistance should be no more than 528K (470K +/- 10 percent is suggested) for either the X or Y pots. This is based on a charge capacitor of 0.047uf, +/- 10 percent, and a maximum time of 16.6 milliseconds for charge to full value, ie. one video frame time.

All potentiometers exhibit a certain amount of "jitter". For acceptable results on a wide base of configurations, several input readings will need to be averaged.

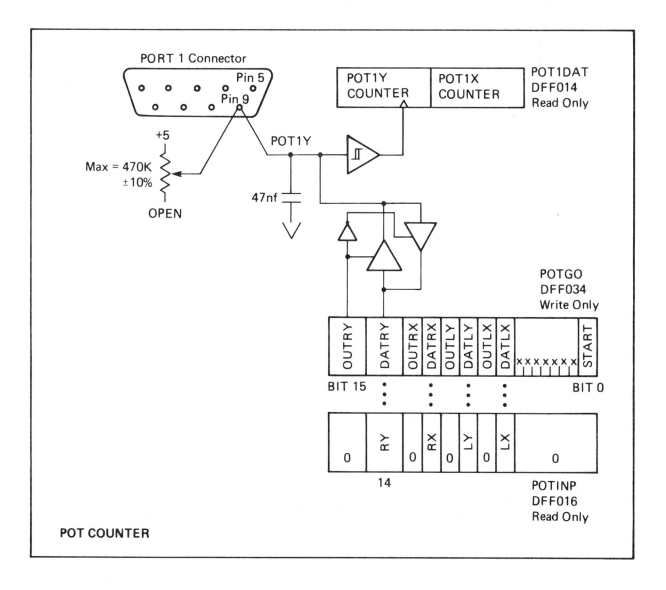

Figure 8-6: Potentiometer Charging Circuit

READING A LIGHT PEN

A light pen can be connected to one of the controller ports. On the A1000, the light pen must be connected to port 1. Changing ports requires a minor internal modification. On the A500 and A2000 the default is port 2. An internal jumper can select port 1. Regardless of the port used, the light pen design is the same.

The signal called "pen-pressed-to-screen" is typically actuated by a switch in the nose of the light pen. Note that this switch is connected to one of the potentiometer inputs and must be read as same as the right or middle button on a mouse.

The principles of light pen operation are as follows:

1. Just as the system exits vertical blank, the capture circuitry for the light pen is automatically enabled.

2. The video beam starts to create the picture, sweeping from left to right for each horizontal line as it paints the picture from the top of the screen to the bottom.

3. The sensors in the light pen see a pulse of light as the video beam passes by. The pen converts this light pulse into an electrical pulse on the "Beam Trigger" line (pin 6).

4. This trigger signal tells the internal circuitry to capture and save the current contents of the beam register, VPOSR. This allows you to determine where the pen was placed by reading the exact horizontal and vertical value of the counter beam at the instant the beam passed the light pen.

Reading the Light Pen Registers

The light pen register is at the same address as the beam counters. The bits are as follows:

VPOSR:	Bit 15	Long frame/short frame. 0=short frame
	Bits 14-1	Chip ID code. Do not depend on value!
	Bit 0	V8 (most significant bit of vertical position)
VHPOSR:	Bits 15-8	V7-V0 (vertical position)
	Bits 7-0	H8-H1 (horizontal position)

The software can refer to this register set as a long word whose address is VPOSR.

The positional resolution of these registers is as follows:

Vertical   1 scan line in non-interlaced mode
2 scan lines in interlaced mode (However, if you know which interlaced frame is under display, you can determine the correct position)

Horizontal   2 low-resolution pixels in either high- or low-resolution

The quality of the light pen will determine the amount of short-term jitter. For most applications, you should average several readings together.

To enable the light pen input, write a 1 into bit 3 of BPLCON0. Once the light pen input is enabled and the light pen issues a trigger signal, the value in VPOSR is frozen. If no trigger is seen, the counters latch at the end of the display field. It is impossible to read the current beam location while the VPOSR register is latched. This freeze is released at the end of internal vertical blanking (vertical position 20). There is no single bit in the system that indicates a light pen trigger. To determine if a trigger has occurred, use one of these methods:

1. Read (long) VPOSR twice.

2. If both values are not the same, the light pen has not triggered since the last top-of-screen (V = 20).

3. If both values are the same, mask off the upper 15 bits of the 32-bit word and compare it with the hex value of $10500 (V=261).

4. If the VPOSR value is greater than $10500, the light pen has not triggered since the last top-of-screen. If the value is less, the light pen has triggered and the value read is the screen position of the light pen.

A somewhat simplified method of determining the truth of the light pen value involves instructing the system software to read the register *only* during the internal vertical blanking period of 0<V20:

1. Read (long) VPOSR once, during the period of 0<V20.

2. Mask off the upper 15 bits of the 32-bit word and compare it with the hex value of $10500 (V=261).

3. If the VPOSR value is greater than $10500, the light pen has not triggered since the last top-of-screen. If the value is less, the light pen has triggered and the value read is the screen position of the light pen.

Note that when the light pen latch is enabled, the VPOSR register may be latched at any time, and cannot be relied on as a counter. This behavior may cause problems with software that attempts to derive timing based on VPOSR ticks.

DIGITAL INPUT/OUTPUT ON THE CONTROLLER PORT

The Amiga can read and interpret many different and nonstandard controllers. The control lines built into the POTGO register (address $DFF034) can redefine the functions of some of the controller port pins.

Table 8-4 is the POTGO register bit description. POTGO ($DFF034) is the write-only address for the pot control register. POTINP ($DFF016) is the read-only address for the pot control register. The pot-control register controls a four-bit bidirectional I/O port that shares the same four pins as the four pot inputs.

Table 8-4: POTGO ($DFF034) and POTINP ($DFF016) Registers

Bit Number	Name	Function
15	OUTRY	Output enable for bit 14 (1=output)
14	DATRY	data for port 2, pin 9
13	OUTRX	Output enable for bit 12
12	DATRX	data for port 2, pin 5
11	OUTLY	Output enable for bit 10
10	DATLY	data for port 1, pin 9 (right mouse button)
09	OUTLX	Output enable for bit 8
08	DATLX	data for port 1, pin 5 (middle mouse button)
07-01	X	chip revision identification number
00	START	Start pots (dump capacitors, start counters)

Instead of using the pot pins as variable-resistive inputs, you can use these pins as a four-bit input/output port. This provides you with two additional pins on each of the two controller ports for general purpose I/O.

If you set the output enable for any pin to a 1, the Amiga disconnects the potentiometer control circuitry from the port, and configures the pin for output. The state of the data bit controls the logic level on the output pin. This register must be written to at the POTGO address, and read from the POTINP address. There are large capacitors on these lines, and it can take up to 300 microseconds for the line to change state.

To use the entire register as an input, sensing the current state of the pot pins, write all 0s to POTGO. Thereafter you can read the current state by using read-only address POTINP. Note that bits set as inputs will be connected to the proportional counters (See the description of the START bit in POTGO).

These lines can also be used for button inputs. A button is a normally open switch that shorts to ground. The Amiga must provide a pull-up resistance on the sense pin. To do this, set the proper pin to output, and drive the line high (set both OUT... and DAT... to 1). Reading POTINP will produce a 0 if the button is pressed, a 1 if it is not.

The joystick fire buttons can also be configured as outputs. CIAADDRA ($BFE201) contains a mask that corresponds one-to-one with the data read register, CIAAPRA ($BFE001). Setting a 1 in the direction position makes the corresponding bit an output. See the 8520 appendix for more details.

Floppy Disk Controller

The built-in disk controller in the system can handle up to four MFM-type devices. Typically these are double-sided, double-density, 3.5" (90mm) or 5.25" disk drives. One 3.5" drive is installed in the basic unit.

The controller is extremely flexible. It can DMA an entire track of raw MFM data into memory in a single disk revolution. Special registers allow the CPU to synchronize with specific data, or read input a byte at a time. The controller can read and write virtually any double-density MFM encoded disk, including the Amiga V1.0 format, IBM PC (MS-DOS) 5.25", IBM PC (MS-DOS) 3.5" and most CP/M™ formatted disks. The controller has provisions for reading and writing most disk using the Group Coded Recording (GCR) method, including Apple II™ disks. With motor speed tricks, the controller can read and write Commodore 1541/1571 format diskettes.

REGISTERS USED BY THE DISK SUBSYSTEM

The disk subsystem uses two ports on the system's 8520 CIA chips, and several registers in the Paula chip:

CIAAPRA	($BFE001)	four input bits for disk sensing
CIABPRB	($BFD100)	eight output bits for disk selection, control and stepping
ADKCON	($DFF09E)	control bits (write only register)
ADKCONR	($DFF010)	control bits (read only register)
DSKPTH	($DFF020)	DMA pointer (32 bits)
DSKLEN	($DFF024)	length of DMA
DSKBYTR	($DFF01A)	Disk data byte and status read
DSKSYNC	($DFF07E)	Disk sync finder; holds a match word

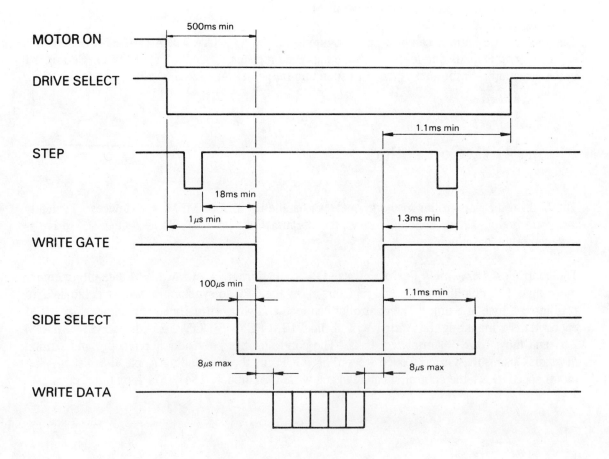

Figure 8-7: Chinon Timing Diagram

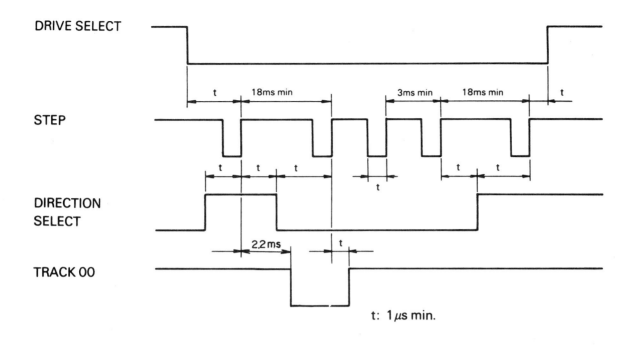

t: 1 μs min.

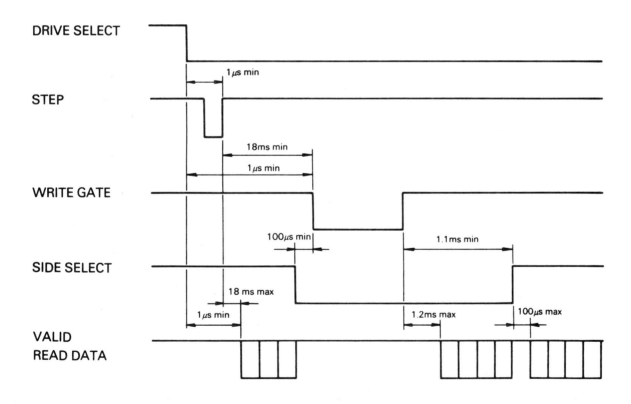

Figure 8-8: Chinon Timing Diagram (cont.)

CIAAPRA/CIABPRB - Disk selection, control and sensing

The following table lists how 8520 chip bits used by the disk subsystem. Bits labeled "PA" are input bits in CIAAPRA ($BFE001). Bits labeled "PB" are output bits located in CIAAPRB ($BFD100). More information on how the 8520 chips operate can be found in Appendix F.

Table 8-5: Disk Subsystem

Bit	Name	Function
PA5	DSKRDY*	Disk ready (active low). The drive will pull this line low when the motor is known to be rotating at full speed. This signal is only valid when the motor is ON, at other times configuration information may obscure the meaning of this input.
PA4	DSKTRACK0*	Track zero detect. The drive will pull this line low when the disk heads are positioned over track zero. Software must not attempt to step outwards when this signal is active. Some drives will refuse to step, others will attempt the step, possibly causing alignment damage. All new drives must refuse to step outward in this condition.
PA3	DSKPROT*	Disk is write protected (active low).
PA2	DSKCHANGE*	Disk has been removed from the drive. The signal goes low whenever a disk is removed. It remains low until a disk is inserted AND a step pulse is received.

Bit	Name	Function
PB7	DSKMOTOR*	Disk motor control (active low). This signal is nonstandard on the Amiga system. Each drive will latch the motor signal at the time its select signal turns on. The disk drive motor will stay in this state until the next time select turns on. DSKMOTOR* also controls the activity light on the front of the disk drive.

All software that selects drives must set up the motor signal *before* selecting any drives. The drive will "remember" the state of its motor when it is not selected. All drive motors turn off after system reset. |

After turning on the motor, software must further wait for one half second (500ms), or for the DSKRDY* line to go low.

PB6	DSKSEL3*	Select drive 3 (active low).

PB5	DSKSEL2*	Select drive 2 (active low).

PB4	DSKSEL1*	Select drive 1 (active low).

PB3	DSKSEL0*	Select drive 0 (internal drive) (active low).

PB2   DSKSIDE   Specify which disk head to use. Zero indicates the upper head. DSKSIDE must be stable for 100 microseconds before writing. After writing, at least 1.3 milliseconds must pass before switching DSKSIDE.

PB1   DSKDIREC   Specify the direction to seek the heads. Zero implies seek towards the center spindle. Track zero is at the outside of the disk. This line must be set up *before* the actual step pulse, with a separate write to the register.

PB0   DSKSTEP*   Step the heads of the disk. This signal must always be used as a quick pulse (high, momentarily low, then high).

The drives used for the Amiga are guaranteed to get to the next track within 3 milliseconds. Some drives will support a much faster rate, others will fail. Loops that decrement a counter to provide delay are **not acceptable**. See Appendix F for a better solution.

When reversing directions, a minimum of 18 milliseconds delay is required from the last step pulse. Settle time for Amiga drives is specified at 15 milliseconds.

FLAG   DSKINDEX*   Disk index pulse ($BFDD00, bit 4). Can be used to create a level 6 interrupt. See Appendix F for details.

Disk DMA Channel Control

Data is normally transferred to the disk by direct memory access (DMA). The disk DMA is controlled by four items:

- Pointer to the area into which or from which the data is to be moved

- Length of data to be moved by DMA

- Direction of data transfer (read/write)

- DMA enable

DSKPTH - Pointer to Data

You specify the 32-bit-wide address from which or to which the data is to be transferred. The lowest bit of the address must be zero, and the buffer must be in CHIP memory. The value must be written as a single long word to the DSKPTH register ($DFF020).

DSKLEN - Length, Direction, DMA Enable

All of the control bits relating to this topic are contained in a write-only register, called DSKLEN:

Table 8-6: DSKLEN Register ($DFF024)

Bit Number	Name	Usage
15	DMAEN	Secondary disk DMA enable
14	WRITE	Disk write (RAM → disk if 1)
13-0	LENGTH	Number of words to transfer

The hardware requires a special sequence in order to start DMA to the disk. This sequence prevents accidental writes to the disk. In short, the DMAEN bit in the DSKLEN register must be turned on twice in order to actually enable the disk DMA hardware. Here is the sequence you should follow:

1. Enable disk DMA in the DMACON register (See Chapter 7 for more information)

2. Set DSKLEN to $4000, thereby forcing the DMA for the disk to be turned off.

3. Put the value you want into the DSKLEN register.

4. Write this value again into the DSKLEN register. This actually starts the DMA.

5. After the DMA is complete, set the DSKLEN register back to $4000, to prevent accidental writes to the disk.

As each data word is transferred, the length value is decremented. After each transfer occurs, the value of the pointer is incremented. The pointer points to the the next word of data to written or read. When the length value counts down to 0, the transfer stops.

The recommended method of reading from the disk is to read an entire track into a buffer and then search for the sector(s) that you want. Using the DSKSYNC register (described below) will guarantee word alignment of the data. With this process you need to read from the disk only once for the entire track. In a high speed loader, the step to the next head can occur while the previous track is processed and checksummed. With this method there are no time-critical sections in reading data, other high-priority subsystems (such as graphics or audio) are be allowed to run.

If you have too little memory for track buffering (or for some other reason decide not to read a whole track at once), the disk hardware supports a limited set of sector-searching facilities. There is a register that may be polled to examine the disk input stream.

There is a hardware bug that causes the last three bits of data sent to the disk to be lost. Also, the last word in a disk-read DMA operation may not come in (that is, one less word may be read than you asked for).

DSKBYTR - Disk Data Byte and Status Read (read-only)

This register is the disk-microprocessor data buffer. In read mode, data from the disk is placed into this register one byte at a time. As each byte is received into the register, the DSKBYT bit is set true. DSKBYT is cleared when the DSKBYTR register is read.

DSKBYTR may be used to synchronize the processor to the disk rotation before issuing a read or write under DMA control.

Table 8-7: DSKBYTR Register

Bit Number	Name	Function
15	DSKBYT	When set, indicates that this register contains a valid byte of data (reset by reading this register).
14	DMAON	Indicates when DMA is actually enabled. All the various DMA bits must be true. This means the DMAEN bit in DKSLEN, and the DSKEN & DMAEN bits in DMACON.
13	DISKWRITE	The disk write bit (in DSKLEN) is enabled.
12	WORDEQUAL	Indicates the DISKSYNC register equals the disk input stream. This bit is true only while the input stream matches the sync register (as little as two microseconds).
11-8		Currently unused; don't depend on read value.
7-0	DATA	Disk byte data.

ADKCON and ADKCONR - Audio and Disk Control Register

ADKCON is the write-only address and ADKCONR is the read-only address for this register. Not all of the bits are dedicated to the disk. Bit 15 of this register allows independent setting or clearing of any bit or bits. If bit 15 is a one on a write, any ones in positions 0-14 will set the corresponding bit. If bit 15 is a zero, any ones will clear the corresponding bit.

Table 8-8: ADKCON and ADKCONR Register

Bit Number	Name	Function
15	SET/CLR	Control bit that allows setting or clearing of individual bits without affecting the rest of the register.
		If bit 15 is a 1, the specified bits are set.
		If bit 15 is a 0, the specified bits are cleared.
14	PRECOMP1	MSB of Precompensation specifier
13	PRECOMP0	LSB of Precompensation specifier
		Value of 00 selects none.
		Value of 01 selects 140 ns.
		Value of 10 selects 280 ns.
		Value of 11 selects 560 ns.
12	MFMPREC	Value of 0 selects GCR Precompensation.
		Value of 1 selects MFM Precompensation.
10	WORDSYNC	Value of 1 enables synchronizing and starting of DMA on disk read of a word. The word on which to synchronize must be written into the DSKSYNC address ($DFF07E). This capability is highly useful.
9	MSBSYNC	Value of 1 enables sync on most significant bit of the input (usually used for GCR).
8	FAST	Value of 1 selects two microseconds per bit cell (usually MFM). Data must be valid raw MFM. 0 selects four microseconds per bit (usually GCR).

The raw MFM data that must be presented to the disk controller will be twice as large as the unencoded data. The following table shows the relationship:

$$1 \rightarrow 01$$
$$0 \rightarrow 10 \quad \text{;if following a 0}$$
$$0 \rightarrow 00 \quad \text{;if following a 1}$$

With clever manipulation, the blitter can be used to encode and decode the MFM.

In one common form of GCR recording, each data byte always has the most significant bit set to a 1. MSBSYNC, when a 1, tells the disk controller to look for this sync bit on every disk byte. When reading a GCR formatted disk, the software must use a translate table called a nybble-izer to assure that data written to the disk does not have too many consecutive 1's or 0's.

DSKSYNC - Disk Input Synchronizer

The DSKSYNC register is used to synchronize the input stream. This is highly useful when reading disks. If the WORDSYNC bit is enabled in ADKCON, no data is transferred until a word is found in the input stream that matches the word in the DSKSYNC register. On read, DMA will start with the following word from the disk. During disk read DMA, the controller will resync every time the word match is found. Typically the DSKSYNC will be set to the magic MFM sync mark value, $4489.

In addition, the DSKSYNC bit in INTREQ is set when the input stream matches the DSKSYNC register. The DSKSYNC bit in INTREQ is independent of the WORDSYNC enable.

DISK INTERRUPTS

The disk controller can issue three kinds of interrupts:

- DSKSYNC (level 5, INTREQ bit 12)—input stream matches the DSKSYNC register.

- DSKBLK (level 1, INTREQ bit 1)—disk DMA has completed.

- INDEX (level 6, 8520 Flag pin)—index sensor triggered.

Interrupts are explained further in the section "Length, Direction, DMA Enable". See Chapter 7, "System Control Hardware," for more information about interrupts. See Appendix F for more information on the 8520.

The Keyboard

The keyboard is interfaced to the system via the serial shift register on one of the 8520 CIA chips. The keyboard data line is connected to the SP pin, the keyboard clock is connected to the CNT pin. Appendix H contains a full description of the interface.

HOW THE KEYBOARD DATA IS RECEIVED

The CNT line is used as a clock for the keyboard. On each transition of this line, one bit of data is clocked in from the keyboard. The keyboard sends this clock when each data bit is stable on the SP line. The clock is an active low pulse. The rising edge of this pulse clocks in the data.

After a data byte has been received from the keyboard, an interrupt from the 8520 is issued to the processor. The keyboard waits for a handshake signal from the system before transmitting any more keystrokes. This handshake is issued by the processor pulsing the SP line low then high. While some keyboards can detect a 1 microsecond handshake pulse, the pulse must be at least 85 microseconds for operation with all models of Amiga keyboards.

If another keystroke is received before the previous one has been accepted by the processor, the keyboard microprocessor holds keys in a 10 keycode type-ahead buffer.

TYPE OF DATA RECEIVED

The keyboard data is *not* received in the form of ASCII characters. Instead, for maximum versatility, it is received in the form of keycodes. These codes include both the down and up transitions of the keys. This allows your software to use both sets of information to determine exactly what is happening on the keyboard.

Here is a list of the hexadecimal values that are assigned to the keyboard. A downstroke of the key transmits the value shown here. An upstroke of the key transmits this value plus $80. The picture of the keyboard at the end of this section shows the positions that correspond to the description in the paragraphs below.

Note that raw keycodes provide positional information *only*, the legend which is printed on top of the keys changes from country to country.

RAW KEYCODES → 00-3F hex

These are key codes assigned to specific positions on the main body of the keyboard. The letters on the tops of these keys are different for each country; not all countries use the QWERTY key layout. These keycodes are best described positionally as shown in Figure 8-9 and Figure 8-10 at the end of the keyboard section. The international keyboards have two more keys that are "cut out" of larger keys on the USA version. These are $30, cut out from the the left shift, and $2B, cut out from the return key.

RAW KEYCODES → 40-5F hex (Codes common to all keyboards)

40	Space
41	Backspace
42	Tab
43	Numeric Pad "ENTER"
44	Return
45	Escape
46	Delete
4C	Cursor up
4D	Cursor down
4E	Cursor right
4F	Cursor left
50-59	Function keys F1-F10
5F	Help

RAW KEYCODES → 60-67 hex (Key codes for qualifier keys:)

60	Left shift
61	Right shift
62	Caps lock
63	Control
64	Left ALT
65	Right ALT
66	Left Amiga (or Commodore key)
67	Right Amiga

F0-FF hex

These key codes are used for keyboard to 68000 communication, and are not associated with a keystroke. They have no key transition flag, and are therefore described completely by 8-bit codes:

    78   Reset warning. CTRL-AMIGA-AMIGA has been pressed. The keyboard
            will wait a maximum of 10 seconds before resetting the machine.
            (Not available on all keyboard models)

    F9   Last key code bad, next key is same code retransmitted

    FA   Keyboard key buffer overflow

    FC   Keyboard self-test fail. Also, the caps-lock LED will blink
            to indicate the source of the error. Once for ROM failure,
            twice for RAM failure and three times if the watchdog timer
            fails to function.

    FD   Initiate power-up key stream (for keys held or stuck at power on)

    FE   Terminate power-up key stream.

These key codes will usually be filtered out by keyboard drivers.

LIMITATIONS OF THE KEYBOARD

The Amiga keyboard is a matrix of rows and columns with a key switch at each intersection (see Appendix H for a diagram of the matrix). Because of this, the keyboard is subject to a phenomenon called "phantom keystrokes." While this is generally not a problem for typing, games may require several keys be independently held down at once. By examining the matrix, you can determine which keys may interfere with each other, and which ones are always safe.

Phantom keystrokes occur when certain combinations of keys pressed are pressed simultaneously. For example, hold the "A" and "S" keys down simultaneously. Notice that "A" and "S" are transmitted. While still holding them down, press "Z". On the original Amiga 1000 keyboard, both the "Z" and a ghost "X" would be generated. Starting with the Amiga 500, the controller was upgraded to notice simple phantom situations like the one above; instead of generating a ghost, the controller will hold off sending any character until the matrix has cleared (releasing "A" or "S" would clear the matrix). Some high-end Amiga keyboards may implement true "N-key rollover," where any combination of keys can be detected simultaneously.

All of the keyboards are designed so that phantoms will not happen during normal typing, only when unusual key combinations like the one just described are pressed. Normally, the keyboard will appear to have "N-key rollover," which means that you will run out of fingers before generating a ghost character.

NOTE

Seven keys are not part of the matrix, and will never contribute to generating phantoms. These keys are: CTRL, the two SHIFT keys, the two Amiga keys, and the two ALT keys.

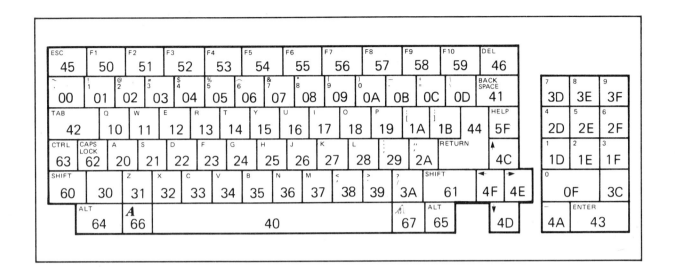

Figure 8-9: The Amiga 1000 Keyboard, Showing Keycodes in Hexadecimal

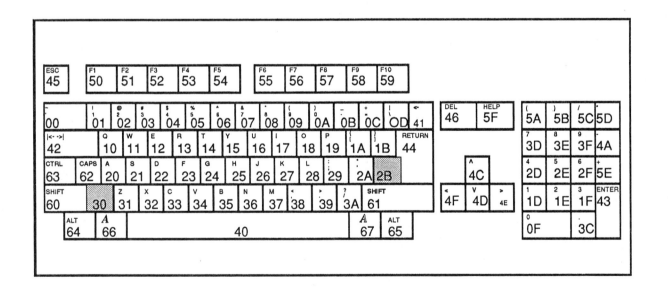

Figure 8-10: The Amiga 500/2000 Keyboard, Showing Keycodes in Hexadecimal

Parallel Input/Output Interface

The general-purpose bi-directional parallel interface is a 25-pin connector on the back panel of the computer. This connector is generally used for a parallel printer.

For each data byte written to the parallel port register, the hardware automatically generates a pulse on the data ready pin. The acknowledge pulse from the parallel device is hooked up to an interrupt. For pin connections and timing, see Appendix E and F.

Serial Interface

A 25-pin connector on the back panel of the computer serves as the general purpose serial interface. This connector can drive a wide range of different peripherals, including an external modem or a serial printer.

For pin connections, see Appendix E.

INTRODUCTION TO SERIAL CIRCUITRY

The Paula custom chip contains a Universal Asynchronous Receiver/Transmitter, or UART. This UART is programmable for any rate from 110 to over 1,000,000 bits per second. It can receive or send data with a programmable length of eight or nine bits.

The UART implementation provides a high degree of software control. The UART is capable of detecting overrun errors, which occur when some other system sends in data faster than you remove it from the data-receive register. There are also status bits and interrupts for the conditions of receive buffer full and transmit buffer empty. An additional status bit is provided that indicates "all bits have been shifted out". All of these topics are discussed below.

SETTING THE BAUD RATE

The rate of transmission (the baud rate) is controlled by the contents of the register named SERPER. Bits 14-0 of SERPER are the baud-rate divider bits.

All timing is done on the basis of a "color clock," which is 279.36ns long on NTSC machines and 281.94ns on PAL machines. If the SERPER divisor is set to the number N, then N+1 color clocks occur between samples of the state of the input pin (for receive) or between transmissions of output bits (for transmit). Thus SERPER=(3,579,545/baud)-1. On a PAL machine, SERPER=(3,546,895/baud)-1. For example, the proper SERPER value for 9600 baud on an NTSC machine is (3,579,545/9600)-1=371.

With a cable of a reasonable length, the maximum reliable rate is on the order of 150,000-250,000 bits per second. Maximum rates will vary between machines. At these high rate it is not possible to handle the overhead of interrupts. The receiving end will need to be in a tight read loop. Through the use of low speed control information and high-speed bursts, a very inexpensive communication network can be built.

SETTING THE RECEIVE MODE

The number of bits that are to be received before the system tells you that the receive register is full may be defined either as eight or nine (this allows for 8 bit transmission with parity). In either case, the receive circuitry expects to see one start bit, eight or nine data bits, and at least one stop bit.

Receive mode is set by bit 15 of the write-only SERPER register. Bit 15 is a 1 if you chose nine data bits for the receive-register full signal, and a 0 if you chose eight data bits. The normal state of this bit for most receive applications is a 0.

CONTENTS OF THE RECEIVE DATA REGISTER

The serial input data-receive register is 16 bits wide. It contains the 8 or 9 bit input data and status bits.

The data is received, one bit at a time, into an internal serial-to-parallel shift register. When the proper number of bit times have elapsed, the contents of this register are transferred to the serial data read register (SERDATR) shown in Table 8-10, and you are signaled that there is data ready for you.

Immediately after the transfer of data takes place, the receive shift register again becomes ready to accept new data. After receiving the receiver-full interrupt, you will have up to one full character-receive time (8 to 10 bit times) to accept the data and clear the interrupt. If the interrupt is not cleared in time, the OVERRUN bit is set.

Table 8-10 shows the definitions of the various bit positions within SERDATR.

Table 8-9: SERDATR / ADKCON Registers

SERDATR

Bit Number	Name	Function
15	OVRUN	OVERRUN bit (Mirror—also appears in the interrupt request register.) Indicates that another byte of data was received before the previous byte was picked up by the processor. To prevent this condition, it is necessary to reset INTF_RBF (bit 11, receive-buffer-full) in INTREQ.
14	RBF	READ BUFFER FULL (Mirror—also appears in the interrupt request register.) When this bit is 1, there is data ready to be picked up by the processor. After reading the contents of this data register, you must reset the INTF_RBF bit in INTREQ to prevent an overrun.
13	TBE	TRANSMIT BUFFER EMPTY (Not a mirror—interrupt occurs when the buffer *becomes* empty.) When bit 14 is a 1, the data in the output data register (SERDAT) has been transferred to the serial output shift register, so SERDAT is ready to accept another output word. This is also true when the buffer *is* empty. This bit is normally used for full-duplex operation.
12	TSRE	TRANSMIT SHIFT REGISTER EMPTY When this bit is a 1, the output shift register has completed its task, all data has been transmitted, and the register is now idle. If you stop writing data into the output register (SERDAT), then this bit will become a 1 after both the word currently in the shift register *and* the word placed into SERDAT have been transmitted. This bit is normally used for half-duplex operation.
11	RXD	Direct read of RXD pin on Paula chip.
10		Not used at this time.
9	STP	Stop bit if 9 data bits are specified for receive.

8	STP	Stop bit if 8 data bits are specified for receive.
		OR
	DB8	9th data bit if 9 bits are specified for receive.
7-0	DB7-DB0	Low 8 data bits of received data. Data is TRUE (data you read is the same polarity as the data expected).

ADKCON

15	SET/CLR	Allows setting or clearing individual bits.
		If bit 15 is a 1 specified bits are set.
		If bit 15 is a 0 specified bits are cleared.
11	UARTBRK	Force the transmit pin to zero.

HOW OUTPUT DATA IS TRANSMITTED

You send data out on the transmit lines by writing into the serial data output register (SERDAT). This register is write-only.

Data will be sent out at the same rate as you have established for the read. Immediately after you write the data into this register, the system will begin the transmission at the baud rate you selected.

At the start of the operation, this data is transferred from SERDAT into an internal serial shift register. When the transfer to the serial shift register has been completed, SERDAT can accept new data; the TBE interrupt signals this fact.

Data will be moved out of the shift register, one bit during each time interval, starting with the least significant bit. The shifting continues until all 1 bits have been shifted out. Any number or combination of data and stop bits may be specified this way.

SERDAT is a 16-bit register that allows you to control the format (appearance) of the transmitted data. To form a typical data sequence, such as one start bit, eight data bits, and one stop bit, you write into SERDAT the contents shown in Figures 8-11 and 8-12.

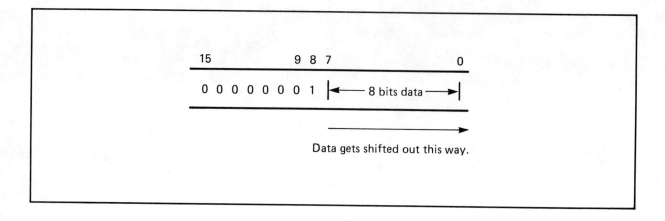

Figure 8-11: Starting Appearance of SERDAT and Shift Register

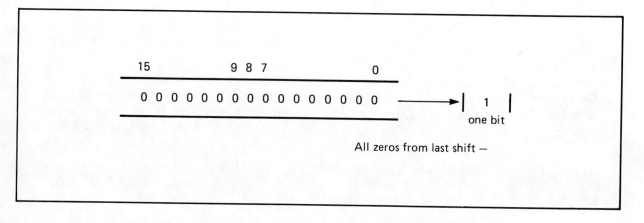

Figure 8-12: Ending Appearance of Shift Register

The register stops shifting and signals "shift register empty" (TSRE) when there is a 1 bit present in the bit-shifted-out position *and* the rest of the contents of the shift register are 0s. When new nonzero contents are loaded into this register, shifting begins again.

SPECIFYING THE REGISTER CONTENTS

The data to be transmitted is placed in the output register (SERDAT). Above the data bits, 1 bits must be added as stop bits. Normally, either one or two stop bits are sent.

The transmission of the start bit is independent of the contents of this register. One start bit is automatically generated before the first data bit (bit 0) is sent.

Writing this register starts the data transmission. If this register is written with all zeros, *no* data transmission is initiated.

Display Output Connections

All Amigas provide a 23-pin connector on the back. This jack contains video outputs and inputs for external genlock devices. Two separate type of RGB video are available on the connector:

- RGB Monitors ("analog RGB"). Provides four outputs; Red (R), Green (G), Blue (B), and Sync (S). They can generate up to 4,096 different colors on-screen simultaneously using the circuitry presently available on the Amiga.

- Digital RGB Monitors. Provides four outputs, distinct from those shown above, named Red (R), Green (G), Blue (B), Half-Intensity (I), and Sync (S). All output levels are logic levels (0 or 1). On some monitors these outputs allow up to 15 possible color combinations, where the values 0000 and 0001 map to the same output value (Half intensity with no color present is the same as full intensity, no color). Some monitors arbitrarily map the 16 combinations to 16 arbitrary colors.

Note that the sync signals from the Amiga are unbuffered. For use with any device that presents a heavy load on the sync outputs, external buffers will be required.

The Amiga 500 and 2000 provide a full-bandwidth monochrome video jack for use with inexpensive monochrome monitors. The Amiga colors are combined into intensities based on the following table:

Red	Green	Blue
30%	60%	10%

The Amiga 1000 provides an RF modulator jack. An adapter is available that allows the Amiga to use a television set for display. Stereo sound is available on the jack, but will generally be combined into monaural sound for the TV set.

The Amiga 1000 provides a color composite video jack. This is suitable for recording directly with a VCR, but the output is not broadcast quaility. For use on a monochrome monitor, the color information often has undesired effects; careful color selection or a modification to the internal circuitry can improve the results. High quality composite adaptors for the A500, A1000, and A2000 plug into the 23 pin RGB port.

The Amiga 2000 provides a special "video slot" that contains many more signals than are available elsewhere: all the 23-pin RGB port signals, the unencoded digital video, light pen, power, audio, colorburst, pixel switch, sync, clock signals, etc.

Appendix A

Register Summary—Alphabetical Order

This appendix contains the definitive summary, in alphabetical order, of the register set and the usages of the individual bits.

The addresses shown here are used by the special chips (called "Agnus", "Denise", and "Paula") for transferring data among themselves. Also, the Copper uses these addresses for writing to the special chip registers. To write to these registers with the 68000, calculate the 68000 address using this formula:

$$68000\ address = (chip\ address) + \$DFF000$$

For example, for the 68000 to write to ADKCON (address = $09E), the address would be $DFF09E. No other access address is valid. Unused registers must not be accessed

All bits marked as "unused" must be written as zeros. The value of any unused read bit must not be trusted. Registers are either *read-only* or *write-only*. Reading a write-only register will trash the register. Writing a read-only register will cause unexpected results.

All of the "pointer" type registers are organized as 32 bits on a long word boundary. These registers may be written with one MOVE.L instruction. The lowest bit of all pointers must be written as zero. The custom chips can only access CHIP memory; using a non-CHIP address will fail (See the AllocMem() documentation or your compiler manual for more information on CHIP memory). Disk data, sprite data, bitplane data, audio data, copper lists and anything that will be blitted or accessed by custom chip DMA must be located in chip memory.

When strobing any register which responds to either a read or a write, (for example copjmp2) be sure to use a MOVE.W, not CLR.W. The CLR instruction causes a read and a clear (two accesses) on a 68000, but only a single access on 68020 processors. This will give different results on different processors.

```
                        Agnus/
                 Read/  Denise/
Register Address Write  Paula        Function
-------- ------- ------ -------      --------

ADKCON   09E     W        P          Audio, disk, control write
ADKCONR  010     R        P          Audio, disk, control read

                 BIT#   USE
                 ----   ------------------------------------
                 15     SET/CLR   Set/clear control bit. Determines if bits
                                  written with a 1 get set or cleared. Bits
                                  written with a zero are always unchanged.
                 14-13  PRECOMP 1-0

                        CODE  PRECOMP VALUE
                        ----  -------------
                        00    none
                        01    140 ns
                        10    280 ns
                        11    560 ns

                 12     MFMPREC   ( 1=MFM precomp 0=GCR precomp)
                 11     UARTBRK    Forces a UART break (clears TXD) if true.
                 10     WORDSYNC   Enables disk read synchronizing on a word
                                  equal to DISK SYNC CODE, located in
                                  address (3F)*2.
                 09 MSBSYNC   Enables disk read synchronizing on the MSB
                                  (most signif bit). Appl type GCR.
                 08 FAST   Disk data clock rate control 1=fast(2us) 0=slow(4us).
                           (fast for MFM, slow for MFM or GCR)

                 07 USE3PN Use audio channel 3 to modulate nothing.
                 06 USE2P3 Use audio channel 2 to modulate period of channel 3.
                 05 USE1P2 Use audio channel 1 to modulate period of channel 2.
                 04 USE0P1 Use audio channel 0 to modulate period of channel 1.

                 03 USE3VN Use audio channel 3 to modulate nothing.
                 02 USE2V3 Use audio channel 2 to modulate volume of channel 3.
                 01 USE1V2 Use audio channel 1 to modulate volume of channel 2.
                 00 USE0V1 Use audio channel 0 to modulate volume of channel 1.

                 NOTE:  If both period and volume are modulated on the
                 same channel, the period and volume will be alternated.
                 First word xxxxxxx V6-V0 , Second word P15-P0 (etc)

AUDxDAT  0AA  W        P   Audio channel x data

                 This register is the audio channel x (x=0,1,2,3)
                 DMA data buffer.  It contains 2 bytes of data that
                 are each 2's complement and are outputted
                 sequentially (with digital-to-analog conversion)
                 to the audio output pins.  (LSB = 3 MV)  The DMA
                 controller automatically transfers data to this
                 register from RAM.  The processor can also write
                 directly to this register.  When the DMA data is
                 finished (words outputted=length) and the data in
                 this register has been used, an audio channel
                 interrupt request is set.
```

```
AUDxLCH     0A0  W    A          Audio channel x location (high 3 bits)
AUDxLCL     0A2  W    A          Audio channel x location (low 15 bits)
```

This pair of registers contains the 18 bit starting address
(location) of audio channel x (x=0,1,2,3) DMA data.
This is not a pointer register and therefore needs
to be reloaded only if a different memory location is to
be outputted.

```
AUDxLEN     0A4  W         P    Audio channel x length
```

This register contains the length (number of words) of
audio channel x DMA data.

```
AUDxPER     0A6  W         P    Audio channel x Period
```

This register contains the period (rate) of
audio channel x DMA data transfer.
The minimum period is 124 color clocks. This means
that the smallest number that should be placed in
this register is 124 decimal. This corresponds to
a maximum sample frequency of 28.86 khz.

```
AUDxVOL     0A8  W         P    Audio channel x volume
```

This register contains the volume setting for
audio channel x. Bits 6,5,4,3,2,1,0 specify 65
linear volume levels as shown below.

Bit#	Use
15-07	Not used
06	Forces volume to max (64 ones, no zeros)
05-00	Sets one of 64 levels (000000=no output (111111=63 1s, one 0)

```
BLTAFWM     044  W    A          Blitter first-word mask for source A
BLTALWM     046  W    A          Blitter last-word mask for source A
```

The patterns in these two registers are ANDed with
the first and last words of each line of data from
source A into the blitter. A zero in any bit
overrides data from source A. These registers
should be set to all 1s for fill mode or for
line-drawing mode.

```
BLTCON0    040  W   A        Blitter control register 0
BLTCON1    042  W   A        Blitter control register 1
```

These two control registers are used together to
control blitter operations. There are two basic
modes, area and line, which are selected by bit
0 of BLTCON1, as shown below.

```
        AREA MODE ("normal")
        ---------------------
        BIT#  BLTCON0      BLTCON1
        ----  -------      -------
        15    ASH3         BSH3
        14    ASH2         BSH2
        13    ASH1         BSH1
        12    ASA0         BSH0
        11    USEA         X
        10    USEB         X
        09    USEC         X
        08    USED         X
        07    LF7          X
        06    LF6          X
        05    LF5          X
        04    LF4          EFE
        03    LF3          IFE
        02    LF2          FCI
        01    LF1          DESC
        00    LF0          LINE(=0)
```

```
ASH3-0   Shift value of A source
BSH3-0   Shift value of B source
USEA     Mode control bit to use source A
USEB     Mode control bit to use source B
USEC     Mode control bit to use source C
USED     Mode control bit to use destination D
LF7-0    Logic function minterm select lines
EFE      Exclusive fill enable
IFE      Inclusive fill enable
FCI      Fill carry input
DESC     Descending (decreasing address) control bit
LINE     Line mode control bit (set to 0)
```

```
BLTCON0 (cont.)   LINE DRAW      LINE MODE (line draw)
BLTCON1 (cont.)   LINE DRAW      -------------------------------
                  LINE DRAW      BIT# BLTCON0      BLTCON1
                  LINE DRAW      ---- -------      -------
                  LINE DRAW      15   START3       TEXTURE3
                  LINE DRAW      14   START2       TEXTURE2
                  LINE DRAW      13   START1       TEXTURE1
                  LINE DRAW      12   START0       TEXTURE0
                  LINE DRAW      11   1            0
                  LINE DRAW      10   0            0
                  LINE DRAW      09   1            0
                  LINE DRAW      08   1            0
                  LINE DRAW      07   LF7          0
                  LINE DRAW      06   LF6          SIGN
                  LINE DRAW      05   LF5          0 (Reserved)
                  LINE DRAW      04   LF4          SUD
                  LINE DRAW      03   LF3          SUL
                  LINE DRAW      02   LF2          AUL
                  LINE DRAW      01   LF1          SING
                  LINE DRAW      00   LF0          LINE (=1)
                  LINE DRAW
                  LINE DRAW      START3-0   Starting point of line
                  LINE DRAW                 (0 thru 15 hex)

                  LINE DRAW      LF7-0     Logic function minterm
                  LINE DRAW      select lines should be preloaded
                  LINE DRAW      with 4A to select the equation
                  LINE DRAW      D=(AC+ABC).  Since A contains a
                  LINE DRAW      single bit true (8000), most bits
                  LINE DRAW      will pass the C field unchanged
                  LINE DRAW      (not A and C), but one bit will
                  LINE DRAW      invert the C field and combine it
                  LINE DRAW      with texture (A and B and not C).
                  LINE DRAW      The A bit is automatically moved
                  LINE DRAW      across the word by the hardware.

                  LINE DRAW      LINE   Line mode control bit (set to 1)
                  LINE DRAW      SIGN   Sign flag
                  LINE DRAW      0      Reserved for new mode
                  LINE DRAW      SING   Single bit per horizontal line for
                  LINE DRAW             use with subsequent area fill
                  LINE DRAW      SUD    Sometimes up or down (=AUD*)
                  LINE DRAW      SUL    Sometimes up or left
                  LINE DRAW      AUL    Always up or left

                  LINE DRAW      The 3 bits above select the octant
                  LINE DRAW      for line drawing:

                  LINE DRAW                 OCT    SUD  SUL  AUL
                  LINE DRAW                 ---    ---  ---  ---
                  LINE DRAW                 0       1    1    0
                  LINE DRAW                 1       0    0    1
                  LINE DRAW                 2       0    1    1
                  LINE DRAW                 3       1    1    1
                  LINE DRAW                 4       1    0    1
                  LINE DRAW                 5       0    1    0
                  LINE DRAW                 6       0    0    0
                  LINE DRAW                 7       1    0    0

                  LINE DRAW      The "B" source is used for
                  LINE DRAW      texturing the drawn lines.
```

BLTDDAT   ---   -   - - -   Blitter destination data register

         This register holds the data resulting from each
         word of blitter operation until it is sent to a
         RAM destination. This is a dummy address and
         cannot be read by the micro. The transfer is
         automatic during blitter operation.

BLTSIZE   058 W   A   Blitter start and size (window width,
                               height)

         This register contains the width and height of
         the blitter operation (in line mode, width must
         = 2, height = line length). Writing to this
         register will start the blitter, and should be
         done last, after all pointers and control
         registers have been initialized.

         BIT# 15,14,13,12,11,10,09,08,07,06,05,04,03,02,01,00
               ----
               h9 h8 h7 h6 h5 h4 h3 h2 h1 h0,w5 w4 w3 w2 w1 w0

         h=height=vertical lines (10 bits=1024 lines max)
         w=width =horizontal pixels (6 bits=64 words=1024 pixels max)

         LINE DRAW   BLTSIZE controls the line length and starts
         LINE DRAW   the line draw when written to. The h field
         LINE DRAW   controls the line length (10 bits gives
         LINE DRAW   lines up to 1024 dots long). The w field
         LINE DRAW   must be set to 02 for all line drawing.

BLTxDAT   074 W   A   Blitter source x data register

         This register holds source x (x=A,B,C) data for
         use by the blitter. It is normally loaded by the
         blitter DMA channel; however, it may also be
         preloaded by the microprocessor.

         LINE DRAW   BLTADAT is used as an index register
         LINE DRAW   and must be preloaded with 8000.
         LINE DRAW   BLTBDAT is used for texture; it must
         LINE DRAW   be preloaded with FF if no texture
         LINE DRAW   (solid line) is desired.

```
BLTxMOD        064  W   A      Blitter modulo x
```

This register contains the modulo for blitter source (x=A,B,C) or destination (x=D). A modulo is a number that is automatically added to the address at the end of each line, to make the address point to the start of the next line. Each source or destination has its own modulo, allowing each to be a different size, while an identical area of each is used in the blitter operation.

```
LINE DRAW     BLTAMOD and BLTBMOD are used as slope
LINE DRAW     storage registers and must be preloaded
LINE DRAW     with the values (4Y-4X) and (4Y)
LINE DRAW     respectively.  Y/X= line slope.
LINE DRAW     BLTCMOD and BLTDMOD must both be
LINE DRAW     preloaded with the width (in bytes)
LINE DRAW     of the image into which the line is
LINE DRAW     being drawn (normally two times the
LINE DRAW     screen width in words).
```

```
BLTxPTH        050  W   A      Blitter pointer to x (high 3 bits)
BLTxPTL        052  W   A      Blitter pointer to x (low 15 bits)
```

This pair of registers contains the 18-bit address of blitter source (x=A,B,C) or destination (x=D) DMA data. This pointer must be preloaded with the starting address of the data to be processed by the blitter. After the blitter is finished, it will contain the last data address (plus increment and modulo).

```
LINE DRAW     BLTAPTL is used as an accumulator
LINE DRAW     register and must be preloaded with
LINE DRAW     the starting value of (2Y-X) where
LINE DRAW     Y/X is the line slope.  BLTCPT and
LINE DRAW     BLTDPT (both H and L) must be
LINE DRAW     preloaded with the starting address
LINE DRAW     of the line.
```

```
BPL1MOD        108  W   A      Bit plane modulo (odd planes)
BPL2MOD        10A  W   A      Bit Plane modulo (even planes)
```

These registers contain the modulos for the odd and even bit planes. A modulo is a number that is automatically added to the address at the end of each line, so that the address then points to the start of the next line.
Since they have separate modulos, the odd and even bit planes may have sizes that are different from each other, as well as different from the display window size.

```
BPLCON0    100  W  A D    Bit plane control register (misc.
                                  control bits)
BPLCON1    102  W    D    Bit plane control register
                                  (horizontal scroll control)
BPLCON2    104  W    D    Bit Plane control register
                                  (video priority control)
```

These **registers** control the operation of the
bit **planes** and various aspects of the display.

BIT#	BPLCON0	BPLCON1	BPLCON2
15	HIRES	X	X
14	BPU2	X	X
13	BPU1	X	X
12	BPU0	X	X
11	HOMOD	X	X
10	DBLPF	X	X
09	COLOR	X	X
08	GAUD	X	X
07	X	PF2H3	X
06	X	PF2H2	PF2PRI
05	X	PF2H1	PF2P2
04	X	PF2H0	PF2P1
03	LPEN	PF1H3	PF2P0
02	LACE	PF1H2	PF1P2
01	ERSY	PF1H1	PF1P1
00	X	PF1H0	PF1P0

```
HIRES=High-resolution (640) mode
BPU  =Bit plane use code 000-110 (NONE through 6 inclusive)
HOMOD=Hold-and-modify mode
DBLPF=Double playfield (PF1=odd PF2=even bit planes)
COLOR=Composite video COLOR enable
GAUD=Genlock audio enable (muxed on BKGND pin
        during vertical blanking
LPEN =Light pen enable (reset on power up)
LACE =Interlace enable (reset on power up)
ERSY =External resync (HSYNC, VSYNC pads become
        inputs) (reset on power up)
PF2PRI=Playfield 2 (even planes) has priority over
        (appears in front of) playfield 1
        (odd planes).
PF2P=Playfield 2 priority code (with respect
        to sprites)
PF1P=Playfield 1 priority code (with respect
        to sprites)
PF2H=Playfield 2 horizontal scroll code
PF1H=Playfield 1 horizontal scroll code
```

```
BPLxDAT      110  W   D     Bit plane x data (parallel-to-serial
                            convert)

             These registers receive the DMA data fetched from
             RAM by the bit plane address pointers described
             above.  They may also be written by either
             microprocessor.  They act as a six-word parallel-
             to-serial buffer for up to six memory bit planes
             (x=1-6).  The parallel-to-serial conversion is
             triggered whenever bit plane #1 is written,
             indicating the completion of all bit planes for
             that word (16 pixels).  The MSB is output first,
             and is, therefore, always on the left.

BPLxPTH      0E0  W   A     Bit plane x pointer (high 3 bits)
BPLxPTL      0E2  W   A     Bit plane x pointer (low 15 bits)

             This pair of registers contains the 18-bit pointer to
             the address of bit-plane x (x=1,2,3,4,5,6) DMA data.
             This pointer must be reinitialized by the processor
             or copper to point to the beginning of bit plane data
             every vertical blank time.

CLXCON       098  W   D     Collision control

             This register controls which bit-planes are
             included (enabled) in collision detection and
             their required state if included.  It also controls
             the individual inclusion of odd-numbered sprites
             in the collision detection by logically OR-ing
             them with their corresponding even-numbered sprite.
```

BIT#	FUNCTION	DESCRIPTION
15	ENSP7	Enable sprite 7 (ORed with sprite 6)
14	ENSP5	Enable sprite 5 (ORed with sprite 4)
13	ENSP3	Enable sprite 3 (ORed with sprite 2)
12	ENSP1	Enable sprite 1 (ORed with sprite 0)
11	ENBP6	Enable bit plane 6 (match required for collision)
10	ENBP5	Enable bit plane 5 (match required for collision)
09	ENBP4	Enable bit plane 4 (match required for collision)
08	ENBP3	Enable bit plane 3 (match required for collision)
07	ENBP2	Enable bit plane 2 (match required for collision)
06	ENBP1	Enable bit plane 1 (match required for collision)
05	MVBP6	Match value for bit plane 6 collision
04	MVBP5	Match value for bit plane 5 collision
03	MVBP4	Match value for bit plane 4 collision
02	MVBP3	Match value for bit plane 3 collision
01	MVBP2	Match value for bit plane 2 collision
00	MVBP1	Match value for bit plane 1 collision

```
             NOTE:  Disabled bit planes cannot prevent
             collisions.  Therefore if all bit planes are
             disabled, collisions will be continuous,
             regardless of the match values.
```

CLXDAT   00E R   D   Collision data register (read and clear)

This address reads (and clears) the collision
detection register. The bit assignments are below.

NOTE: Playfield 1 is all odd-numbered enabled
      bit planes. Playfield 2 is all even-numbered
      enabled bit planes

```
BIT#    COLLISIONS REGISTERED
-----   --------------------------
15      not used
14      Sprite 4 (or 5) to sprite 6 (or 7)
13      Sprite 2 (or 3) to sprite 6 (or 7)
12      Sprite 2 (or 3) to sprite 4 (or 5)
11      Sprite 0 (or 1) to sprite 6 (or 7)
10      Sprite 0 (or 1) to sprite 4 (or 5)
09      Sprite 0 (or 1) to sprite 2 (or 3)
08      Playfield 2 to sprite 6 (or 7)
07      Playfield 2 to sprite 4 (or 5)
06      Playfield 2 to sprite 2 (or 3)
05      Playfield 2 to sprite 0 (or 1)
04      Playfield 1 to sprite 6 (or 7)
03      Playfield 1 to sprite 4 (or 5)
02      Playfield 1 to sprite 2 (or 3)
01      Playfield 1 to sprite 0 (or 1)
00      Playfield 1 to playfield 2
```

COLORxx   180 W   D   Color table xx

There are 32 of these registers (xx=00-31) and they
are sometimes collectively called the "color
palette." They contain 12-bit codes representing
red, green, and blue colors for RGB systems.
One of these registers at a time is selected
(by the BPLxDAT serialized video code)
for presentation at the RGB video output pins.
The table below shows the color register bit usage.

```
BIT# 15,14,13,12,11,10,09,08,07,06,05,04,03,02,01,00
     -----------  -----------  -----------  -----------
RGB  X  X  X  X   R3 R2 R1 R0  G3 G2 G1 G0  B3 B2 B1 B0
```

B=blue, G=green, R=red,

COP1LCH   080 W   A   Copper first location register
                           (high 3 bits)
COP1LCL   082 W   A   Copper first location register
                           (low 15 bits)
COP2LCH   084 W   A   Copper second location register
                           (high 3 bits)
COP2LCL   086 W   A   Copper second location register
                           (low 15 bits)

These registers contain the jump addresses
described above.

COPCON   02E   W   A   Copper control register

          This is a 1-bit register that when set true, allows
          the Copper to access the blitter hardware. This
          bit is cleared by power-on reset, so that the
          Copper cannot access the blitter hardware.

          BIT#   NAME   FUNCTION
          ----   -------   -------------------
          01   CDANG   Copper danger mode. Allows Copper
                            access to blitter if true.

COPINS   08C   W   A   Copper instruction fetch identify

          This is a dummy address that is generated by the
          Copper whenever it is loading instructions into
          its own instruction register. This actually occurs
          every Copper cycle except for the second (IR2)
          cycle of the MOVE instruction. The three types
          of instructions are shown below.

          MOVE   Move immediate to destination.
          WAIT   Wait until beam counter is equal to, or
                  greater than. (keeps Copper off of bus
                  until beam position has been reached).
          SKIP   Skip if beam counter is equal to or greater
                  than (skips following MOVE instruction unless
                  beam position has been reached).

	MOVE		WAIT UNTIL		SKIP IF	
BIT#	IR1	IR2	IR1	IR2	IR1	IR2
15	X	RD15	VP7	BFD *	VP7	BFD *
14	X	RD14	VP6	VE6	VP6	VE6
13	X	RD13	VP5	VE5	VP5	VE5
12	X	RD12	VP4	VE4	VP4	VE4
11	X	RD11	VP3	VE3	VP3	VE3
10	X	RD10	VP2	VE2	VP2	VE2
09	X	RD09	VP1	VE1	VP1	VE1
08	DA8	RD08	VP0	VE0	VP0	VE0
07	DA7	RD07	HP8	HE8	HP8	HE8
06	DA6	RD06	HP7	HE7	HP7	HE7
05	DA5	RD05	HP6	HE6	HP6	HE6
04	DA4	RD04	HP5	HE5	HP5	HE5
03	DA3	RD03	HP4	HE4	HP4	HE4
02	DA2	RD02	HP3	HE3	HP3	HE3
01	DA1	RD01	HP2	HE2	HP2	HE2
00	0	RD00	1	0	1	1

IR1=First instruction register
IR2=Second instruction register
DA =Destination address for MOVE instruction. Fetched
    during IR1 time, used during IR2 time on RGA bus.
RD =RAM data moved by MOVE instruction at IR2 time
    directly from RAM to the address given by the
    DA field.
VP =Vertical beam position comparison bit.
HP =Horizontal beam position comparison bit.
VE =Enable comparison (mask bit).
HE =Enable comparison (mask bit).

* NOTE BFD=Blitter finished disable. When this bit
         is true, the Blitter Finished flag will
         have no effect on the Copper. When this
         bit is zero, the Blitter Finished flag
         must be true (in addition to the rest of
         the bit comparisons) before the Copper
         can exit from its wait state or skip
         over an instruction. Note that the V7
         comparison cannot be masked.

The Copper is basically a two-cycle machine that
requests the bus only during odd memory cycles
(4 memory cycles per instruction). This prevents
collisions with display, audio, disk, refresh, and
sprites, all of which use only even cycles. It
therefore needs (and has) priority over only the
blitter and microprocessor.

There are only three types of instructions:
MOVE immediate, WAIT until, and SKIP if. All
instructions (except for WAIT) require two bus
cycles (and two instruction words). Since only
the odd bus cycles are requested, four memory
cycle times are required per instruction
(memory cycles are 280 ns.)

COPINS (cont.)   There are two indirect jump registers, COP1LC and
                  COP2LC. These are 18-bit pointer registers whose
                  contents are used to modify the program counter for
                  initialization or jumps. They are transferred to
                  the program counter whenever strobe addresses
                  COPJMP1 or COPJMP2 are written. In addition,
                  COP1LC is automatically used at the beginning of
                  each vertical blank time.

                  It is important that one of the jump registers be
                  initialized and its jump strobe address hit after
                  power-up but before Copper DMA is initialized.
                  This insures a determined startup address and state.

COPJMP1   088 S A   Copper restart at first location
COPJMP2   08A S A   Copper restart at second location

                  These addresses are strobe addresses. When written
                  to, they cause the Copper to jump indirect using
                  the address contained in the first or second
                  location registers described below. The Copper
                  itself can write to these addresses, causing its
                  own jump indirect.

```
DDFSTOP      094   W   A       Display data fetch stop (horiz. position)
DDFSTRT      092   W   A       Display data fetch start (horiz. position)
```

These registers control the horizontal timing of the
beginning and end of the bit plane DMA display data
fetch. The vertical bit plane DMA timing is identical
to the display windows described above.
The bit plane modulos are dependent on the bit plane
horizontal size and on this data-fetch window size.

Register bit assignment
```
------------------------
BIT#  15,14,13,12,11,10,09,08,07,06,05,04,03,02,01,00
      -------------------------------------------------
USE    X  X  X  X  X  X  X  X H8 H7 H6 H5 H4 H3  X  X
```

(X bits should always be driven with 0 to maintain
upward compatibility)

The tables below show the start and stop timing for
different register contents.

```
DDFSTRT (left edge of display data fetch)
------------------------------------------
      PURPOSE           H8,H7,H6,H5,H4
------------------      ---------------
Extra wide (max) *      0  0  1  0  1
Wide                    0  0  1  1  0
Normal                  0  0  1  1  1
Narrow                  0  1  0  0  0

DDFSTOP (right edge of display data fetch)
------------------------------------------
      PURPOSE           H8,H7,H6,H5,H4
------------------      ---------------
Narrow                  1  1  0  0  1
Normal                  1  1  0  1  0
Wide (max)              1  1  0  1  1
```

```
DIWSTOP      090   W   A       Display window stop (lower right
                                 vertical-horizontal position)
DIWSTRT      08E   W   A       Display window start (upper left
                                 vertical-horizontal position)
```

These registers control display window size and
position by locating the upper left and lower right
corners.

```
BIT# 15,14,13,12,11,10,09,08,07,06,05,04,03,02,01,00
     -------------------------------------------------
USE  V7 V6 V5 V4 V3 V2 V1 V0 H7 H6 H5 H4 H3 H2 H1 H0
```

DIWSTRT is vertically restricted to the upper 2/3
of the display (V8=0) and horizontally restricted to
the left 3/4 of the display (H8=0).

DIWSTOP is vertically restricted to the lower 1/2
of the display (V8=/=V7) and horizontally restricted
to the right 1/4 of the display (H8=1).

```
DMACON     096  W   A D P   DMA control write (clear or set)
DMACONR    002  R   A   P   DMA control (and blitter status) read
```

This register controls all of the DMA channels and
contains blitter DMA status bits.

```
BIT#   FUNCTION    DESCRIPTION
----   --------    ----------------------------------------
15     SET/CLR     Set/clear control bit. Determines
                   if bits written with a 1 get set or
                   cleared.  Bits written with a zero
                   are unchanged.
14     BBUSY       Blitter busy status bit (read only)
13     BZERO       Blitter logic  zero status bit
                   (read only).
12     X
11     X
10     BLTPRI      Blitter DMA priority
                   (over CPU micro) (also called
                   "blitter nasty") (disables /BLS
                   pin, preventing micro from
                   stealing any bus cycles while
                   blitter DMA is running).
09     DMAEN       Enable all DMA below
08     BPLEN       Bit plane DMA enable
07     COPEN       Copper DMA enable
06     BLTEN       Blitter DMA enable
05     SPREN       Sprite DMA enable
04     DSKEN       Disk DMA enable
03     AUD3EN      Audio channel 3 DMA enable
02     AUD2EN      Audio channel 2 DMA enable
01     AUD1EN      Audio channel 1 DMA enable
00     AUD0EN      Audio channel 0 DMA enable
```

```
DSKBYTR    01A  R       P   Disk data byte and status read
```

This register is the disk-microprocessor data
buffer. Data from the disk (in read mode) is
loaded into this register one byte at a time, and
bit 15 (DSKBYT) is set true.

```
BIT#
----   --------    ----------------------------------------
15     DSKBYT      Disk byte ready (reset on read)
14     DMAON       Mirror of bit 15 (DMAEN) in DSKLEN,
                   ANDed with Bit09 (DMAEN) in DMACON
13     DISKWRITE   Mirror of bit 14 (WRITE) in DSKLEN
12     WORDEQUAL   This bit true only while the
                   DSKSYNC register equals the data
                   from disk.
11-08  X           Not used
07-00  DATA        Disk byte data
```

```
DSKDAT      026  W      P   Disk DMA data write
DSKDATR     008  ER     P   Disk DMA data read (early read dummy
                                address)
```

This register is the disk DMA data buffer. It
contains two bytes of data that are either sent
(written) to or received (read) from the disk.
The write mode is enabled by bit 14 of the LENGTH
register. The DMA controller automatically
transfers data to or from this register and RAM,
and when the DMA data is finished (length=0) it
causes a disk block interrupt. See interrupts below.

```
DSKLEN      024  W      P   Disk length
```

This register contains the length (number of words)
of disk DMA data. It also contains two control
bits, a DMA enable bit, and a DMA direction
(read/write) bit.

```
BIT#   FUNCTION        DESCRIPTION
----   --------        -----------------------------------
15     DMAEN           Disk DMA enable
14     WRITE           Disk write (RAM to disk) if 1
13-0   LENGTH          Length (# of words) of DMA data.
```

```
DSKPTH      020  W   A   Disk pointer (high 3 bits)
DSKPTL      022  W   A   Disk pointer (low 15 bits)
```

This pair of registers contains the 18-bit
address of disk DMA data. These address registers
must be initialized by the processor or Copper
before disk DMA is enabled.

```
DSKSYNC     07E  W      P   Disk sync register
```

holds the match code for disk read synchronization.
See ADKCON bit 10.

```
INTENA      09A  W       P    Interrupt enable bits (clear or set bits)
INTENAR     01C  R       P    Interrupt enable bits (read)
```

This register contains interrupt enable bits. The bit
assignment for both the request and enable registers
is given below.

BIT#	FUNCT	LEVEL	DESCRIPTION
15	SET/CLR		Set/clear control bit. Determines if bits written with a 1 get set or cleared. Bits written with a zero are always unchanged.
14	INTEN		Master interrupt (enable only, no request)
13	EXTER	6	External interrupt
12	DSKSYN	5	Disk sync register (DSKSYNC) matches disk data
11	RBF	5	Serial port receive buffer full
10	AUD3	4	Audio channel 3 block finished
09	AUD2	4	Audio channel 2 block finished
08	AUD1	4	Audio channel 1 block finished
07	AUD0	4	Audio channel 0 block finished
06	BLIT	3	Blitter finished
05	VERTB	3	Start of vertical blank
04	COPER	3	Copper
03	PORTS	2	I/O ports and timers
02	SOFT	1	Reserved for software-initiated interrupt
01	DSKBLK	1	Disk block finished
00	TBE	1	Serial port transmit buffer empty

```
INTREQ      09C  W       P    Interrupt request bits (clear or set)
INTREQR     01E  R       P    Interrupt request bits (read)
```

This register contains interrupt request bits (or
flags). These bits may be polled by the processor;
if enabled by the bits listed in the next register,
they may cause processor interrupts. Both a set and
clear operation are required to load arbitrary data
into this register. These status bits are not
automatically reset when the interrupt is serviced,
and must be reset when desired by writing to this
address. The bit assignments are identical to the
enable register below.

```
JOY0DAT    00A   R   D   Joystick-mouse 0 data (left vertical,
                              horizontal)
JOY1DAT    00C   R   D   Joystick-mouse 1 data (right vertical,
                              horizontal)
```

These addresses each read a pair of 8-bit mouse
counters. 0=left controller pair, 1=right
controller pair (four counters total). The bit
usage for both left and right addresses is shown
below. Each counter is clocked by signals from
two controller pins. Bits 1 and 0 of each counter
may be read to determine the state of these two
clock pins. This allows these pins to double as
joystick switch inputs.

Mouse counter usage:
(pins 1,3=Yclock, pins 2,4=Xclock)

```
BIT# 15,14,13,12,11,10,09,08  07,06,05,04,03,02,01,00
     -----------------------  -----------------------
0DAT Y7 Y6 Y5 Y4 Y3 Y2 Y1 Y0  X7 X6 X5 X4 X3 X2 X1 X0
1DAT Y7 Y6 Y5 Y4 Y3 Y2 Y1 Y0  X7 X6 X5 X4 X3 X2 X1 X0
```

The following table shows the mouse/joystick
connector pin usage. The pins (and their functions)
are sampled (multiplexed) into the DENISE chip
during the clock times shown in the table.
This table is for reference only and should
not be needed by the programmer. (Note that the
joystick functions are all "active low" at the
connector pins.)

| | | | Sampled by DENISE | | |
| Conn | Joystick | Mouse | | | |
Pin	Function	Function	Pin	Name	Clock
L1	FORW*	Y	38	M0V	at CCK
L3	LEFT*	YQ	38	M0V	at CCK*
L2	BACK*	X	9	M0H	at CCK
L4	RIGH*	XQ	9	M0H	at CCK*
R1	FORW*	Y	39	M1V	at CCK
R3	LEFT*	YQ	39	M1V	at CCK*
R2	BACK*	X	8	M1H	at CCK
R4	RIGH*	XQ	8	M1H	at CCK*

After being sampled, these connector pin signals
are used in quadrature to clock the mouse counters.
The LEFT and RIGHT joystick functions (active high)
are directly available on the Y1 and X1 bits of
each counter. In order to recreate the FORWARD
and BACK joystick functions, however, it is
necessary to logically combine (exclusive OR)
the lower two bits of each counter.
This is illustrated in the following table.

To detect	Read these counter bits
Forward	Y1 xor Y0 (BIT#09 xor BIT#08)
Left	Y1
Back	X1 xor X0 (BIT#01 xor BIT#00)
Right	X1

```
JOYTEST      036  W     D     Write to all four joystick-mouse counters
                                 at once.

                        Mouse counter write test data:

                        BIT#  15,14,13,12,11,10,09,08   07,06,05,04,03,02,01,00
                        ------------------------------   ------------------------
                        0DAT  Y7 Y6 Y5 Y4 Y3 Y2 xx xx   X7 X6 X5 X4 X3 X2 xx xx
                        1DAT  Y7 Y6 Y5 Y4 Y3 Y2 xx xx   X7 X6 X5 X4 X3 X2 xx xx

POT0DAT      012  R     P     Pot counter data left pair (vert,horiz)
POT1DAT      014  R     P     Pot counter data right pair (vert,horiz)

                        These addresses each read a pair of 8-bit pot counters.
                        (Four counters total.) The bit assignment for both
                        addresses is shown below. The counters are stopped by
                        signals from two controller connectors (left-right)
                        with two pins each.

                        BIT#  15,14,13,12,11,10,09,08   07,06,05,04,03,02,01,00
                        -----  ------------------------   ------------------------
                        RIGHT Y7 Y6 Y5 Y4 Y3 Y2 Y1 Y0   X7 X6 X5 X4 X3 X2 X1 X0
                        LEFT  Y7 Y6 Y5 Y4 Y3 Y2 Y1 Y0   X7 X6 X5 X4 X3 X2 X1 X0

                              CONNECTORS              PAULA
                              --------------------    ------------------
                              Loc. Dir. Sym  Pin      Pin#   Pin Name
                              ---- ---- ---  ----     ----   --------
                              RIGHT  Y   RY    9       36     (POT1Y)
                              RIGHT  X   RX    5       35     (POT1X)
                              LEFT   Y   LY    9       33     (POT0Y)
                              LEFT   X   LX    5       32     (POT0X)

POTGO        034  W     P     Pot port data write and start.

POTGOR       016  R     P     Pot port data read (formerly called POTINP).

                        This register controls a 4-bit bi-directional I/O port
                        that shares the same four pins as the four pot counters
                        above.

                        BIT#  FUNCT   DESCRIPTION
                        ----  --------------------------------------------
                        15    OUTRY   Output enable for Paula pin 36
                        14    DATRY   I/O data Paula pin 36
                        13    OUTRX   Output enable for Paula pin 35
                        12    DATRX   I/O data Paula pin 35
                        11    OUTLY   Output enable for Paula pin 33
                        10    DATLY   I/O data Paula pin 33
                        09    OUTLX   Output enable for Paula pin 32
                        08    DATLX   I/O data Paula pin 32
                        07-01 0       Reserved for chip ID code (presently 0)
                        00    START   Start pots (dump capacitors, start
                                        counters)

REFPTR       028  W  A        Refresh pointer

                        This register is used as a dynamic RAM refresh
                        address generator. It is writeable for test
                        purposes only, and should never be written by
                        the microprocessor.
```

```
SERDAT    030  W       P    Serial port data and stop bits write
                                 (transmit data buffer)

              This address writes data to a transmit data buffer.
              Data from this buffer is moved into a serial shift
              register for output transmission whenever it is
              empty.  This sets the interrupt request TBE
              (transmit buffer empty). A stop bit must be
              provided as part of the data word. The length of
              the data word is set by the position of the stop
              bit.

              BIT# 15,14,13,12,11,10,09,08,07,06,05,04,03,02,01,00
                   ------------------------------------------------
              USE   0  0  0  0  0  0  S D8 D7 D6 D5 D4 D3 D2 D1 D0

              Note:  S = stop bit = 1, D = data bits.

SERDATR   018  R       P    Serial port data and status read
                                 (receive data buffer)

              This address reads data from a receive data buffer.
              Data in this buffer is loaded from a receiving
              shift register whenever it is full.  Several
              interrupt request bits are also read at this
              address, along with the data, as shown below.

              BIT#  SYM           FUNCTION
              ----  ----          ------------------------
              15    OVRUN         Serial port receiver overrun.
                                  Reset by resetting bit 11 of
                                  INTREQ.
              14    RBF           Serial port receive buffer full
                                  (mirror).
              13    TBE           Serial port transmit buffer
                                  empty (mirror).
              12    TSRE          Serial port transmit shift
                                  register empty.
                                  Reset by loading into buffer.
              11    RXD           RXD pin receives UART serial
                                  data for direct bit test by
                                  the microprocessor.
              10    0             Not used
              09    STP           Stop bit
              08    STP-DB8       Stop bit if LONG, data bit if
                                  not.
              07    DB7           Data bit
              06    DB6           Data bit
              05    DB5           Data bit
              04    DB4           Data bit
              03    DB3           Data bit
              02    DB2           Data bit
              01    DB1           Data bit
              00    DB0           Data bit
```

```
SERPER        032  W       P    Serial port period and control

                       This register contains the control bit LONG referred to
                       above, and a 15-bit number defining the serial port
                       baud rate. If this number is N, then the baud rate is
                       1 bit every (N+1)*.2794  microseconds.

                       BIT#   SYM      FUNCTION
                       -----  ----     ----------------
                       15     LONG     Defines serial receive as 9-bit word.
                       14-00  RATE     Defines baud rate=1/((N+1)*.2794 microsec.)

SPRxCTL       142  W    A D    Sprite x vert stop position and control data
SPRxPOS       140  W    A D    Sprite x vert-horiz start position data

                       These two registers work together as position, size and
                       feature sprite-control registers.  They are usually loaded
                       by the sprite DMA channel during horizontal blank;
                       however, they may be loaded by either processor at any time.
                       SPRxPOS register:

                       BIT#   SYM      FUNCTION
                       ----   ----     ------------------------------
                       15-08  SV7-SV0  Start vertical value. High bit(SV8) is
                                       in SPRxCTL register below.
                       07-00  SH8-SH1  Start horizontal value. Low bit(SH0) is
                                       in SPRxCTL register below.

                       SPRxCTL register (writing this address disables sprite
                                          horizontal comparator circuit):

                       BIT#   SYM       FUNCTION
                       ----   --------  ---------------------------------
                       15-08  EV7-EV0   End (stop) vertical value low 8 bits
                       07     ATT       Sprite attach control bit (odd sprites)
                       06-04  X         Not used
                       02     SV8       Start vertical value high bit
                       01     EV8       End (stop) vertical value high bit
                       00     SH0       Start horizontal value low bit

SPRxDATA      144  W       D    Sprite x image data register A
SPRxDATB      146  W       D    Sprite x image data register B

                       These registers buffer the sprite image data. They are
                       usually loaded by the sprite DMA channel but may be
                       loaded by either processor at any time.  When a
                       horizontal comparison occurs, the buffers are dumped
                       into shift registers and serially outputted to the
                       display, MSB first on the left.

                       NOTE: Writing to the A buffer enables (arms) the sprite.
                       Writing to the SPRxCTL register disables the sprite.
                       If enabled, data in the A and B buffers will be outputted
                       whenever the beam counter equals the sprite horizontal
                       position value in the SPRxPOS register.

SPRxPOS       see SPRxCTL
```

```
SPRxPTH      120  W   A       Sprite x pointer (high 3 bits)
SPRxPTL      122  W   A       Sprite x pointer (low 15 bits)

                  This pair of registers contains the 18-bit address
                  of sprite x (x=0,1,2,3,4,5,6,7) DMA data. These address
                  registers must be initialized by the processor or Copper
                  every vertical blank time.

STREQU       038  S   D       Strobe for horizontal sync with VB
                                 and EQU
STRHOR       03C  S   D P     Strobe for horizontal sync
STRLONG      03E  S   D       Strobe for identification of long
                                 horizontal line

                  One of the first three strobe addresses above is
                  placed on the destination address bus during the
                  first refresh time slot.  The fourth strobe shown
                  above is used during the second refresh time slot of
                  every other line to identify lines with long counts
                  (228).  There are four refresh time slots, and any
                  not used for strobes will leave a null (FF) address
                  on the destination address bus.

STRVBL       03A  S   D       Strobe for horizontal sync with VB
                                 (vertical blank)

VHPOSR       006  R   A       Read vertical and horizontal position of
                                 beam or lightpen
VHPOSW       02C  W   A       Write vertical and horizontal position
                                 of beam or lightpen

             BIT# 15,14,13,12,11,10,09,08,07,06,05,04,03,02,01,00
                  -------------------------------------------------
             USE  V7 V6 V5 V4 V3 V2 V1 V0,H8 H7 H6 H5 H4 H3 H2 H1

             RESOLUTION = 1/160 of screen width (280 ns)

VPOSR        004  R   A       Read vertical most significant bit
                                 (and frame flop)
VPOSW        02A  W   A       Write vertical most significant bit
                                 (and frame flop)

             BIT# 15,14,13,12,11,10,09,08,07,06,05,04,03,02,01,00
                  -------------------------------------------------
             USE  LOF-- -- -- -- -- -- --,-- -- -- -- -- -- -- V8

             LOF=Long frame (auto toggle control bit in BPLCON0)
```

Appendix B

Register Summary—Address Order

This appendix contains information about the register set in address order.

The following codes and abbreviations are used in this appendix:

    &   Register used by DMA channel only.

    %   Register used by DMA channel usually, processors sometimes.

    +   Address register pair. Must be an even address pointing to chip memory.

    *   Address not writable by the Copper.

    ~   Address not writable by the Copper unless the "copper danger bit", COPCON is set true.

A,D,P
A=Agnus chip, D=Denise chip, P=Paula chip.

W,R
W=write-only; R=read-only,

ER Early read. This is a DMA data transfer to RAM, from either the disk or the blitter. RAM timing requires data to be on the bus earlier than microprocessor read cycles. These transfers are therefore initiated by Agnus timing, rather than a read address on the destination address bus.

S Strobe (write address with no register bits). Writing the register causes the effect.

PTL,PTH
Chip memory pointer that addresses DMA data. Must be reloaded by a processor before use (vertical blank for bit-plane and sprite pointers, and prior to starting the blitter for blitter pointers).

LCL,LCH
Chip memory location (starting address) of DMA data. Used to automatically restart pointers, such as the Copper program counter (during vertical blank) and the audio sample counter (whenever the audio length count is finished).

MOD
15-bit modulo. A number that is automatically added to the memory address at the end of each line to generate the address for the beginning of the next line. This allows the blitter (or the display window) to operate on (or display) a window of data that is smaller than the actual picture in memory (memory map). Uses 15 bits, plus sign extend.

```
--------------------------------------------------------------------------
NAME        ADD   R/W CHIP      FUNCTION
--------------------------------------------------------------------------
BLTDDAT   & *000  ER  A         Blitter destination early read (dummy address)
DMACONR     *002  R   A    P    DMA control (and blitter status) read
VPOSR       *004  R   A         Read vert most signif. bit (and frame flop)
VHPOSR      *006  R   A         Read vert and horiz. position of beam
DSKDATR   & *008  ER       P    Disk data early read (dummy address)
JOY0DAT     *00A  R     D        Joystick-mouse 0 data (vert,horiz)
JOY1DAT     *00C  R     D        Joystick-mouse 1 data (vert,horiz)
CLXDAT      *00E  R     D        Collision data register (read and clear)
ADKCONR     *010  R        P    Audio, disk control register read
POT0DAT     *012  R        P    Pot counter pair 0 data (vert,horiz)
POT1DAT     *014  R        P    Pot counter pair 1 data (vert,horiz)
POTGOR      *016  R        P    Pot port data read (formerly POTINP)
SERDATR     *018  R        P    Serial port data and status read
DSKBYTR     *01A  R        P    Disk data byte and status read
INTENAR     *01C  R        P    Interrupt enable bits read
INTREQR     *01E  R        P    Interrupt request bits read
DSKPTH    + *020  W   A         Disk pointer (high 3 bits)
DSKPTL    + *022  W   A         Disk pointer (low 15 bits)
DSKLEN      *024  W        P    Disk length
DSKDAT    & *026  W        P    Disk DMA data write
REFPTR    & *028  W   A         Refresh pointer
VPOSW       *02A  W   A         Write vert most signif. bit (and frame flop)
VHPOSW      *02C  W   A         Write vert and horiz position of beam
COPCON      *02E  W   A         Coprocessor control register (CDANG)
SERDAT      *030  W        P    Serial port data and stop bits write
SERPER      *032  W        P    Serial port period and control
POTGO       *034  W        P    Pot port data write and start
JOYTEST     *036  W     D        Write to all four joystick-mouse counters at once
STREQU    & *038  S     D        Strobe for horiz sync with VB and EQU
STRVBL    & *03A  S     D        Strobe for horiz sync with VB (vert. blank)
STRHOR    & *03C  S     D P      Strobe for horiz sync
STRLONG   & *03E  S     D        Strobe for identification of long horiz. line.
BLTCON0     ~040  W   A         Blitter control register 0
BLTCON1     ~042  W   A         Blitter control register 1
BLTAFWM     ~044  W   A         Blitter first word mask for source A
BLTALWM     ~046  W   A         Blitter last word mask for source A
BLTCPTH   + ~048  W   A         Blitter pointer to source C (high 3 bits)
BLTCPTL   + ~04A  W   A         Blitter pointer to source C (low 15 bits)
BLTBPTH   + ~04C  W   A         Blitter pointer to source B (high 3 bits)
BLTBPTL   + ~04E  W   A         Blitter pointer to source B (low 15 bits)
BLTAPTH   + ~050  W   A         Blitter pointer to source A (high 3 bits)
BLTAPTL   + ~052  W   A         Blitter pointer to source A (low 15 bits)
BLTDPTH   + ~054  W   A         Blitter pointer to destination D (high 3 bits)
BLTDPTL   + ~056  W   A         Blitter pointer to destination D (low 15 bits)
BLTSIZE     ~058  W   A         Blitter start and size (window width, height)
            ~05A
            ~05C
            ~05E
BLTCMOD     ~060  W   A         Blitter modulo for source C
BLTBMOD     ~062  W   A         Blitter modulo for source B
BLTAMOD     ~064  W   A         Blitter modulo for source A
BLTDMOD     ~066  W   A         Blitter modulo for destination D
            ~068
            ~06A
            ~06C
            ~06E
BLTCDAT   % ~070  W   A         Blitter source C data register
BLTBDAT   % ~072  W   A         Blitter source B data register
BLTADAT   % ~074  W   A         Blitter source A data register
```

		~076				
		~078				
		~07A				
		~07C				
DSKSYNC		~07E	W		P	Disk sync pattern register for disk read
COP1LCH	+	080	W	A		Coprocessor first location register (high 3 bits)
COP1LCL	+	082	W	A		Coprocessor first location register (low 15 bits)
COP2LCH	+	084	W	A		Coprocessor second location register (high 3 bits)
COP2LCL	+	086	W	A		Coprocessor second location register (low 15 bits)
COPJMP1		088	S	A		Coprocessor restart at first location
COPJMP2		08A	S	A		Coprocessor restart at second location
COPINS		08C	W	A		Coprocessor instruction fetch identify
DIWSTRT		08E	W	A		Display window start (upper left vert-horiz position)
DIWSTOP		090	W	A		Display window stop (lower right vert.-horiz. position)
DDFSTRT		092	W	A		Display bit plane data fetch start (horiz. position)
DDFSTOP		094	W	A		Display bit plane data fetch stop (horiz. position)
DMACON		096	W	A D P		DMA control write (clear or set)
CLXCON		098	W	D		Collision control
INTENA		09A	W		P	Interrupt enable bits (clear or set bits)
INTREQ		09C	W		P	Interrupt request bits (clear or set bits)
ADKCON		09E	W		P	Audio, disk, UART control
AUD0LCH	+	0A0	W	A		Audio channel 0 location (high 3 bits)
AUD0LCL	+	0A2	W	A		Audio channel 0 location (low 15 bits)
AUD0LEN		0A4	W		P	Audio channel 0 length
AUD0PER		0A6	W		P	Audio channel 0 period
AUD0VOL		0A8	W		P	Audio channel 0 volume
AUD0DAT	&	0AA	W		P	Audio channel 0 data
		0AC				
		0AE				
AUD1LCH	+	0B0	W	A		Audio channel 1 location (high 3 bits)
AUD1LCL	+	0B2	W	A		Audio channel 1 location (low 15 bits)
AUD1LEN		0B4	W		P	Audio channel 1 length
AUD1PER		0B6	W		P	Audio channel 1 period
AUD1VOL		0B8	W		P	Audio channel 1 volume
AUD1DAT	&	0BA	W		P	Audio channel 1 data
		0BC				
		0BE				
AUD2LCH	+	0C0	W	A		Audio channel 2 location (high 3 bits)
AUD2LCL	+	0C2	W	A		Audio channel 2 location (low 15 bits)
AUD2LEN		0C4	W		P	Audio channel 2 length
AUD2PER		0C6	W		P	Audio channel 2 period
AUD2VOL		0C8	W		P	Audio channel 2 volume
AUD2DAT	&	0CA	W		P	Audio channel 2 data
		0CC				
		0CE				
AUD3LCH	+	0D0	W	A		Audio channel 3 location (high 3 bits)
AUD3LCL	+	0D2	W	A		Audio channel 3 location (low 15 bits)
AUD3LEN		0D4	W		P	Audio channel 3 length
AUD3PER		0D6	W		P	Audio channel 3 period
AUD3VOL		0D8	W		P	Audio channel 3 volume
AUD3DAT	&	0DA	W		P	Audio channel 3 data

```
              ODC
              ODE
BPL1PTH   +   OEO    W    A       Bit plane 1 pointer (high 3 bits)
BPL1PTL   +   OE2    W    A       Bit plane 1 pointer (low 15 bits)
BPL2PTH   +   OE4    W    A       Bit plane 2 pointer (high 3 bits)
BPL2PTL   +   OE6    W    A       Bit plane 2 pointer (low 15 bits)
BPL3PTH   +   OE8    W    A       Bit plane 3 pointer (high 3 bits)
BPL3PTL   +   OEA    W    A       Bit plane 3 pointer (low 15 bits)
BPL4PTH   +   OEC    W    A       Bit plane 4 pointer (high 3 bits)
BPL4PTL   +   OEE    W    A       Bit plane 4 pointer (low 15 bits)
BPL5PTH   +   OFO    W    A       Bit plane 5 pointer (high 3 bits)
BPL5PTL   +   OF2    W    A       Bit plane 5 pointer (low 15 bits)
BPL6PTH   +   OF4    W    A       Bit plane 6 pointer (high 3 bits)
BPL6PTL   +   OF6    W    A       Bit plane 6 pointer (low 15 bits)
              OF8
              OFA
              OFC
              OFE
BPLCON0       100    W    A D     Bit plane control register (misc. control bits)
BPLCON1       102    W      D     Bit plane control reg. (scroll value PF1, PF2)
BPLCON2       104    W      D     Bit plane control reg. (priority control)
              106
BPL1MOD       108    W    A       Bit plane modulo (odd planes)
BPL2MOD       10A    W    A       Bit Plane modulo (even planes)
              10C
              10E
BPL1DAT   &   110    W      D     Bit plane 1 data (parallel-to-serial convert)
BPL2DAT   &   112    W      D     Bit plane 2 data (parallel-to-serial convert)
BPL3DAT   &   114    W      D     Bit plane 3 data (parallel-to-serial convert)
BPL4DAT   &   116    W      D     Bit plane 4 data (parallel-to-serial convert)
BPL5DAT   &   118    W      D     Bit plane 5 data (parallel-to-serial convert)
BPL6DAT   &   11A    W      D     Bit plane 6 data (parallel-to-serial convert)
              11C
              11E
```

```
SPR0PTH    +   120   W   A         Sprite 0 pointer (high 3 bits)
SPR0PTL    +   122   W   A         Sprite 0 pointer (low 15 bits)
SPR1PTH    +   124   W   A         Sprite 1 pointer (high 3 bits)
SPR1PTL    +   126   W   A         Sprite 1 pointer (low 15 bits)
SPR2PTH    +   128   W   A         Sprite 2 pointer (high 3 bits)
SPR2PTL    +   12A   W   A         Sprite 2 pointer (low 15 bits)
SPR3PTH    +   12C   W   A         Sprite 3 pointer (high 3 bits)
SPR3PTL    +   12E   W   A         Sprite 3 pointer (low 15 bits)
SPR4PTH    +   130   W   A         Sprite 4 pointer (high 3 bits)
SPR4PTL    +   132   W   A         Sprite 4 pointer (low 15 bits)
SPR5PTH    +   134   W   A         Sprite 5 pointer (high 3 bits)
SPR5PTL    +   136   W   A         Sprite 5 pointer (low 15 bits)
SPR6PTH    +   138   W   A         Sprite 6 pointer (high 3 bits)
SPR6PTL    +   13A   W   A         Sprite 6 pointer (low 15 bits)
SPR7PTH    +   13C   W   A         Sprite 7 pointer (high 3 bits)
SPR7PTL    +   13E   W   A         Sprite 7 pointer (low 15 bits)
SPR0POS    %   140   W   A D       Sprite 0 vert-horiz start position
                                     data
SPR0CTL    %   142   W   A D       Sprite 0 vert stop position and
                                     control data
SPR0DATA   %   144   W     D       Sprite 0 image data register A
SPR0DATB   %   146   W     D       Sprite 0 image data register B
SPR1POS    %   148   W   A D       Sprite 1 vert-horiz start position
                                     data
SPR1CTL    %   14A   W   A D       Sprite 1 vert stop position and
                                     control data
SPR1DATA   %   14C   W     D       Sprite 1 image data register A
SPR1DATB   %   14E   W     D       Sprite 1 image data register B
SPR2POS    %   150   W   A D       Sprite 2 vert-horiz start position
                                     data
SPR2CTL    %   152   W   A D       Sprite 2 vert stop position and
                                     control data
SPR2DATA   %   154   W     D       Sprite 2 image data register A
SPR2DATB   %   156   W     D       Sprite 2 image data register B
SPR3POS    %   158   W   A D       Sprite 3 vert-horiz start position
                                     data
SPR3CTL    %   15A   W   A D       Sprite 3 vert stop position and
                                     control data
SPR3DATA   %   15C   W     D       Sprite 3 image data register A
SPR3DATB   %   15E   W     D       Sprite 3 image data register B
SPR4POS    %   160   W   A D       Sprite 4 vert-horiz start position
                                     data
SPR4CTL    %   162   W   A D       Sprite 4 vert stop position and
                                     control data
SPR4DATA   %   164   W     D       Sprite 4 image data register A
SPR4DATB   %   166   W     D       Sprite 4 image data register B
SPR5POS    %   168   W   A D       Sprite 5 vert-horiz start position
                                     data
SPR5CTL    %   16A   W   A D       Sprite 5 vert stop position and
                                     control data
SPR5DATA   %   16C   W     D       Sprite 5 image data register A
SPR5DATB   %   16E   W     D       Sprite 5 image data register B
```

SPR6POS	%	170	W	A D	Sprite 6 vert–horiz start position data
SPR6CTL	%	172	W	A D	Sprite 6 vert stop position and control data
SPR6DATA	%	174	W	D	Sprite 6 image data register A
SPR6DATB	%	176	W	D	Sprite 6 image data register B
SPR7POS	%	178	W	A D	Sprite 7 vert–horiz start position data
SPR7CTL	%	17A	W	A D	Sprite 7 vert stop position and control data
SPR7DATA	%	17C	W	D	Sprite 7 image data register A
SPR7DATB	%	17E	W	D	Sprite 7 image data register B
COLOR00		180	W	D	Color table 00
COLOR01		182	W	D	Color table 01
COLOR02		184	W	D	Color table 02
COLOR03		186	W	D	Color table 03
COLOR04		188	W	D	Color table 04
COLOR05		18A	W	D	Color table 05
COLOR06		18C	W	D	Color table 06
COLOR07		18E	W	D	Color table 07
COLOR08		190	W	D	Color table 08
COLOR09		192	W	D	Color table 09
COLOR10		194	W	D	Color table 10
COLOR11		196	W	D	Color table 11
COLOR12		198	W	D	Color table 12
COLOR13		19A	W	D	Color table 13
COLOR14		19C	W	D	Color table 14
COLOR15		19E	W	D	Color table 15
COLOR16		1A0	W	D	Color table 16
COLOR17		1A2	W	D	Color table 17
COLOR18		1A4	W	D	Color table 18
COLOR19		1A6	W	D	Color table 19
COLOR20		1A8	W	D	Color table 20
COLOR21		1AA	W	D	Color table 21
COLOR22		1AC	W	D	Color table 22
COLOR23		1AE	W	D	Color table 23
COLOR24		1B0	W	D	Color table 24
COLOR25		1B2	W	D	Color table 25
COLOR26		1B4	W	D	Color table 26
COLOR27		1B6	W	D	Color table 27
COLOR28		1B8	W	D	Color table 28
COLOR29		1BA	W	D	Color table 29
COLOR30		1BC	W	D	Color table 30
COLOR31		1BE	W	D	Color table 31
RESERVED		1110X			
RESERVED		1111X			
NO–OP (NULL)		1FE			

Appendix C

Custom Chip Pin Allocation List

NOTE: * Means an active low signal.

AGNUS PIN ASSIGNMENT

PIN #	DESIGNATION	FUNCTION	DEFINITION
01-09	D8-D0	Data bus lines 8 to 0	I/O
10	VCC	+5 Volt	I
11	RES*	System reset	I
12	INT3*	Interrupt level 3	O
13	DMAL	DMA request line	I
14	BLS*	Blitter slowdown	I
15	DBR*	Data bus request	O
16	ARW*	Agnus RAM write	O
17-24	RGA8-RGA1	Register address bus 8-1	I/O
25	CCK	Color clock	I
26	CCKQ	Color clock delay	I
27	VSS	Ground	I
28-36	DRA0-DRA8	DRAM address bus 0 to 8	O
37	LP*	Light pen input	I
38	VSY*	Vertical sync	I/O
39	CSY*	Composite sync	O
40	HSY*	Horizontal sync	I/O
41	VSS	Ground	I
42-48	D15-D9	Data bus lines 15 to 9	I/O

DENISE PIN ASSIGNMENT

PIN #	DESIGNATION	FUNCTION	DEFINITION
01-07	D6-D0	Data bus lines 6 to 0	I/O
08	M1H	Mouse 1 horizontal	I
09	M0H	Mouse 0 horizontal	I
10-17	RGA8-RGA1	Register address bus 8-1	I
18	BURST*	Color burst	O
19	VCC	+5 Volt	I
20-23	R0-R3	Video red bits 0-3	O
24-27	B0-B3	Video blue bits 0-3	O
28-31	G0-G3	Video green bits 0-3	O
32	N/C	Not connected	N/C
33	ZD*	Background indicator	O
34	N/C	Not connected	N/C
35	7M	7.15909 MHZ	I
36	CCK	Color clock	I
37	VSS	Ground	I
38	M0V	Mouse 0 vertical	I
39	M1V	Mouse 1 vertical	I
40-48	D15-D7	Data bus lines 15 to 7	I/O

```
                  PAULA PIN ASSIGNMENT
                  --------------------

PIN #          DESIGNATION       FUNCTION                    DEFINITION
-----          -----------       --------                    ----------
01-07          D8-D2             Data bus lines 8 to 2        I/O
08             VSS               Ground                       I
09-10          D1-D0             Data bus lines 1 and 0       I/O
11             RES*              System reset                 I
12             DMAL              DMA request line             O
13-15          IPL0*-IPL2        Interrupt lines 0-2          O
16             INT2*             Interrupt level 2            I
17             INT3*             Interrupt level 3            I
18             INT6*             Interrupt level 6            I
19-26          RGA8-RGA1         Register address bus 8-1     I
27             VCC               +5 Volt                      I
28             CCK               Color clock                  I
29             CCKQ              Color clock delay            I
30             AUDB              Right audio                  O
31             AUDA              Left audio                   O
32             POT0X             Pot 0X                       I/O
33             POT0Y             Pot 0Y                       I/O
34             VSSANA            Analog ground                I
35             POT1X             Pot 1X                       I/O
36             POT1Y             Pot 1Y                       I/O
37             DKRD*             Disk read data               I
38             DKWD*             Disk write data              O
39             DKWE              Disk write enable            O
40             TXD               Serial transmit data         O
41             RXD               Serial receive data          I
42-48          D15-D9            Data bus lines 15 to 9       I/O
```

FAT AGNUS PIN ASSIGNMENT

PIN #	DESIGNATION	FUNCTION	DEFINITION
01-14	RD15-RD2	Register bus lines 15 to 2	I/O
17	INT3*	Blitter ready interrupt	O
18	DMAL	Request audio/disk DMA	I
18	RD1	Register bus line 1	I/O
18	RST*	Reset	I
19	BLS*	Blitter slowdown	I
20	DBR*	Data bus request	O
21	RRW	DRAM Write/Read	O
22	PRW	Processor Write/Read	I
23	RGEN*	RG Enable	I
24	AS*	Address Strobe	I
25	RAMEN*	RAM Enable	I
26-33	RGA8-RGA1	Register address bus 8-1	O
34	28MHZ	Master clock	I
35	XCLK	Alternate master clock	I
36	XCLKEN*	Master clock enable	I
37	CDAC*	Inverted shifted 7MHZ clk	O
38	7MHZ	28MHZ clk divided by four	O
39	CCKQ	Color clock delay	O
40	CCK	Color clock	O
41	TEST	Test - access registers	I
43-51	MA0-MA8	Output bus lines 0 to 8	O
52	LDS*	Lower data strobe	I
53	UDS*	Upper data strobe	I
54	CASL*	Column addr strobe lower	O
55	CASU*	Column addr strobe upper	O
56	RAS1*	Row address strobe one	O
57	RAS0*	Row address strobe zero	O
59-77	A19-A1	Address bus lines 19 to 1	I
78	LP*	Light pen	O
79	VSY*	Vertical synch	I/O
80	CSY*	Composite video synch	O
81	HSY*	Horizontal synch	I/O
84	RD0	Register bus line 0	I/O

Appendix D

System Memory Map

A true software memory map, showing system utilization of the various sections of RAM and free space is not provided, or possible with the Amiga. All memory is dynamically allocated by the memory manager, and the actual locations may change from release-to-release, machine-to-machine or boot-to-boot (see the exec/AllocMem function for details). To find the locations of system structures software must use the defined access procedures, starting by fetching the address of the exec.library from location 4; the only absolute memory location in the system. All software is written so that it can be loaded and relocated anywhere in memory by the loader. What follows is the general layout of memory areas withing the current generation of Amiga computers.

ADDRESS RANGE	NOTES
000000-03FFFF	256K Bytes of chip RAM
040000-07FFFF	256K bytes of chip RAM (option card)
080000-0FFFFF	512K Extended chip RAM (to 1 MB).
100000-1FFFFF	Reserved. Do not use.
200000-9FFFFF	Primary 8 MB Auto-config space.
A00000-BEFFFF	Reserved. Do not use.
BFD000-BFDF00	8520-B (access at even-byte addresses only)
BFE001-BFEF01	8520-A (access at odd-byte addresses only)

The underlined digit chooses which of the 16 internal registers of the 8520 is to be accessed. See Appendix F.

C00000-DFEFFF	Reserved. Do not use.
C00000-D7FFFF	Internal expansion memory.
D80000-DBFFFF	Reserved. Do not use.
DC0000-DCFFFF	Real time clock.
DFF000-DFFFFF	Chip registers. See Appendix A and Appendix B.
E00000-E7FFFF	Reserved. Do not use.
E80000-E8FFFF	Auto-config space. Boards appear here before the system relocates them to their final address.
E90000-EFFFFF	Secondary auto-config space (usually 64K I/O boards).
F00000-FBFFFF	Reserved. Do not use.
FC0000-FFFFFF	256K System ROM.

Appendix E

Interfaces

This appendix consists of four distinct parts, related to the way in which the Amiga talks to the outside world.

The first part specifies the pinouts of the externally accessible connectors and the power available at each connector. It does not, however, provide timing or loading information.

The second part briefly describes the functions of those pins whose purpose may not be evident.

The third part contains a list of the connections for certain internal connectors, notably the disk.

The fourth part specifies how various signals relate to the available ports of the 8520. This information enables the programmer to relate the port addresses to the outside-world items (or internal control signals) that are to be affected.

The third and fourth parts are primarily for the use of the systems programmer and should generally not be utilized by applications programmers.

Systems software normally is configured to handle the setting of particular signals, no matter how the physical connections may change. In other words, if you have a version of the system software that matches the revision level of the machine (normally a true condition), when you ask that a particular bit be set, you don't care which port that bit is connected to. Thus, applications programmers should rely on system documentation rather than going directly to the ports.

NOTE

In a multitasking operating system, many different tasks may be competing for the use of the system resources. Applications programmers should follow the established rules for resource access in order to assure compatibility of their software with the system.

************** PART 1 - OUTSIDE WORLD CONNECTORS ********************

This is a list of the connections to the outside world on the Amiga.

RS232 and MIDI Port

PIN	RS232	A1000	A500/ A2000	CBM PCs	HAYES	DESCRIPTION
1	GND	GND	GND	GND	GND	FRAME GROUND
2	TXD	TXD	TXD	TXD	TXD	TRANSMIT DATA
3	RXD	RXD	RXD	RXD	RXD	RECEIVE DATA
4	RTS	RTS	RTS	RTS	-	REQUEST TO SEND
5	CTS	CTS	CTS	CTS	CTS	CLEAR TO SEND
6	DSR	DSR	DSR	DSR	DSR	DATA SET READY
7	GND	GND	GND	GND	GND	SYSTEM GROUND
8	CD	CD	CD	DCD	DCD	CARRIER DETECT
9	-	-	+12v	+12v	-	+ 12 VOLT POWER
10	-	-	-12v	-12v	-	- 12 VOLT POWER
11	-	-	AUDO	-	-	AUDIO OUTPUT
12	S.SD	-	-	-	SI	SPEED INDICATE
13	S.CTS	-	-	-	-	
14	S.TXD	-5Vdc	-	-	-	- 5 VOLT POWER
15	TXC	AUDO	-	-	-	AUDIO OUT OF AMIGA
16	S.RXD	AUDI	-	-	-	AUDIO IN TO AMIGA
17	RXC	EB	-	-	-	BUFFERED PORT CLOCK 716kHz
18	-	INT2*	AUDI	-	-	INTERRUPT LINE TO AMIGA
19	S.RTS	-	-	-	-	
20	DTR	DTR	DTR	DTR	DTR	DATA TERMINAL READY
21	SQD	+5	-	-	-	+ 5 VOLT POWER
22	RI	-	RI	RI	RI	RING INDICATOR
23	SS	+12Vdc	-	-	-	+12 VOLT POWER
24	TXC1	C2*	-	-	-	3.58 MHZ CLOCK
25	-	RESB*	-	-	-	BUFFERED SYSTEM RESET

```
Parallel (Centronics) Port
--------------------------

PIN     1000            500/2000        Commodore PCs
---     ----            --------        -------------
1       DRDY*           STROBE*         STROBE*
2       Data 0          Data 0          Data 0
3       Data 1          Data 1          Data 1
4       Data 2          Data 2          Data 2
5       Data 3          Data 3          Data 3
6       Data 4          Data 4          Data 4
7       Data 5          Data 5          Data 5
8       Data 6          Data 6          Data 6
9       Data 7          Data 7          Data 7
10      ACK*            ACK*            ACK*
11      BUSY (data)     BUSY            BUSY
12      POUT (clk)      POUT            POUT
13      SEL             SEL             SEL
14      GND             +5v pullup      AUTOFDXT
15      GND             NC              ERROR*
16      GND             RESET*          INIT*
17      GND             GND             SLCT IN*
18-22   GND             GND             GND
23      + 5             GND             GND
24      NC              GND             GND
25      Reset*          GND             GND


KEYBOARD ...RJ11
----------------

        A1000           A2000
        -----           -----
1       +5 Volts        KCLK
2       CLOCK           KDAT
3       DATA            NC
4       GND             GND
5                       +5 Volts

Not Applicable to the A500.


Video ...DB23 MALE
------------------
For A500, A1000, A2000 unless otherwise stated

1    XCLK*              13   GNDRTN (Return for XCLKEN*)
2    XCLKEN*            14   ZD*
3    RED                15   C1*
4    GREEN              16   GND
5    BLUE               17   GND
6    DI                 18   GND
7    DB                 19   GND
8    DG                 20   GND
9    DR                 21   A1000/2000    -5 VOLT POWER
10   CSYNC*                  A500          -12 VOLT POWER
11   HSYNC*             22   +12 VOLT POWER
12   VSYNC*             23   +5 VOLT POWER
```

```
RF Monitor ...8 PIN DIN  (J2)  A1000 only
-------------------------------------------

1   N.C.
2   GND
3   AUDIO LEFT
4   COMP VIDEO
5   GND
6   N.C.
7   +12 VOLT POWER
8   AUDIO RIGHT


DISK EXTERNAL ...DB23 FEMALE
----------------------------

For A500, A1000, and A2000 with A2000 differences noted.

1   RDY*                       13   SIDEB*
2   DKRD*                      14   WPRO*
3   GND                        15   TK0*
4   GND                        16   DKWEB*
5   GND                        17   DKWDB*
6   GND                        18   STEPB*
7   GND                        19   DIRB
8   MTRXD*                     20   SEL3B*   A2000 not used (1)
9   SEL2B*   A2000 SEL3B* (1)  21   SEL1B*   A2000 SEL2B* (1)
10  DRESB*                     22   INDEX*
11  CHNG*                      23   +12
12  +5

(1) SEL1B* is not drive 1, but rather the first external drive.  Not
    all select lines may be implemented.
```

RAMEX ...60 PIN EDGE (.156) (P1) A1000 only

1	gnd	A	gnd
2	D15	B	D14
3	+5	C	+5
4	D12	D	D13
5	gnd	E	gnd
6	D11	F	D10
7	+5	H	+5
8	D8	J	D9
9	gnd	K	gnd
10	D7	L	D6
11	+5	M	+5
12	D4	N	D5
13	gnd	P	gnd
14	D3	R	D2
15	+5	S	+5
16	D0	T	D1
17	gnd	U	gnd
18	DRA4	V	DRA3
19	DRA5	W	DRA2
20	DRA6	X	DRA1
21	DRA7	Y	DRA0
22	gnd	Z	gnd
23	RAS*	AA	RRW*
24	gnd	BB	gnd
25	gnd	CC	gnd
26	CASU0*	DD	CASU1*
27	gnd	EE	gnd
28	CASL0*	FF	CASL1*
29	+5	HH	+5
30	+5	JJ	+5

EXPANSION ...86 PIN EDGE (.1) (P2)

PIN	A500	A1000	A2000	A2000b	FUNCTION
1	x	x	x	x	ground
2	x	x	x	x	ground
3	x	x	x	x	ground
4	x	x	x	x	ground
5	x	x	x	x	+5VDC
6	x	x	x	x	+5VDC
7	x	x	x	x	No Connect
8	x	x	x	x	-5VDC
9	x	x			No Connect
			x	x	28MHz Clock
10	x	x	x	x	+12VDC
11	x	x	x		No Connect
				x	/COPCFG (Configuration Out)
12	x	x	x	x	CONFIG IN, Grounded
13	x	x	x	x	Ground
14	x	x	x	x	/C3 Clock
15	x	x	x	x	CDAC Clock
16	x	x	x	x	/C1 Clock
17	x	x	x	x	/OVR
18	x	x	x	x	RDY
19	x	x	x	x	/INT2
20		x			/PALOPE
	x		x		No Connect
				x	/BOSS
21	x	x	x	x	A5
22	x	x	x	x	/INT6
23	x	x	x	x	A6
24	x	x	x	x	A4
25	x	x	x	x	ground
26	x	x	x	x	A3
27	x	x	x	x	A2
28	x	x	x	x	A7
29	x	x	x	x	A1
30	x	x	x	x	A8
31	x	x	x	x	FC0
32	x	x	x	x	A9
33	x	x	x	x	FC1
34	x	x	x	x	A10
35	x	x	x	x	FC2
36	x	x	x	x	A11
37	x	x	x	x	Ground
38	x	x	x	x	A12
39	x	x	x	x	A13
40	x	x	x	x	/IPL0
41	x	x	x	x	A14
42	x	x	x	x	/IPL1
43	x	x	x	x	A15
44	x	x	x	x	/IPL2
45	x	x	x	x	A16
46	x	x	x	x	BEER*
47	x	x	x	x	A17
48	x	x	x	x	/VPA
49	x	x	x	x	Ground
50	x	x	x	x	E Clock

```
EXPANSION ...86 PIN EDGE (.1) (P2)          (cont.)
-----------------------------------------------------
```

PIN	A500	A1000	A2000	A2000b	FUNCTION
51	x	x	x	x	/VMA
52	x	x	x	x	A18
53	x	x	x	x	RST
54	x	x	x	x	A19
55	x	x	x	x	/HLT
56	x	x	x	x	A20
57	x	x	x	x	A22
58	x	x	x	x	A21
59	x	x	x	x	A23
60	x	x	x		/BR
				x	/CBR
61	x	x	x	x	Ground
62	x	x	x	x	/BGACK
63	x	x	x	x	D15
64	x	x	x		/BG
				x	/CBG
65	x	x	x	x	D14
66	x	x	x	x	/DTACK
67	x	x	x	x	D13
68	x	x	x	x	R/W
69	x	x	x	x	D12
70	x	x	x	x	/LDS
71	x	x	x	x	D11
72	x	x	x	x	/UDS
73	x	x	x	x	Ground
74	x	x	x	x	/AS
75	x	x	x	x	D0
76	x	x	x	x	D10
77	x	x	x	x	D1
78	x	x	x	x	D9
79	x	x	x	x	D2
80	x	x	x	x	D8
81	x	x	x	x	D3
82	x	x	x	x	D7
83	x	x	x	x	D4
84	x	x	x	x	D6
85	x	x	x	x	Ground
86	x	x	x	x	D5

```
JOY STICKS ...DB9 male
----------------------
```

USAGE	JOYSTICK	MOUSE
1	FORWARD*	(MOUSE V)
2	BACK*	(MOUSE H)
3	LEFT*	(MOUSE VQ)
4	RIGHT*	(MOUSE HQ)
5	POT X	(or button 3 ... if used)
6	FIRE*	(or button 1)
7	+5	
8	GND	
9	POT Y	(or button 2)

PARALLEL INTERFACE CONNECTOR SPECIFICATION

The 25-pin D-type connector with pins (DB25P=male for the A1000, female for A500/A2000 and IBM compatibles) at the rear of the Amiga is nominally used to interface to parallel printers. In this capacity, data flows from the Amiga to the printer. This interface may also be used for input or bidirectional data transfers. The implementation is similar to Centronics, but the pin assignment and drive characteristics vary significantly from that specification (see Pin Assignment). Signal names correspond to those used in the other places in this appendix, when possible.

PARALLEL CONNECTOR PIN ASSIGNMENT (J8)

NAME	DIR	NOTES
DRDY*	O	Output-data-ready signal to parallel device in output mode, used in conjunction with ACK* (pin 10) for a two-line asynchronous handshake. Functions as input data accepted from Amiga in input mode (similar to ACK* in output mode). See timing diagrams in the following section.
D0	I/O	+
D1	I/O	|
D2	I/O	|
D3	I/O	| D0-D7 comprise an eight-bit bidirectional bus
D4	I/O	| for communication with parallel devices,
D5	I/O	| nominally, a printer.
D6	I/O	|
D7	I/O	+
ACK*	I	Output-data-acknowledge from parallel device in output mode, used in conjunction with DRDY* (pin 1) for a two-line asynchronous handshake. Functions as input-data-ready from parallel device in input mode (similar to DRDY* in output mode). See timing diagrams. The 8520 can be programmed to conditionally generate a level 2 interrupt to the 68000 whenever the ACK* input goes active.
BUSY	I/O	This is a general purpose I/O pin also connected to a serial data I/O pin (serial clock on pin 12). Note: Nominally used to indicate printer buffer full.
POUT	I/O	This is a general purpose I/O pin to a serial clock I/O pin (serial data on pin 11). Note: Nominally used to indicate printer paper out.
SEL	I/O	This is a general purpose I/O pin. Note: nominally a select output from the parallel device to the Amiga. On the A500/A2000 also shared with RS232 "ring indicator" signal.
RESET*	O	Amiga system reset

PARALLEL CONNECTOR INTERFACE TIMING, OUTPUT CYCLE

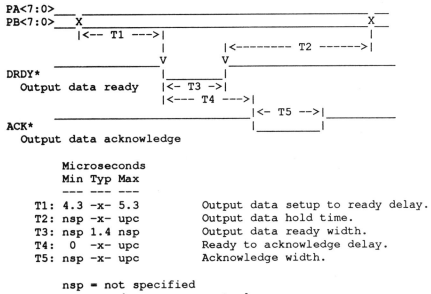

```
PA<7:0>___  _____  ___
PB<7:0>___X  ___                                          X__
         |<-- T1 --->|                                    |
         |           |          |<-------- T2 ------>|
         _____V          V_____
DRDY*                 |_____|                    |
  Output data ready   |<- T3 ->|                      |
                      |<--- T4 --->|
         _____|<- T5 -->|_____
ACK*                                          |_____|
  Output data acknowledge

          Microseconds
          Min Typ Max
          --- --- ---
    T1: 4.3 -x- 5.3       Output data setup to ready delay.
    T2: nsp -x- upc       Output data hold time.
    T3: nsp 1.4 nsp       Output data ready width.
    T4:  0  -x- upc       Ready to acknowledge delay.
    T5: nsp -x- upc       Acknowledge width.

          nsp = not specified
          upc = under program control
```

PARALLEL CONNECTOR INTERFACE TIMING, INPUT CYCLE

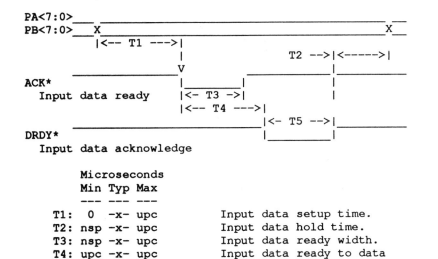

```
PA<7:0>___  _____  ___
PB<7:0>___X  ___                                          X__
         |<-- T1 --->|                                    |
         |           |              T2 -->|<----->|
         _____V              _____|_____
ACK*                  |_____|                |
  Input data ready    |<- T3 ->|                  |
                      |<-- T4 --->|
         _____|<- T5 -->|_____
DRDY*                                         |_____|
  Input data acknowledge

          Microseconds
          Min Typ Max
          --- --- ---
    T1:  0  -x- upc       Input data setup time.
    T2: nsp -x- upc       Input data hold time.
    T3: nsp -x- upc       Input data ready width.
    T4: upc -x- upc       Input data ready to data
                            acknowledge delay.
    T5: nsp 1.4 nsp       Input data acknowledge width.

          nsp = not specified
          upc = under program control
```

SERIAL INTERFACE CONNECTOR SPECIFICATION

This 25-pin D-type connector with sockets (DB25S=female) is used to
interface to RS-232-C standard signals. Signal names correspond to
those used in other places in this appendix, when possible.

WARNING: Pins on the RS232 connector other than these standard ones
described below may be connected to power or other non-RS232 standard
signals. When making up RS232 cables, connect only those pins actually
used for a particular application. Avoid generic 25-connector "straight-
thru" cables.

SERIAL INTERFACE CONNECTOR PIN ASSIGNMENT (J6)

        RS-232-C

NAME   DIR STD NOTES
----   --- --- ---------------------------
FGND   y   Frame ground -- do not tie to signal ground
TXD   O   y   Transmit data
RXD   I   y   Receive data
RTS   O   y   Request to send
CTS   I   y   Clear to send
DSR   I   y   Data set ready
GND   y   Signal ground -- do not tie to frame ground
CD   I   y   Carrier detect
-5V   n*   50 ma maximum   *** WARNING -5V ***
AUDO   O   n*   Audio output from left (channels 0, 3) port,
                  intended to send audio to the modem.
AUDI   I   n*   Audio input to right (channels 1, 2) port,
                  intended to receive audio from the modem; this
                  input is mixed with the analog output of the
                  right (channels 1, 2). It is not digitized or
                  used by the computer in any way.
DTR   O   y   Data terminal ready.
RI   I   y   Ring Indicator (A500/A2000 only) shared with printer
                  "select" signal.
RESB*   O   n*   Amiga system reset.

NOTES:
     n*: See warning above
     See part 1 of this appendix for pin numbers.

SERIAL INTERFACE CONNECTOR TIMING

Maximum operating frequency is 19.2 KHz. Refer to EIA standard
RS-232-C for operating and installation specifications.
A rate of 31.25 KHz will be supported through the use of a MIDI adapter.

Modem control signals (CTS, RTS, DTR, DSR, CD) are completely under
software control. The modem control lines have no hardware affect
on and are completely asynchronous to TXD and RXD.

SERIAL INTERFACE CONNECTOR ELECTRICAL CHARACTERISTICS

OUTPUTS	MIN	TYP	MAX		
Vo(-):	-13.2	-x-	-2.5	V	Negative output voltage range
Vo(+):	8.0	-x-	13.2	V	Positive output voltage range
Io:	-x-	-x-	10.0	ma	Output current

INPUTS	MIN	TYP	MAX		
Vi(+):	3.0	-x-	25.0	V	Positive input voltage range
Vi(-):	-25.0	-x-	0.5	V	Negative input voltage range
Vhys:	-x-	1.0	-x-	V	Input hysteresis voltage
Ii:	0.3	-x-	10.0	ma	Input current

Unconnected inputs are interpreted the same as positive input voltages.

GAME CONTROLLER INTERFACE CONNECTOR SPECIFICATION

The two 9-pin D-type connectors with pins (male) are used to
interface to four types of devices:

1. Mouse or trackball, 3 buttons max.
2. Digital joystick, 2 buttons max.
3. Proportional (pot or proportional joystick), 2 buttons max.
4. Light pen, including pen-pressed-to-screen button.

The connector pin assignments are discussed in sections organized
by similar hardware and/or software operating requirements as shown
in the previous list. Signal names follow those used elsewhere
in this appendix, when possible.

J11 is the right controller port connector (JOY1DAT, POT1DAT).
J12 is the left controller port connector (JOY0DAT, POT0DAT).

NOTE: While most of the hardware discussed below is directly
   accessible, hardware should be accessed through ROM kernel software.
   This will keep future hardware changes transparent to the user.

GAME CONTROLLER INTERFACE TO MOUSE/TRACKBALL QUADRATURE INPUTS

A mouse or trackball is a device that translates planar motion into
pulse trains. Quadrature techniques are employed to preserve the
direction as well as magnitude of displacement. The registers JOY0DAT
and JOY1DAT become counter registers, with y displacement in the high
byte and x in the low byte. Movement causes the following action:

          Up: y decrements
          Down: y increments
          Right: x increments
          Left: x decrements

To determine displacement, JOYxDAT is read twice with corresponding x
and y values subtracted (careful, modulo 128 arithmetic). Note that
if either count changes by more than 127, both distance and direction
become ambiguous. There is a relationship between the sampling
interval and the maximum speed (that is, change in distance) that
can be resolved as follows:

          Velocity < Distance(max) / SampleTime

          Velocity < SQRT(DeltaX**2 + DeltaY**2) / SampleTime

For an Amiga with a 200 count-per-inch mouse sampling during each
vertical blanking interval, the maximum velocity in either the X or Y
direction becomes:

          Velocity < (128 Counts * 1 inch/200 Counts) / .017 sec = 38 in/sec

which should be sufficient for most users.

NOTE: The Amiga software is designed to do mouse update cycles during
    vertical blanking. The horizontal and vertical counters are always
    valid and may be read at any time.

CONNECTOR PIN USAGE FOR MOUSE/TRACKBALL QUADRATURE INPUTS

PIN	MNEMONIC	DESCRIPTION	HARDWARE REGISTER/NOTES
1	V	Vertical pulses	JOY[0/1]DAT<15:8>
2	H	Horizontal pulses	JOY[0/1]DAT(7:0>
3	VQ	Vertical quadrature pulses	JOY[0/1]DAT<15:8>
4	HQ	Horizontal quadrature pulses	JOY[0/1]DAT<7:0>
5	UBUT*	Unused mouse button	See Proportional Inputs.
6	LBUT*	Left mouse button	See Fire Button.
7	+5V	+5V, current limited	
8	Ground		
9	RBUT*	Right mouse button	See Proportional Inputs.

GAME PORT INTERFACE TO DIGITAL JOYSTICKS

A joystick is a device with four normally opened switches arranged 90
degrees apart. The JOY[0/1]DAT registers become encoded switch input
ports as follows:

        Forward: bit#9 xor bit#8
        Left: bit#9
        Back: bit#1 xor bit#0
        Right: bit#1

Data is encoded to facilitate the mouse/trackball operating mode.

NOTE: The right and left direction inputs are also designed to be
  right and left buttons, respectively, for use with proportional
  inputs. In this case, the forward and back inputs are not used,
  while right and left become button inputs rather than joystick inputs.

The JOY[0/1]DAT registers are always valid and may be read at any time.

CONNECTOR PIN USAGE FOR DIGITAL JOYSTICK INPUTS

PIN	MNEMONIC	DESCRIPTION	HARDWARE REGISTER/NOTES
1	FORWARD*	Forward joystick switch	JOY[0/1]DAT<9 xor 8>
2	BACK*	Back joystick switch	JOY[0/1]DAT(1 xor 0>
3	LEFT*	Left joystick switch	JOY[0/1]DAT<9>
4	RIGHT*	Right joystick switch	JOY[0/1]DAT<1>
5	Unused		
6	FIRE*	Left mouse button	See Fire Button.
7	+5V	125ma max, 200ma surge	Total both ports.
8	Ground		
9	Unused		

GAME PORT INTERFACE TO FIRE BUTTONS

The fire buttons are normally opened switches routed to the 8520
adapter PRA0 as follows:

        PRA0 bit 7 = Fire* left controller port
        PRA0 bit 6 = Fire* right controller port

Before reading this register, the corresponding bits of the data
direction register must be cleared to define input mode:

        DDRA0<7:6> cleared as appropriate

NOTE: Do not disturb the settings of other bits in DDRA0 (Use of ROM
  kernel calls is recommended).

Fire buttons are always valid and may be read at any time.

CONNECTOR PIN USAGE FOR FIRE BUTTON INPUTS

```
PIN     MNEMONIC    DESCRIPTION
---     --------    -----------
1       -x-
2       -x-
3       -x-
4       -x-
5       -x-
6       FIRE*       Left mouse button/fire button
7       -x-
8       ground
9       -x-
```

GAME PORT INTERFACE TO PROPORTIONAL CONTROLLERS

Resistive (potentiometer) element linear taper proportional
controllers are supported up to 528k Ohms max (470k +/- 10%
recommended). The JOY[0/1]DAT registers contain digital
translation values for y in the high byte and x in the low byte.
A higher count value indicates a higher external resistance.
The Amiga performs an integrating analog-to-digital conversion
as follows:

   1. For the first 7 (NTSC) or 8 (PAL) horizontal display lines,
   the analog input capacitors are discharged and the positions
   counters reflected in the POT[0/1]DAT registers are held reset.

   For the remainder of the display field, the input capacitors are
   allowed to recharge through the resistive element in the external
   control device.

   2. The gradually increasing voltage is continuously compared to
   an internal reference level while counter keeps track of the
   number of lines since the end of the reset interval.

   3. When the input voltage finally exceeds the internal threshold
   for a given input channel, the current counter value is latched
   into the POT[0/1]DAT register corresponding to that channel.

   4. During the vertical blanking interval, the software examines
   the resulting POT[0/1]DAT register values and interprets the
   counts in terms of joystick position.

NOTE: The POTY and POTX inputs are designated as "right mouse button" and
"unused mouse button" respectively. An opened switch corresponds to high
resistance, a closed switch to a low resistance. The buttons are also
available in POTGO and POTINP registers. It is recommended that
ROM kernel calls be used for future hardware compatibility.

It is important to realize that the proportional controller is more of a
"pointing" device than an absolute position input. It is up to the
software to provide the calibration, range limiting and averaging functions
needed to support the application's control requirements.

The POT[0/1]DAT registers are typically read during video blanking,
but MAY be available prior to that.

CONNECTOR PIN USAGE FOR PROPORTIONAL INPUTS

PIN	MNEMONIC	DESCRIPTION	HARDWARE REGISTER/NOTES
1	XBUT	Extra Button	
2	Unused		
3	LBUT*	Left button	See Digital Joystick
4	RBUT*	Right button	See Digital Joystick
5	POTX	X analog in	POT[0/1]DAT<7:0>, POTGO, POTINP
6	Unused		
7	+5V	125ma max, 200 ma surge	
8	Ground		
9	POTY	Y analog in	POT[0,1]DAT<15:8>, POTGO, POTINP

GAME PORT INTERFACE TO LIGHT PEN

A light pen is an optoelectronic device whose light-sensitive portion
is placed in proximity to a CRT. As the electron beam sweeps past the
light pen, a trigger pulse is generated which can be enabled to latch the
horizontal and vertical beam positions. There is no hardware bit to
indicate this trigger, but this can be determined in the two ways
as shown in chapter 8, "Interface Hardware."

Light pen position is usually read during blanking, but MAY be available
prior to that.

CONNECTOR PIN USAGE FOR LIGHT PEN INPUTS

PIN	MNEMONIC	DESCRIPTION	HARDWARE REGISTER/NOTES
1	Unused		
2	Unused		
3	Unused		
4	Unused		
5	LPENPR*	Light pen pressed	See Proportional Inputs
6	LPENTG*	Light pen trigger	VPOSR, VHPOSR
7	+5V	125ma max, 200 ma surge	Both ports
8	Ground		
9	Unused		

Note: depending on the maker, the light pen input may be either.

EXTERNAL DISK INTERFACE CONNECTOR SPECIFICATION

The 23-pin D-type connector with sockets (DB23S) at the rear of the
Amiga is nominally used to interface to MFM devices.

EXTERNAL DISK CONNECTOR PIN ASSIGNMENT (J7)

PIN	NAME	DIR	NOTES
1	RDY*	I/O	If motor on, indicates disk installed and up to speed. If motor not on, identification mode. See below.
2	DKRD*	I	MFM input data to Amiga.
3	GND		
4	GND		
5	GND		
6	GND		
7	GND		
8	MTRXD*	OC	Motor on data, clocked into drive's motor-on flip-flop by the active transition of SELxB*. Guaranteed setup time is 1.4 usec. Guaranteed hold time is 1.4 usec.
9	SEL2B*	OC	Select drive 2.*
10	DRESB*	OC	Amiga system reset. Drives should reset their motor-on flip-flops and set their write-protect flip-flops.
11	CHNG*	I/O	Note: Nominally used as an open collector input. Drive's change flop is set at power up or when no disk is not installed. Flop is reset when drive is selected and the head stepped, but only if a disk is installed.
12	+5V		270 ma maximum; 410 ma surge. When below 3.75V, drives are required to reset their motor-on flops, and set their write-protect flops.
13	SIDEB*	O	Side 1 if active, side 0 if inactive
14	WPRO*	I/O	Asserted by selected, write-protected disk.
15	TK0*	I/O	Asserted by selected drive when read/write head is positioned over track 0.
16	DKWEB*	OC	Write gate (enable) to drive.
17	DKWDB*	OC	MFM output data from Amiga.
18	STEPB*	OC	Selected drive steps one cylinder in the direction indicated by DIRB.
19	DIRB	OC	Direction to step the head. Inactive to step towards center of disk (higher-numbered tracks).
20	SEL3B*	OC	Select drive 3. *
21	SEL1B*	OC	Select drive 1. *
22	INDEX*	I/O	Index is a pulse generated once per disk revolution, between the end and beginning of cylinders. The 8520 can be programmed to conditionally generate a level 6 interrupt to the 68000 whenever the INDEX* input goes active.
23	+12V		160 ma maximum; 540 ma surge.

* Note: the drive select lines are shifted as they pass through
       a string of daisy chained devices. Thus the signal that appears
       as drive 2 select at the first drive shows up as drive 1 select
       at the second drive and so on...

EXTERNAL DISK CONNECTOR IDENTIFICATION MODE

An identification mode is provided for reading a 32-bit serial
identification data stream from an external device. To initialize
this mode, the motor must be turned on, then off. See pin 8,
MTRXD* for a discussion of how to turn the motor on and off. The
transition from motor on to motor off reinitializes the serial
shift register.
After initialization, the SELxB* signal should be left in the
inactive state.
Now enter a loop where SELxB* is driven active, read serial input
data on RDY* (pin 1), and drive SELxB* inactive. Repeat this loop
a total of 32 times to read in 32 bits of data. The most significant
bit is received first.

EXTERNAL DISK CONNECTOR DEFINED IDENTIFICATIONS

$0000 0000 - no drive present.
$FFFF FFFF - Amiga standard 3.25 diskette.
$5555 5555 - 48 TPI double-density, double-sided.

As with other peripheral ID's, users should contact Commodore-Amiga
for ID assignment.
The serial input data is active low and must therefore be inverted
to be consistent with the above table.

EXTERNAL DISK CONNECTOR LIMITATIONS

1. The total cable length, including daisy chaining, must not exceed
    1 meter.

2. A maximum of 3 external devices may reside on this interface,
    but specific implementations may support fewer external devices.

3. Each device must provide a 1000-Ohm pull-up resistor on those
    outputs driven by an open-collector device on the Amiga
    (pins 8-10, 16-21).

4. The system provides power for only the first external device in the
    daisy chains.

```
************** PART 3 - INTERNAL CONNECTORS ********************


DISK INTERNAL ...34 PIN RIBBON   (J10)
--------------------------------------

1   GND              18   DIRB
2   CHNG*            19   GND
3   GND              20   STEPB*
4   MTR0D*(led)      21   GND
5   GND              22   DKWDB*
6   N.C.             23   GND
7   GND              24   DKWEB*
8   INDEX*           25   GND
9   GND              26   TK0*
10  SEL0B*           27   GND
11  GND              28   WPRO*
12  N.C.             29   GND
13  GND              30   DKRD*
14  N.C.             31   GND
15  GND              32   SIDEB*
16  MTR0D*           33   GND
17  GND              34   RDY*



DISK INTERNAL POWER ...4 PIN STRAIGHT   (J13)
---------------------------------------------

1   +12   (some drives are +5 only)
2   GND
3   GND
4   +5
```

```
********** PART 4 - PORT SIGNAL ASSIGNMENTS FOR 8520 ***********

Address BFFR01  data bits 7-0   (A12*) (int2)
--------------------------------------------------


PA7..game port 1, pin 6 (fire button*)
PA6..game port 0, pin 6 (fire button*)
PA5..RDY*        disk ready*
PA4..TK0*        disk track 00*
PA3..WPRO*       write protect*
PA2..CHNG*       disk change*
PA1..LED*        led light (0=bright) / audio filter control (A500 & A2000)
PA0..OVL         ROM/RAM overlay bit

SP...KDAT        keyboard data
CNT..KCLK        keyboard clock
PB7..P7          data 7
PB6..P6          data 6
PB5..P5          data 5       Centronics parallel interface
PB4..P4          data 4             data
PB3..P3          data 3
PB2..P2          data 2
PB1..P1          data 1
PB0..P0   data 0

PC...drdy*                    Centronics control
F....ack*




Address BFDRFE  data bits 15-8   (A13*) (int6)
--------------------------------------------------


PA7..com line DTR*, driven output
PA6..com line RTS*, driven output
PA5..com line carrier detect*
PA4..com line CTS*
PA3..com line DSR*
PA2..SEL         Centronics control
PA1..POUT  +--- paper out -------------+
PA0..BUSY  | +--busy      -------------+ |
           | |                         | |
SP...BUSY  | +- commodore serial bus + |
CNT..POUT  +----commodore serial bus --+

PB7..MTR*        motor
PB6..SEL3*       select external 3rd drive
PB5..SEL2*       select external 2nd drive
PB4..SEL1*       select external 1st drive
PB3..SEL0*       select internal drive
PB2..SIDE*       side select*
PB1..DIR         direction
PB0..STEP*       step*

PC...not used
F....INDEX*      disk index pulse*
```

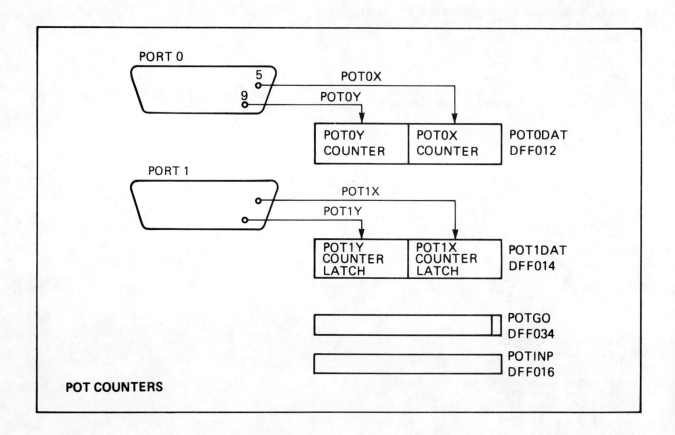

POT COUNTERS

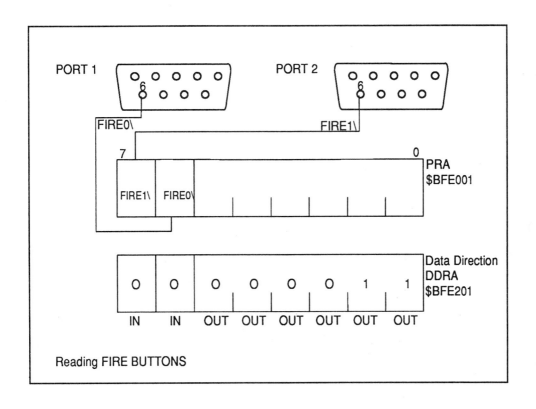

Reading FIRE BUTTONS

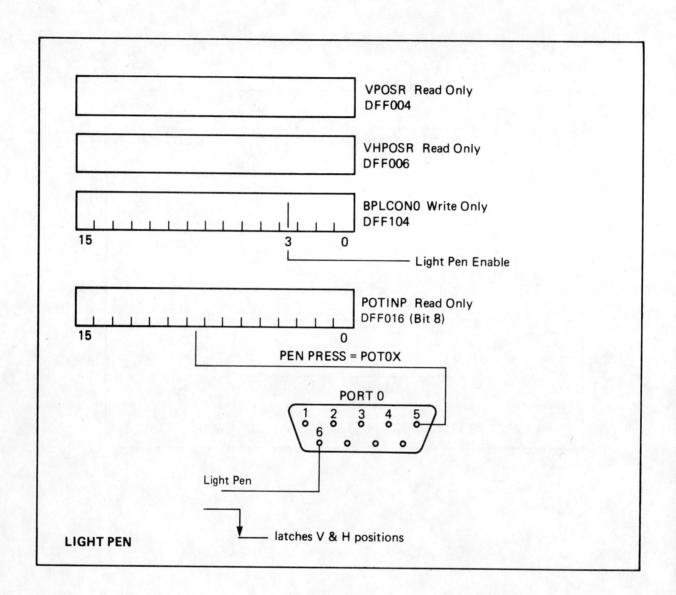

VPOSR Read Only
DFF004

VHPOSR Read Only
DFF006

BPLCON0 Write Only
DFF104

15   3   0

└── Light Pen Enable

POTINP Read Only
DFF016 (Bit 8)

15   0

PEN PRESS = POT0X

PORT 0

Light Pen

latches V & H positions

LIGHT PEN

316 Appendix E

Appendix F

Complex Interface Adapters

This appendix contains information about the 8520 peripheral interface adapters.

8520 Complex Interface Adaptor (CIA) Chips

Each Amiga system contains two 8520 Complex Interface Adaptor (CIA) chips. Each chip has 16 general purpose input/output pins, plus a serial shift register, three timers, an output pulse pin and an edge detection input. In the Amiga system various tasks are assigned to the chip's capabilities.

CIAA Address Map

```
------------------------------------------------------------------------
Byte      Register                    Data bits
Address   Name       7     6     5     4     3     2     1     0
------------------------------------------------------------------------
BFE001    pra        /FIR1 /FIR0 /RDY /TK0  /WPRO /CHNG /LED  OVL
BFE101    prb        Parallel port
BFE201    ddra       Direction for port A (BFE001);1=output (set to 0x03)
BFE301    ddrb       Direction for port B (BFE101);1=output (can be in or out)
BFE401    talo       CIAA timer A low byte (.715909 Mhz NTSC; .709379 Mhz PAL)
BFE501    tahi       CIAA timer A high byte
BFE601    tblo       CIAA timer B low byte (.715909 Mhz NTSC; .709379 Mhz PAL)
BFE701    tbhi       CIAA timer B high byte
BFE801    todlo      50/60 Hz event counter bits 7-0 (VSync or line tick)
BFE901    todmid     50/60 Hz event counter bits 15-8
BFEA01    todhi      50/60 Hz event counter bits 23-16
BFEB01               not used
BFEC01    sdr        CIAA serial data register (connected to keyboard)
BFED01    icr        CIAA interrupt control register
BFEE01    cra        CIAA control register A
BFEF01    crb        CIAA control register B
```

Note: CIAA can generate interrupt INT2.

CIAB Address Map

```
------------------------------------------------------------------------
Byte      Register                    Data bits
Address   Name       7     6     5     4     3     2     1     0
------------------------------------------------------------------------
BFD000    pra        /DTR  /RTS  /CD   /CTS  /DSR  SEL   POUT  BUSY
BFD100    prb        /MTR  /SEL3 /SEL2 /SEL1 /SEL0 /SIDE DIR   /STEP
BFD200    ddra       Direction for Port A (BFD000);1 = output (set to 0xFF)
BFD300    ddrb       Direction for Port B (BFD100);1 = output (set to 0xFF)
BFD400    talo       CIAB timer A low byte (.715909 Mhz NTSC; .709379 Mhz PAL)
BFD500    tahi       CIAB timer A high byte
BFD600    tblo       CIAB timer B low byte (.715909 Mhz NTSC; .709379 Mhz PAL)
BFD700    tbhi       CIAB timer B high byte
BFD800    todlo      Horizontal sync event counter bits 7-0
BFD900    todmid     Horizontal sync event counter bits 15-8
BFDA00    todhi      Horizontal sync event counter bits 23-16
BFDB00               not used
BFDC00    sdr        CIAB serial data register (unused)
BFDD00    icr        CIAB interrupt control register
BFDE00    cra        CIAB Control register A
BFDF00    crb        CIAB Control register B
```

Note: CIAB can generate INT6.

Chip Register Map

Each 8520 has 16 registers that you may read or write. Here is the list of registers and the access address of each within the memory space dedicated to the 8520:

```
                         Register
RS3  RS2  RS1  RS0       #(hex)   NAME     MEANING
--------------------------------------------------------------------
 0    0    0    0          0      pra      Peripheral data register A
 0    0    0    1          1      prb      Peripheral data register B
 0    0    1    0          2      ddra     Data direction register A
 0    0    1    1          3      ddrb     Direction register B
 0    1    0    0          4      talo     Timer A low register
 0    1    0    1          5      tahi     Timer A high register
 0    1    1    0          6      tblo     Timer B low register
 0    1    1    1          7      tbhi     Timer B high register
 1    0    0    0          8      todlow   Event LSB
 1    0    0    1          9      todmid   Event 8-15
 1    0    1    0          A      todhi    Event MSB
 1    0    1    1          B               No connect
 1    1    0    0          C      sdr      Serial data register
 1    1    0    1          D      icr      Interrupt control register
 1    1    1    0          E      cra      Control register A
 1    1    1    1          F      crb      Control register B
--------------------------------------------------------------------
```

```
SOFTWARE NOTE:

The operating system kernel has already allocated the use of
several of the 8520 timers.

    CIAA, timer A    -- Keyboard  (used continuously to handshake
                        keystrokes).  NOT AVAILABLE.
    CIAA, timer B    -- Virtual timer device (used continuously
                        whenever system Exec is in control; used
                        for task switching, interrupts and timing).
    CIAA, TOD        -- 50/60 Hz timer used by timer.device. The
                        A1000 uses power line tick.  The A500 uses
                        vertical sync.  The A2000 has a jumper
                        selection.

    CIAB, timer A    -- not used
    CIAB, timer B    -- not used
    CIAB, TOD        -- graphics.library video beam follower.  This
                        timer counts at the horizontal sync rate,
                        and is used to syncronize graphics events
                        to the video beam.

    Note that previous editions of this chart were incorrect.
--------------------------------------------------------------------
```

Register Functional Description

I/O PORTS (PRA, PRB, DDRA, DDRB)

Ports A and B each consist of an 8-bit peripheral data register (PR) and an 8-bit data direction register (DDR). If a bit in the DDR is set to a 1, the corresponding bit position in the PR becomes an output. If a DDR bit is set to a 0, the corresponding PR bit is defined as an input.

When you READ a PR register, you read the actual current state of the I/O pins (PA0-PA7, PB0-PB7, regardless of whether you have set them to be inputs or outputs.

Ports A and B have passive pull-up devices as well as active pull-ups, providing both CMOS and TTL compatibility. Both ports have two TTL load drive capability.

In addition to their normal I/O operations, ports PB6 and PB7 also provide timer output functions.

HANDSHAKING

Handshaking occurs on data transfers using the PC output pin and the FLAG input pin. PC will go low on the third cycle after a port B access. This signal can be used to indicate "data ready" at port B or "data accepted" from port B. Handshaking on 16-bit data transfers (using both ports A and B) is possible by always reading or writing port A first. FLAG is a negative edge-sensitive input that can be used for receiving the PC output from another 8520 or as a general- purpose interrupt input. Any negative transition on FLAG will set the FLAG interrupt bit.

REG	NAME	D7	D6	D5	D4	D3	D2	D1	D0
0	PRA	PA7	PA6	PA5	PA4	PA3	PA2	PA1	PA0
1	PRB	PB7	PB6	PB5	PB4	PB3	PB2	PB1	PB0
2	DDRA	DPA7	DPA6	DPA5	DPA4	DPA3	DPA2	DPA1	DPA0
3	DDRB	DPB7	DPB6	DPB5	DPB4	DPB3	DPB2	DPB1	DPB0

INTERVAL TIMERS (TIMER A, TIMER B)

Each interval timer consists of a 16-bit read-only timer counter and a 16-bit write-only timer latch. Data written to the timer is latched into the timer latch, while data read from the timer is the present contents of the timer counter.

The latch is also called a prescalar in that it represents the countdown value which must be counted before the timer reaches an underflow (no more counts) condition. This latch (prescalar) value is a divider of the input clocking frequency. The timers can be used independently or linked for extended operations. Various timer operating modes allow generation of long time delays, variable width pulses, pulse trains, and variable frequency waveforms. Utilizing the CNT input, the timers can count external pulses or measure frequency, pulse width, and delay times of external signals.

Each timer has an associated control register, providing independent control over each of the following functions:

Start/Stop

A control bit allows the timer to be started or stopped by the microprocessor at any time.

PB on/off

A control bit allows the timer output to appear on a port B output line (PB6 for timer A and PB7 for timer B). This function overrides the DDRB control bit and forces the appropriate PB line to become an output.

Toggle/pulse

A control bit selects the output applied to port B while the PB on/off bit is ON. On every timer underflow, the output can either toggle or generate a single positive pulse of one cycle duration. The toggle output is set high whenever the timer is started, and set low by RES.

One-shot/continuous

A control bit selects either timer mode. In one-shot mode, the timer will count down from the latched value to zero, generate an interrupt, reload the latched value, then stop. In continuous mode, the timer will count down from the latched value to zero, generate an interrupt, reload the latched value, and repeat the procedure continuously.

In one-shot mode, a write to timer-high (register 5 for timer A, register 7 for Timer B) will transfer the timer latch to the counter and initiate counting regardless of the start bit.

Force load

A strobe bit allows the timer latch to be loaded into the timer counter at any time, whether the timer is running or not.

INPUT MODES

Control bits allow selection of the clock used to decrement the timer. Timer A can count 02 clock pulses or external pulses applied to the CNT pin. Timer B can count 02 pulses, external CNT pulses, timer A underflow pulses, or timer A underflow pulses while the CNT pin is held high.

The timer latch is loaded into the timer on any timer underflow, on a force load, or following a write to the high byte of the pre- scalar while the timer is stopped. If the timer is running, a write to the high byte will load the timer latch but not the counter.

BIT NAMES on READ-Register

REG	NAME	D7	D6	D5	D4	D3	D2	D1	D0
4	TALO	TAL7	TAL6	TAL5	TAL4	TAL3	TAL2	TAL1	TAL0
5	TAHI	TAH7	TAH6	TAH5	TAH4	TAH3	TAH2	TAH1	TAH0
6	TBLO	TBL7	TBL6	TBL5	TBL4	TBL3	TBL2	TBL1	TBL0
7	TBHI	TBH7	TBH6	TBH5	TBH4	TBH3	TBH2	TBH1	TBH0

BIT NAMES on WRITE-Register

REG	NAME	D7	D6	D5	D4	D3	D2	D1	D0
4	TALO	PAL7	PAL6	PAL5	PAL4	PAL3	PAL2	PAL1	PAL0
5	TAHI	PAH7	PAH6	PAH5	PAH4	PAH3	PAH2	PAH1	PAH0
6	TBLO	PBL7	PBL6	PBL5	PBL4	PBL3	PBL2	PBL1	PBL0
7	TBHI	PBH7	PBH6	PBH5	PBH4	PBH3	PBH2	PBH1	PBH0

Time of Day Clock

TOD consists of a 24-bit binary counter. Positive edge transitions on this pin cause the binary counter to increment. The TOD pin has a passive pull-up on it.

A programmable alarm is provided for generating an interrupt at a desired time. The alarm registers are located at the same addresses as the corresponding TOD registers. Access to the alarm is governed by a control register bit. The alarm is write-only; any read of a TOD address will read time regardless of the state of the ALARM access bit.

A specific sequence of events must be followed for proper setting and reading of TOD. TOD is automatically stopped whenever a write to the register occurs. The clock will not start again until after a write to the LSB event register. This assures that TOD will always start at the desired time.

Since a carry from one stage to the next can occur at any time with respect to a read operation, a latching function is included to keep all TOD information constant during a read sequence. All TOD registers latch on a read of MSB event and remain latched until after a read of LSB event. The TOD clock continues to count when the output registers are latched. If only one register is to be read, there is no carry problem and the register can be read "on the fly" provided that any read of MSB event is followed by a read of LSB Event to disable the latching.

BIT NAMES for WRITE TIME/ALARM or READ TIME

```
REG  NAME
---  ----
 8   LSB Event   E7   E6   E5   E4   E3   E2   E1   E0
 9   Event 8-15  E15  E14  E13  E12  E11  E10  E9   E8
 A   MSB Event   E23  E22  E21  E20  E19  E18  E17  E16

WRITE
CRB7 = 0
CRB7 = 1 ALARM
```

Serial Shift Register (SDR)

The serial port is a buffered, 8-bit synchronous shift register. A control bit selects input or output mode. In the Amiga system one shift register is used for the keyboard, and the other is unassigned. Note that the RS-232 compatible serial port is controlled by the Paula chip; see chapter 8 for details.

INPUT MODE

In input mode, data on the SP pin is shifted into the shift register on the rising edge of the signal applied to the CNT pin. After eight CNT pulses, the data in the shift register is dumped into the serial data register and an interrupt is generated.

OUTPUT MODE

In the output mode, Timer A is used as the baud rate generator. Data is shifted out on the SP pin at 1/2 the underflow rate of Timer A. The maximum baud rate possible is 02 divided by 4, but the maximum usable baud rate will be determined by line loading and the speed at which the receiver responds to input data.

To begin transmission, you must first set up Timer A in continuous mode, and start the timer. Transmission will start following a write to the serial data register. The clock signal derived from Timer A appears as an output on the CNT pin. The data in the serial data register will be loaded into the shift register, then shifted out to the SP pin when a CNT pulse occurs. Data shifted out becomes valid on the next falling edge of CNT and remains valid until the next falling edge.

After eight CNT pulses, an interrupt is generated to indicate that more data can be sent. If the serial data register was reloaded with new information prior to this interrupt, the new data will automatically be loaded into the shift register and transmission will continue.

If no further data is to be transmitted after the eighth CNT pulse, CNT will return high and SP will remain at the level of the last data bit transmitted.

SDR data is shifted out MSB first. Serial input data should appear in this same format.

BIDIRECTIONAL FEATURE

The bidirectional capability of the shift register and CNT clock allows many 8520s to be connected to a common serial communications bus on which one 8520 acts as a master, sourcing data and shift clock, while all other 8520 chips act as slaves.   Both CNT and SP outputs are open drain to allow such a common bus. Protocol for master/slave selection can be transmitted over the serial bus or via dedicated handshake lines.

```
REG   NAME      D7    D6    D5    D4    D3    D2    D1    D0
---   ----      ----  ----  ----  ----  ----  ----  ----  ----
C     SDR       S7    S6    S5    S4    S3    S2    S1    S0
```

Interrupt Control Register (ICR)

There are five sources of interrupts on the 8520:

> -Underflow from Timer A (timer counts down past 0)
> -Underflow from Timer B
> -TOD alarm
> -Serial port full/empty
> -Flag

A single register provides masking and interrupt information. The interrupt control register consists of a write-only MASK register and a read-only DATA register. Any interrupt will set the corresponding bit in the DATA register. Any interrupt that is enabled by a 1-bit in that position in the MASK will set the IR bit (MSB) of the DATA register and bring the IRQ pin low. In a multichip system, the IR bit can be polled to detect which chip has generated an interrupt request.

When you read the DATA register, its contents are cleared (set to 0), and the IRQ line returns to a high state. Since it is cleared on a read, you must assure that your interrupt polling or interrupt service code can preserve and respond to all bits which may have been set in the DATA register at the time it was read. With proper preservation and response, it is easily possible to intermix polled and direct interrupt service methods.

You can set or clear one or more bits of the MASK register without affecting the current state of any of the other bits in the register. This is done by setting the appropriate state of the MSBit, which is called the set/clear bit. In bits 6-0, you yourself form a mask that specifies which of the bits you wish to affect. Then, using bit 7, you specify HOW the bits in corresponding positions in the mask are to be affected.

- If bit 7 is a 1, then any bit 6-0 in your own mask byte which is set to a 1 sets the corresponding bit in the MASK register. Any bit that you have set to a 0 causes the MASK register bit to remain in its current state.

- If bit 7 is a 0, then any bit 6-0 in your own mask byte which is set to a 1 clears the corresponding bit in the MASK register. Again, any 0 bit in your own mask byte causes no change in the contents of the corresponding MASK register bit.

If an interrupt is to occur based on a particular condition, then that corresponding MASK bit must be a 1.

Example: Suppose you want to set the Timer A interrupt bit (enable the Timer A interrupt), but want to be sure that all other interrupts are cleared. Here is the sequence you can use:

```
INCLUDE "hardware/cia.i"
XREF    _ciaa                       ; From amiga.lib
lea     _ciaa,a0                    ; Defined in amiga.lib
move.b  #%01111110,ciaicr(a0)
```

MSB is 0, means clear any bit whose value is 1 in the rest of the byte

```
INCLUDE "hardware/cia.i"
XREF    _ciaa                       ; From amiga.lib
lea     _ciaa,a0                    ; Defined in amiga.lib
move.b  #%10000001,ciaicr(a0)
```

MSB is 1, means set any bit whose value is 1 in the rest of the byte (do not change any values wherein the written value bit is a zero)

READ INTERRUPT CONTROL REGISTER

REG	NAME	D7	D6	D5	D4	D3	D2	D1	D0
D	ICR	IR	0	0	FLG	SP	ALRM	TB	TA

WRITE INTERRUPT CONTROL MASK

REG	NAME	D7	D6	D5	D4	D3	D2	D1	D0
D	ICR	S/C	x	x	FLG	SP	ALRM	TB	TA

Control Registers

There are two control registers in the 8520, CRA and CRB. CRA is associated with Timer A and CRB is associated with Timer B. The format of the registers is as follows:

CONTROL REGISTER A

```
BIT   NAME      FUNCTION

 0    START     1 = start Timer A, 0 = stop Timer A.
                This bit is automatically reset (= 0) when
                underflow occurs during one-shot mode.

 1    PBON      1 = Timer A output on PB6, 0 = PB6 is normal operation.

 2    OUTMODE   1 = toggle, 0 = pulse.

 3    RUNMODE   1 = one-shot mode, 0 = continuous mode.

 4    LOAD      1 = force load (this is a strobe input, there is no
                data storage;  bit 4 will always read back a zero
                and writing a 0 has no effect.)

 5    INMODE    1 = Timer A counts positive CNT transitions,
                0 = Timer A counts 02 pulses.

 6    SPMODE    1 = Serial port=output (CNT is the source of the shift
                clock)
                0 = Serial port=input  (external shift clock is
                required)

 7    UNUSED
```

BIT MAP OF REGISTER CRA

REG#	NAME	UNUSED	SPMODE	INMODE	LOAD	RUNMODE	OUTMODE	PBON	START
E	CRA	unused	0=input	0=02	1=force	0=cont.	0=pulse	0=PB6OFF	0=stop
		unused	1=output	1=CNT	load	1=one-	1=toggle	1=PB6ON	1=start
					(strobe)	shot			

|<-------- Timer A Variables ------------------>|

All unused register bits are unaffected by a write and forced to 0 on a read.

CONTROL REGISTER B:

BIT	NAME	FUNCTION
0	START	1 = start Timer B, 0 = stop Timer B. This bit is automatically reset (= 0) when underflow occurs during one-shot mode.
1	PBON	1 = Timer B output on PB7, 0 = PB7 is normal operation.
2	OUTMODE	1 = toggle, 0 = pulse.
3	RUNMODE	1 = one-shot mode, 0 = continuous mode.
4	LOAD	1 = force load (this is a strobe input, there is no data storage; bit 4 will always read back a zero and writing a 0 has no effect.)
6,5	INMODE	Bits CRB6 and CRB5 select one of four possible input modes for Timer B, as follows:

CRB6	CRB5	Mode Selected
0	0	Timer B counts 02 pulses
0	1	Timer B counts positive CNT transitions
1	0	Timer B counts Timer A underflow pulses
1	1	Timer B counts Timer A underflow pulses while CNT pin is held high.

BIT	NAME	FUNCTION
7	ALARM	1 = writing to TOD registers sets Alarm
		0 = writing to TOD registers sets TOD clock. Reading TOD registers always reads TOD clock, regardless of the state of the Alarm bit.

BIT MAP OF REGISTER CRB

```
REG
  #  NAME ALARM     INMODE     LOAD     RUNMODE  OUTMODE   PBON     START

  F  CRB  0=TOD     00=02      1=force  0=cont.  0=pulse  0=PB7OFF 0=stop
          1=Alarm   01=CNT        load  1=one-   1=toggle 1=PB7ON  1=start
                    10=Timer A (strobe) shot
                    11=CNT+
                       Timer A

                    |<---------------Timer B Variables--------------->|
```

All unused register bits are unaffected by a write and forced to 0 on a read.

Port Signal Assignments

This part specifies how various signals relate to the available ports of the 8520. This information enables the programmer to relate the port addresses to the outside-world items (or internal control signals) which are to be affected. This part is primarily for the use of the systems programmer and should generally not be used by applications programmers. Systems software normally is configured to handle the setting of particular signals, no matter how the physical connections may change.

NOTE

In a multi-tasking operating system, many different tasks may be competing for the use of the system resources. Applications programmers should follow the established rules for resource access in order to assure compatibility of their software with the system.

```
Address BFEr01  data bits 7-0  (A12*) (INT2)

PA7..game port 1, pin 6 (fire button*)
PA6..game port 0, pin 6 (fire button*)
PA5..RDY*          disk ready*
PA4..TK0*          disk track 00*
PA3..WPRO*         write protect*
PA2..CHNG*         disk change*
PA1..LED*          led light (0=bright)
PA0..OVL           memory overlay bit
SP...KDAT          keyboard data
CNT..KCLK
PB7..P7        data 7
PB6..P6        data 6
PB5..P5        data 5        Centronics parallel interface
PB4..P4        data 4             data
PB3..P3   data 3
PB2..P2        data 2
PB1..P1        data 1
PB0..P0        data 0
PC...drdy*             centronics control
F....ack*


Address BFDr00  data bits 15-8   (A13*) (INT6)

PA7..com line DTR*, driven output
PA6..com line RTS*, driven output
PA5..com line carrier detect*
PA4..com line CTS*
PA3..com line DSR*
PA2..SEL           centronics control
PA1..POUT          paper out ---+
PA0..BUSY          busy     ---+ |
                              | |
SP...BUSY          commodore -+ |
CNT..POUT          commodore ---+


PB7..MTR*          motor
PB6..SEL3*         select external 3rd drive
PB5..SEL2*         select external 2nd drive
PB4..SEL1*         select external 1st drive
PB3..SEL0*         select internal drive
PB2..SIDE*         side select*
PB1..DIR           direction
PB0..STEP*         step*  (3.0 milliseconds minimum)

PC...not used
F....INDEX*        disk index*
```

```
; A complete 8520 timing example.  This blinks the power light at (exactly)
; 3 milisecond intervals.  It takes over the machine, so watch out!
;
; The base Amiga crytal frequecies are:
;          NTSC    28.63636  MHz
;          PAL     28.37516  MHz
;
; The two 16 bit timers on the 8520 chips each count down at 1/10 the CPU
; clock, or 0.715909 MHz.  That works out to 1.3968255 microseconds per count.
; Under PAL the countdown is slightly slower, 0.709379 MHz.
;
; To wait 1/100 second would require waiting 10,000 microseconds.
; The timer register would be set to (10,000 / 1.3968255 = 7159).
;
; To wait 3 miliseconds would require waiting 3000 microsecsonds.
; The register would be set to (3000 / 1.3968255 = 2148).
;
        INCLUDE "hardware/cia.i"
        INCLUDE "hardware/custom.i"
;
        XREF    _ciaa
        XREF    _ciab
        XREF    _custom
;
        lea     _custom,a3              ; Base of custom chips
        lea     _ciaa,a4                ; Get base address if CIA-A
;
        move.w  #$7fff,dmacon(a3)       ; Kill all chip interrupts
;
;----Setup, only do once
;----This sets all bits needed for timer A one-shot mode.
        move.b  ciacra(a4),d0           ;Set control register A on CIAA
        and.b   #%11000000,d0           ;Don't trash bits we are not
        or.b    #%00001000,d0           ;using...
        move.b  d0,ciacra(a4)
        move.b  #%01111111,ciaicr(a4)   ;Clear all 8520 interrupts
;
;----Set time (low byte THEN high byte)
;----And the low order with $ff
;----Shift the high order by 8
;
TIME    equ     2148
        move.b  #(TIME&$FF),ciatalo(a4)
        move.b  #(TIME>>8),ciatahi(a4)
;
;----Wait for the timer to count down
busy_wait:
        btst.b  #0,ciaicr(a4)           ;Wait for timer expired flag
        beq.s   busy_wait
        bchg.b  #CIAB_LED,ciapra(a4)    ;Blink light
        bset.b  #0,ciacra(a4)           ;Restart timer
        bra.s   busy_wait

        END
```

Hardware Connection Details

The system hardware selects the CIAs when the upper three address bits are 101. Furthermore, CIAA is selected when A12 is low, A13 high; CIAB is selected when A12 is high, A13 low. CIAA communicates on data bits 7-0, CIAB communicates on data bits 15-8.

Address bits A11, A10, A9, and A8 are used to specify which of the 16 internal registers you want to access. This is indicated by ''r'' in the address. All other bits are don't cares. So, CIAA is selected by the following binary address: 101x xxxx xx01 rrrr xxxx xxx0. CIAB address: 101x xxxx xx10 rrrr xxxx xxx1

With future expansion in mind, we have decided on the following addresses: CIAA = BFEr01; CIAB = BFDr00. Software must use byte accesses to these address, and no other.

INTERFACE SIGNALS

Clock input

The 02 clock is a TTL compatible input used for internal device operation and as a timing reference for communicating with the system data bus. On the Amiga, this is connected to the 68000 ''E'' clock. The ''E'' clock runs at 1/10 of the CPU clock. This works out to .715909 Mhz for NTSC or .709379 Mhz for PAL.

CS - chip-select input

The CS input controls the activity of the 8520. A low level on CS while 02 is high causes the device to respond to signals on the R/W and address (RS) lines. A high on CS prevents these lines from controlling the 8520. The CS line is normally activated (low) at 02 by the appropriate address combination.

R/W - read/write input

The R/W signal is normally supplied by the microprocessor and controls the direction of data transfers of the 8520. A high on R/W indicates a read (data transfer out of the 8520), while a low indicates a write (data transfer into the 8520).

RS3-RS0 - address inputs

The address inputs select the internal registers as described by the register map.

DB7-DB0 - data bus inputs/outputs

The eight data bus output pins transfer information between the 8520 and the system data bus. These pins are high impedance inputs unless CS is low and R/W and 02 are high, to read the device. During this read, the data bus output buffers are enabled, driving the data from the selected register onto the system data bus.

IRQ - interrupt request output

IRQ is an open drain output normally connected to the processor interrupt input. An external pull-up resistor holds the signal high, allowing multiple IRQ outputs to be connected together. The IRQ output is normally off (high impedance) and is activated low as indicated in the functional description.

RES - reset input

A low on the RES pin resets all internal registers. The port pins are set as inputs and port registers to zero (although a read of the ports will return all highs because of passive pull-ups). The timer control registers are set to zero and the timer latches to all ones. All other registers are reset to zero.

Appendix G

AUTOCONFIG™

The AUTOCONFIG™ protocol is designed to allow the dynamic assignment of available address slots to expansion boards, eliminating the need for user configuration via jumpers. Upon reset, each board appears in turn at $E80000, with readable identification information, most of which is in one's complement format, stored in the high nibbles of the first $40 words ($80 bytes) of the board. This identification information includes the size of the board, its address space preferences, type of board (memory or other), and a unique Hardware Manufacturer Number assigned by Commodore Amiga Technical Support, West Chester, Pennsylvania.

Each board contains configuration hardware including an address latch appearing in the nibble at offset $0048 and the nibble at offset $004a. When A23 through A16 of the assigned board base address are written to this register, the board latches and appears at the assigned address, then passes a signal called CONFIG-OUT that causes the next board to appear at $E80000. To make certain types of boards less expensive, an expansion board's write registers may be organized as either a byte-wide register or two nibble-wide registers. If the register is nibble-wide then it must latch the low nibble of the assigned address (at $4A) until the high nibble (at $48) is written. This allows the following algorithm to work with either type of board:

> Write the low order address nibble to offset $4A
> Write the entire address byte to offset $48

Alternatively, many boards can be asked to "shut-up" (pass CONFIG-OUT and stop responding) by writing to offset $004c of the board. A bit in the nibble at offset $0008 flags whether a board supports shut-up.

All commercial expansion slot boards for the Amiga must implement the AUTOCONFIG protocol. More in-depth machine-specific information on the design and implementation of AUTO-CONFIG boards is available from Commodore Amiga Technical Support.

The Amiga operating system contains support for matching up disk-based drivers with AUTO-CONFIG boards. Since 1.3, the OS also supports initialization of onboard ROM driver software. As a general rule, applications should not attempt to AUTOCONFIG expansion peripherals, but rather should allow the Amiga system software to handle all automatic configuration. Many boards contain registers which once activated could do irreparable damage, for example, data on a user's hard disk could be lost if the board had been configured improperly.

However, certain types of low level stand-alone applications may need to configure hardware such as RAM boards without using the Amiga operating system. Such applications should only configure expansion RAM boards (boards which ask to be added to the free memory list) and known dedicated boards designed for specific applications. All other boards should be shut-up if the board supports shut-up, or configured and ignored if shut-up is not supported. (There are many boards which do not support shut-up). Configuration of boards should only be attempted by applications which take over the whole machine at reset. Presence of an AUTOCONFIG board waiting for configuration is determined by comparing the nibbles appearing at the initial AUTOCONFIG address with the valid values for such nibbles in the specifications.

The AUTOCONFIG spec requires that boards be configured on boundaries that match their space requirements. For example, a 1 MB memory board should be configured on a 1 MB boundary. There are two exceptions to this rule: boards with a 4 MB address space are capable of being placed at $200000 and $600000 as well as being placed on 4 MB boundaries; 8 MB boards can be placed at $200000. These exceptions are necessary because the 8 MB space reserved for expansion in the current machine begins at $200000.

Debugging AUTOCONFIG Boards

If there is a defect in your configuration information, your board may be ignored, may shut-up or may crash in a way that makes diagnosis difficult. There is a simple trick allows you to test the configuration information. Cut the CONFIGIN* line to your board and wire a switch into the line. Wire in the switch such that when it is set one way, the CONFIGIN* line will pass through from the bus to the board. This allows the board to respond to the AUTOCONFIG process. When the switch is set the other way, it should be wired such that the input to the board is forced high. This will disable the AUTOCONFIG of the board.

Set the switch so that the CONFIGIN* line is forced high, then bring up the system. Your board will be invisible to the system software. Activate a debugger, and flip the switch. Your board should now respond at the normal $E80000 address. Your view of the board is identical to what the operating system sees when configuring your board. You can compare the bits with the expected values.

NOTE

The board to be debugged must be the last board in the system (closest to the PC slots, away from the power supply.) Boards downstream of the board to be debugged will not be configured by the system.

Address Specification Table

The following table describes the board identification information and AUTOCONFIG registers which appear in the first $80 bytes of an AUTOCONFIG board at configuration time.

NOTES

- Identification information is stored in the high nibbles of the even (word) addresses at the start of an AUTOCONFIG board. For example, the first two words of a board might contain $Cxxx 1xxx. The valid information in these first two words would be the $C (high nibble of the word at offset $00), then the $1 (high nibble of the word at offset $02). Much of the information is interpreted by combining several nibbles, with low to high address nibbles containing high to low order parts of the resulting value.

- All nibbles of information, except for those at offsets $00/02 and $40/42, are stored in an inverted (one's complement) form and must be exclusive OR'd with $F before interpreting them according to the table below. Unused nibbles (the three other nibbles in each word) may not be assumed to contain any particular value. All values written to the AUTOCON-FIG area, including the assigned address, are written uninverted.

- All addresses are shown here as offsets from the base address $E80000 where boards appear at configuration time, so offset $02 is at $E80002, offset $04 at $E80004, etc.

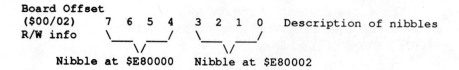

```
Board Offset
($00/02)     7  6  5  4    3  2  1  0    Description of nibbles
R/W info     _____/    _____/
                 \/            \/
       Nibble at $E80000    Nibble at $E80002
```

Figure G-1: How to read the Address Specification Table

NOTE

The bit numbering (7 6 5 4 3 2 1 0) is for use when two nibbles are to be interpreted together as a byte. Physically, each nibble is the high nibble of the word at its address (ie. bits 15 14 13 12).

Table G-1: Address Specification Table

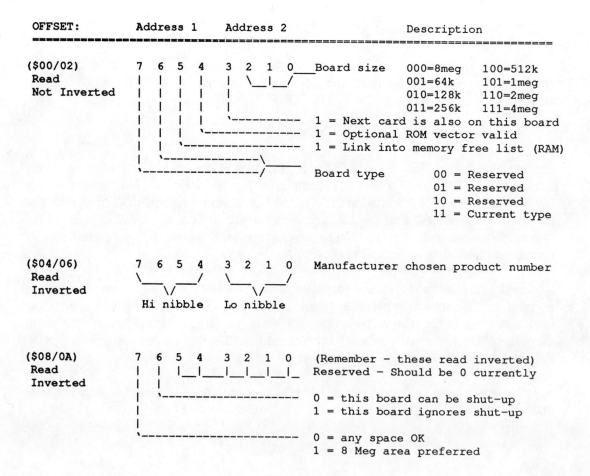

```
OFFSET:          Address 1      Address 2            Description
============================================================================

($00/02)     7  6  5  4    3  2  1  0   Board size   000=8meg    100=512k
Read         |  |  |  |    |  \__|__/                001=64k     101=1meg
Not Inverted |  |  |  |    |                         010=128k    110=2meg
             |  |  |  |    |                         011=256k    111=4meg
             |  |  |  |    '---------- 1 = Next card is also on this board
             |  |  |  '------------- 1 = Optional ROM vector valid
             |  |  '-------------- 1 = Link into memory free list (RAM)
             |  '--------------\____
             '-----------------/    Board type      00 = Reserved
                                                    01 = Reserved
                                                    10 = Reserved
                                                    11 = Current type


($04/06)     7  6  5  4    3  2  1  0   Manufacturer chosen product number
Read         _____/    _____/
Inverted         \/            \/
             Hi nibble     Lo nibble


($08/0A)     7  6  5  4    3  2  1  0   (Remember - these read inverted)
Read         |  |  |__|__|__|__|__|__   Reserved - Should be 0 currently
Inverted     |  |
             |  '-------------------- 0 = this board can be shut-up
             |                        1 = this board ignores shut-up
             |
             '-------------------- 0 = any space OK
                                   1 = 8 Meg area preferred
```

```
OFFSET:          Address 1    Address 2           Description    (cont.)
============================================================================

($0C/0E)         7  6  5  4   3  2  1  0
Read             |__|__|__|___|__|__|__|_   Reserved - must be 0
Inverted


($10/12)         7  6  5  4   3  2  1  0    High byte of unique hardware
Read             \____ ____/  \____ ____/   manufacturer number assigned
Inverted              \/           \/       to manufacturer.
                 Hi nibble    Lo nibble     (Not developer number!)

($14/16)         7  6  5  4   3  2  1  0    Low byte of unique hardware
Read             \____ ____/  \____ ____/   manufacturer number assigned
Inverted              \/           \/       to manufacturer.
                 Hi nibble    Lo nibble     (Not developer number!)
```

NOTE

Manufacturer number is assigned by Commodore Amiga Technical Support in West Chester, Pennsylvania (CATS). Contact CATS for further information.

```
($18/1A)         7  6  5  4   3  2  1  0    Optional serial #, first byte (msb)
($1C/1E)         7  6  5  4   3  2  1  0    Optional serial #, second byte
($20/22)         7  6  5  4   3  2  1  0    Optional serial #, third byte
($24/26)         7  6  5  4   3  2  1  0    Optional serial #, fourth byte (lsb)
Read
Inverted


($28/2A)         7  6  5  4   3  2  1  0    High byte of optional ROM vector.
Read             \____ ____/  \____ ____/
Inverted              \/           \/
                 Hi nibble    Lo nibble


($2C/2E)         7  6  5  4   3  2  1  0    Low byte of optional ROM vector.
Read             \____ ____/  \____ ____/   If the ``ROM vector valid'' bit
Inverted              \/           \/       is set in nibble $00 at the start
                 Hi nibble    Lo nibble     of the board, then this optional
                                            ROM vector is the offset from the
                                            board base to ROM driver structures.


($30/32)         7  6  5  4   3  2  1  0    Read - Reserved, must be 00
R/W                                         Write - optional reset of
Inverted                                    board base register to
                                            pre-configuration address


($34/36)         7  6  5  4   3  2  1  0    Reserved, must be 00
($38/3A)         7  6  5  4   3  2  1  0    Reserved, must be 00
($3C/3E)         7  6  5  4   3  2  1  0    Reserved, must be 00
Inverted
```

```
OFFSET:          Address 1    Address 2              Description   (cont.)
=================================================================================

($40/42)         7  6  5  4   3  2  1  0    Write                  Read
R/W              |  |  |  |   |  |  |  |
Not Inverted     |  |  |  |   |  |  |  '-   Interrupt enable       Interrupt enable
                 |  |  |  |   |  |  '----   User definable         Undefined
                 |  |  |  |   |  '-------   Local reset            Must be 0
                 |  |  |  |   '----------   User definable         Undefined
                 |  |  |  '--------------   User definable         INT2 pending
                 |  |  '-----------------   User definable         INT6 pending
                 |  '--------------------   User definable         INT7 pending
                 '-----------------------   User definable         Board pulling INT
```

NOTE

Use of the $40/42 registers is an optional feature which can be implemented by boards which generate interrupts. They make it possible for board-specific interrupt servers to determine if the current interrupt is being generated by their board, or by some other hardware using the same interrupt line.

```
($44/46)         7  6  5  4   3  2  1  0    Reserved, read must be 00
R/W                                         Write undefined
Inverted


($48/4A)         7  6  5  4   3  2  1  0    Base address register, write only.
Write Only       \____ ____/  \____ ____/   These bits are compared with A23
Not Inverted          \/            \/       through A16 (or fewer) to determine
                 Hi nibble    Lo nibble     the base address of the board.


($4C/4E)         7  6  5  4   3  2  1  0    Optional shut-up register.
Write Only       \____ ____/               Any write to $4C will cause
                      \/                     board to pass CONFIG-OUT and
                      '------------------    and then never respond again
                                            to any address, until RESET.
                                            A bit in nibble $08 flags
                                            whether the board can be shut-up.


($50 through $7E)                           Reserved, must be 00
Inverted
```

Remember that all nibbles except $00/02 and $40/42 will actually appear inverted from the values in the above table. For example, a "must be 0" nibble will appear as $F, and flags and hex values will also be inverted (i.e. a value of $1 will read as $E, etc).

```
/*
 *  Examine all AUTOCONFIG(tm) boards in the system
 */
#include "exec/types.h"
#include "libraries/configvars.h"


struct Library    *OpenLibrary();
struct ConfigDev *FindConfigDev();
struct Library    *ExpansionBase;


void main()
{
struct ConfigDev *myCD=0;

ExpansionBase=OpenLibrary("expansion.library",0L);

while(myCD=FindConfigDev(myCD,-1L,-1L))  /* search for any ConfigDev */
    {
    printf("\n---ConfigDev structure found at location $%lx---\n",myCD);

    /* These values are read directly from the board */
    printf("er_Manufacturer          =");
        printf("%d,",myCD->cd_Rom.er_Manufacturer);
        printf("$%x,",myCD->cd_Rom.er_Manufacturer);
        printf("(~$%4x)\n",~myCD->cd_Rom.er_Manufacturer);

    printf("er_Product               =");
        printf("%d,",myCD->cd_Rom.er_Product);
        printf("$%x,",myCD->cd_Rom.er_Product);
        printf("(~$%x)\n",~myCD->cd_Rom.er_Product);

    printf("er_Type                    =$%x\n",myCD->cd_Rom.er_Type);

    printf("er_Flags                   =");
        printf("$%x\n",myCD->cd_Rom.er_Flags);

    /* These values are generated when the AUTOCONFIG(tm) software
     * relocates the board
     */
    printf("cd_BoardAddr              =$%lx\n",myCD->cd_BoardAddr);
    printf("cd_BoardSize              =$%lx (%ldK)\n",
           myCD->cd_BoardSize,((ULONG)myCD->cd_BoardSize)/1024);

    printf("cd_Flags                   =$%x\n",myCD->cd_Flags);
    }
CloseLibrary(ExpansionBase);
}
```

Appendix H

Keyboard

This appendix contains the keyboard interface specification for A1000, A500 and A2000.

The keyboard plugs into the Amiga computer via a cable with four primary connections. The four wires provide 5-volt power, ground, and signals called KCLK (keyboard clock) and KDAT (keyboard data). KCLK is unidirectional and always driven by the keyboard; KDAT is driven by both the keyboard and the computer. Both signals are open-collector; there are pullup resistors in both the keyboard (inside the keyboard microprocessor) and the computer.

Keyboard Communications

The keyboard transmits 8-bit data words serially to the main unit. Before the transmission starts, both KCLK and KDAT are high. The keyboard starts the transmission by putting out the first data bit (on KDAT), followed by a pulse on KCLK (low then high); then it puts out the second data bit and pulses KCLK until all eight data bits have been sent. After the end of the last KCLK pulse, the keyboard pulls KDAT high again.

When the computer has received the eighth bit, it must pulse KDAT low for at least 1 (one) microsecond, as a handshake signal to the keyboard. The handshake detection on the keyboard end will typically use a hardware latch. *The keyboard must be able to detect pulses greater than or equal to 1 microsecond. Software MUST pulse the line low for 85 microseconds to ensure compatibility with all keyboard models.*

All codes transmitted to the computer are rotated one bit before transmission. The transmitted order is therefore 6-5-4-3-2-1-0-7. The reason for this is to transmit the up/down flag last, in order to cause a key-up code to be transmitted in case the keyboard is forced to restore lost sync (explained in more detail below).

The KDAT line is active low; that is, a high level (+5V) is interpreted as 0, and a low level (0V) is interpreted as 1.

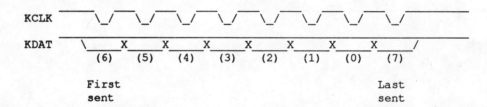

The keyboard processor sets the KDAT line about 20 microseconds before it pulls KCLK low. KCLK stays low for about 20 microseconds, then goes high again. The processor waits another 20 microseconds before changing KDAT.

Therefore, the bit rate during transmission is about 60 microseconds per bit, or 17 kbits/sec.

Keycodes

Each key has a keycode associated with it (see accompanying table). Keycodes are always 7 bits long. The eighth bit is a "key-up"/"key-down" flag; a 0 (high level) means that the key was pushed down, and a 1 (low level) means the key was released (the CAPS LOCK key is different -- see below).

For example, here is a diagram of the "B" key being pushed down. The keycode for "B" is $35 = 00110101; due to the rotation of the byte, the bits transmitted are 01101010.

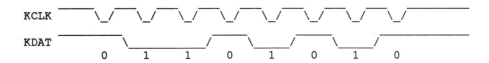

In the next example, the "B" key is released. The keycode is still $35, except that bit 7 is set to indicate "key-up," resulting in a code of $B5 = 10110101. After rotating, the transmission will be 01101011:

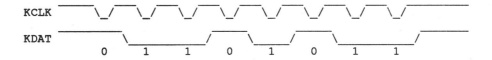

"CAPS LOCK" Key

This key is different from all the others in that it generates a keycode only when it is pushed down, never when it is released. However, the up/down bit is still used. When pushing the CAPS LOCK key turns on the CAPS LOCK LED, the up/down bit will be 0; when pushing CAPS LOCK shuts off the LED, the up/down bit will be 1.

"Out-of-Sync" Condition

Noise or other glitches may cause the keyboard to get out of sync with the computer. This means that the keyboard is finished transmitting a code, but the computer is somewhere in the middle of receiving it.

If this happens, the keyboard will not receive its handshake pulse at the end of its transmission. If the handshake pulse does not arrive within 143 ms of the last clock of the transmission, the keyboard will assume that the computer is still waiting for the rest of the transmission and is therefore out of sync. The keyboard will then attempt to restore sync by going into "resync mode." In this mode, the keyboard clocks out a 1 and waits for a handshake pulse. If none arrives within 143 ms, it clocks out another 1 and waits again. This process will continue until a handshake pulse arrives.

Once sync is restored, the keyboard will have clocked a garbage character into the computer. That is why the key-up/key-down flag is always transmitted last. Since the keyboard clocks out 1's to restore sync, the garbage character thus transmitted will appear as a key release, which is less dangerous than a key hit.

Whenever the keyboard detects that it has lost sync, it will assume that the computer failed to receive the keycode that it had been trying to transmit. Since the computer is unable to detect lost sync, it is the keyboard's responsibility to inform the computer of the disaster. It does this by transmitting a "lost sync" code (value $F9 = 11111001) to the computer. Then it retransmits the code that had been garbled.

NOTE

The only reason to transmit the "lost sync" code to the computer is to alert the software that something may be screwed up. The "lost sync" code does not help the recovery process, because the garbage keycode can't be deleted, and the correct key code could simply be retransmitted without telling the computer that there was an error in the previous one.

Power-Up Sequence

There are two possible ways for the keyboard to be powered up under normal circumstances: <1> the computer can be turned on with the keyboard plugged in, or <2> the keyboard can be plugged into an already "on" computer. The keyboard and computer must handle either case without causing any upset.

The first thing the keyboard does on power-up is to perform a self-test. This involves a ROM checksum test, simple RAM test, and watchdog timer test. Whenever the keyboard is powered up (or restarted -- see below), it must not transmit anything until it has achieved synchronization with the computer. The way it does this is by slowly clocking out 1 bits, as described above, until it receives a handshake pulse.

If the keyboard is plugged in before power-up, the keyboard may continue this process for several minutes as the computer struggles to boot up and get running. The keyboard must continue clocking out 1s for however long is necessary, until it receives its handshake.

If the keyboard is plugged in after power-up, no more than eight clocks will be needed to achieve sync. In this case, however, the computer may be in any state imaginable but must not be adversely affected by the garbage character it will receive. Again, because it receives a key release, the damage should be minimal. The keyboard driver must anticipate this happening and handle it, as should any application that uses raw keycodes.

NOTE

The keyboard must not transmit a "lost sync" code after re-synchronizing due to a power-up or restart; only after re-synchronizing due to a handshake time-out.

Once the keyboard and computer are in sync, the keyboard must inform the computer of the results of the self-test. If the self-test failed for any reason, a "selftest failed" code (value $FC = 11111100) is transmitted (the keyboard does not wait for a handshake pulse after sending the "selftest failed" code). After this, the keyboard processor goes into a loop in which it blinks the CAPS LOCK LED to inform the user of the failure. The blinks are coded as bursts of one, two, three, or four blinks, approximately one burst per second:

One blink	ROM checksum failure.
Two blinks	RAM test failed.
Three blinks	Watchdog timer test failed.
Four blinks	A short exists between two row lines or one of the seven special keys (not implemented).

If the self-test succeeds, then the keyboard will proceed to transmit any keys that are currently down. First, it sends an "initiate power-up key stream" code (value $FD = 11111101), followed by the key codes of all depressed keys (with keyup/down set to "down" for each key). After all keys are sent (usually there won't be any at all), a "terminate key stream" code (value $FE = 11111110) is sent. Finally, the CAPS LOCK LED is shut off. This marks the end of the start-up sequence, and normal processing commences.

The usual sequence of events will therefore be: power-up; synchronize; transmit "initiate power-up key stream" ($FD); transmit "terminate key stream" ($FE).

Reset Warning

NOTE

Available on some A1000 and A2000 keyboards. You cannot rely on this feature for all Amigas.

The keyboard has the additional task of resetting the computer on the command of the user. The user initiates Reset Warning by simultaneously pressing the CTRL key and the two "AMIGA" keys.

The keyboard responds to this input by syncing up any pending transmit operations. The keyboard then sends a "reset warning" to the Amiga. This action alerts the Amiga software to finish up any pending operations (such as disk DMA) and prepare for reset.

A specific sequence of operations ensure that the Amiga is in a state where it can respond to the reset warning. The keyboard sends two actual "reset warning" keycodes. The Amiga must handshake to the first code like any normal keystroke, else the keyboard goes directly to Hard Reset. On the second "reset warning" code the Amiga must drive KDAT low within 250 milliseconds, else the keyboard goes directly to Hard Reset. If the all the tests are passed, the Amiga has 10 full seconds to do emergency processing. When the Amiga pulls KDAT high again, the keyboard finally asserts hard reset.

If the Amiga fails to pull KDAT high within 10 seconds, Hard Reset is asserted anyway.

Hard Reset

NOTE

This happens after Reset Warning. Valid for all keyboards except the Amiga 500.

The keyboard Hard Resets the Amiga by pulling KCLK low and starting a 500 millisecond timer. When one or more of the keys is released AND 500 milliseconds have passed, the keyboard will release KCLK. 500 milliseconds is the minimum time KCLK must be held low. The maximum KCLK time depends on how long the user holds the three keys down.

NOTE

Circuitry on the Amiga motherboard detects the 500 millisecond KCLK pulse.

After releasing KCLK, the keyboard jumps to its start-up code (internal RESET). This will initialize the keyboard in the same way as cold power-on.

NOTE

The keyboard must resend the "powerup key stream"!

Special Codes

The special codes that the keyboard uses to communicate with the main unit are summarized here.

NOTE

The special codes are 8-bit numbers; there is no up/down flag associated with them. However, the transmission bit order is the same as previously described.

```
Code       Name          Meaning
---------------------------------------------------------------
78         Reset warning.  CTRL-AMIGA  AIGA has been hit -
           computer will be reset in 10 seconds. (see text)
F9         Last key code bad, next code is the same code
              retransmitted (used when keyboard and main unit
              get out of sync).
FA         Keyboard output buffer overflow
FB         Unused (was controller failure)
FC         Keyboard selftest failed
FD         Initiate power-up key stream (keys pressed at powerup)
FE         Terminate power-up key stream
FF         Unused (was interrupt)
```

Matrix Table

Column	Row 5 (Bit 7)	Row 4 (Bit 6)	Row 3 (Bit 5)	Row 2 (Bit 4)	Row 1 (Bit 3)	Row 0 (Bit 2)
15 (PD.7)	(spare) (0E)	(spare) (1C)	(spare) (2C)	(spare) (47)	(spare) (48)	(spare) (49)
14 (PD.6)	* note 1 (5D)	\<SHIFT\> note 2 (30)	CAPS LOCK (62)	TAB (42)	~ ` (00)	ESC (45)
13 (PD.5)	+ note 1 (5E)	Z (31)	A (20)	Q (10)	! 1 (01)	(note 1 (5A)
12 (PD.4)	9 note 3 (3F)	X (32)	S (21)	W (11)	@ 2 (02)	F1 (50)
11 (PD.3)	6 note 3 (2F)	C (33)	D (22)	E (12)	# 3 (03)	F2 (51)
10 (PD.2)	3 note 3 (1F)	V (34)	F (23)	R (13)	$ 4 (04)	F3 (52)
9 (PD.1)	. note 3 (3C)	B (35)	G (24)	T (14)	% 5 (05)	F4 (53)
8 (PD.0)	8 note 3 (3E)	N (36)	H (25)	Y (15)	^ 6 (06)	F5 (54)
7 (PC.7)	5 note 3 (2E)	M (37)	J (26)	U (16)	& 7 (07)	) note 1 (5B)
6 (PC.6)	2 note 3 (1E)	< , (38)	K (27)	I (17)	* 8 (08)	F6 (55)
5 (PC.5)	ENTER note 3 (43)	> . (39)	L (28)	O (18)	(9 (09)	/ note 1 (5C)

```
         Row 5     Row 4     Row 3     Row 2     Row 1     Row 0
Column   (Bit 7)   (Bit 6)   (Bit 5)   (Bit 4)   (Bit 3)   (Bit 2)
       +-------+-------+-------+-------+-------+-------+
  4    |   7   |   ?   |   :   |   P   |   )   |  F7   |
(PC.4) |note 3 |   /   |   ;   |       |   0   |       |
       |  (3D) |  (3A) |  (29) |  (19) |  (0A) |  (56) |
       +-------+-------+-------+-------+-------+-------+
  3    |   4   |(spare)|   "   |   {   |   _   |  F8   |
(PC.3) |note 3 |   [   |   '   |   [   |   -   |       |
       |  (2D) |  (3B) |  (2A) |  (1A) |  (0B) |  (57) |
       +-------+-------+-------+-------+-------+-------+
  2    |   1   | SPACE | <RET> |   }   |   +   |  F9   |
(PC.2) |note 3 |  BAR  |note 2 |   ]   |   =   |       |
       |  (1D) |  (40) |  (2B) |  (1B) |  (0C) |  (58) |
       +-------+-------+-------+-------+-------+-------+
  1    |   0   | BACK  |  DEL  |RETURN |       |  F10  |
(PC.1) |note 3 | SPACE |       |       |   \   |       |
       |  (0F) |  (41) |  (46) |  (44) |  (0D) |  (59) |
       +-------+-------+-------+-------+-------+-------+
  0    |   -   | CURS  | CURS  | CURS  | CURS  | HELP  |
(PC.0) |note 3 | DOWN  | RIGHT | LEFT  |  UP   |       |
       |  (4A) |  (4D) |  (4E) |  (4F) |  (4C) |  (5F) |
       +-------+-------+-------+-------+-------+-------+
```

note 1: A500 and A2000 keyboards only (numeric pad)
note 2: International keyboards only (these keys are cutouts of the
        larger key on the US ASCII version.)   The key that generates
        $30 is cut out of the left shift key. Key $2B is cut out of
        return. These keys are labeled with country-specific markings.
note 3: Numeric pad.

The following table shows which keys are independently readable. These keys never generate
ghosts or phantoms.

```
    (Bit 6) (Bit 5) (Bit 4) (Bit 3) (Bit 2) (Bit 1) (Bit 0)
  +-------+-------+-------+-------+-------+-------+-------+
  | LEFT  | LEFT  | LEFT  | CTRL  | RIGHT | RIGHT | RIGHT |
  | AMIGA | ALT   | SHIFT |       | AMIGA | ALT   | SHIFT |
  | (66)  | (64)  | (60)  | (63)  | (67)  | (65)  | (61)  |
  +-------+-------+-------+-------+-------+-------+-------+
```

Appendix I

External Disk Connector Interface Specification

General

The 23-pin female connector at the rear of the main computer unit is used to interface to and control devices that generate and receive MFM data. This interface can be reached either as a resource or under the control of a driver. The following pages describe the interface in both cases.

Summary Table

Pin #	Name	Note	
1	RDY-	I/O	ID and ready
2	DKRD-	I	MFM input
3	GRND	G	-
4	GRND	G	-
5	GRND	G	-
6	GRND	G	-
7	GRND	G	-
8	MTRXD-	O	Motor control.
9	SEL2B-	O*	Select drive 2
10	DRESB-	O	Reset
11	CHNG-	I/O	Disk changed
12	+5v	PWR	540 mA average 870 mA surge
13	SIDEB-	O	Side 1 if low
14	WRPRO-	I/O	Write protect
15	TK0-	I/O	Track 0
16	DKWEB-	O	Write gate
17	DKWDB-	O	Write data
18	STEPB-	O	Step
19	DIRB	O	Direction (high is out)
20	SEL3B-	O*	Select drive 3
21	SEL1B-	O*	Select drive 1
22	INDEX-	I/O	Index
23	+12v	PWR	120 mA average 370 mA surge

Key to Class:

G   ground, note connector shield grounded.

I   input pulled up to 5v by 1K ohm.

I/O   input in driver, but bidirectional input (1k pullup)

O   output pulled though 1K to 5v

O*   output, separates resources.

PWR   available for external use, but currently used up by external drive.

Signals When Driving a Disk

The following describes the interface under driver control.

SEL1B-, SEL2B-, SEL3B-

Select lines for the three external disk drives active low.

TK0-

A selected drive pulls this signal low whenever its read-write head is on track 00.

RDY-

When a disk drive's motor is on, this line indicates the selected disk is installed and rotating at speed. The driver ignores this signal. When the motor is off this is used as a ID data line. See below.

WPRO- (Pin #14)

A selected drive pulls this signal low whenever it has a write-protected diskette installed.

INDEX- (Pin #22)

A selected drive pulses this signal low once for each revolution of its motor.

SIDEB- (Pin #13)

The system drives this signal to all disk drives—low for side 1, high for side 0.

STEPB- (Pin #18)

Pulsed to step the selected drive's head.

DIRB (Pin #19)

The system drives this signal high or low to tell the selected drive which way to step when the STEPB- pulse arrives. Low means step in (to higher-numbered track); high means step out.

DKRD- (Pin #2)

A selected drive will put out read data on this line.

DKWDB- (Pin #17)

The system drives write data to all disks via this signal. The data is only written when DKWEB- is active (low). Data is written only to selected drives.

DKWEB- (Pin #16)

This signal causes a selected drive to start writing data (provided by DKWDB-) onto the disk.

CHNG- (Pin #11)

A selected drive will drive this signal low whenever its internal "disk change" latch is set. This latch is set when the drive is first powered on, or whenever there is no diskette in the drive. To reset the latch, the system must select the drive, and step the head. Of course, the latch will not reset if there is no diskette installed.

MTRXD- (Pin #8)

This is the motor control line for all four disk drives. When the system wants to turn on a disk drive motor, it first deselects the drive (if selected), pulls MTRXD- low, and selects the drive. To turn the motor off, the system deselects the drive, pulls MTRXD- high, and selects the drive. The system will always set MTRXD- at least 1.4 microseconds before it selects the drive, and will not change MTRXD- for at least 1.4 microseconds after selecting the drive. All external drives must have logic equivalent to a D flip-flop, whose D input is the MTRXD- signal, and whose clock input is activated by the off-to-on (high-to-low) transition of its SELxB- signal. As noted above, both the setup and hold times of MTRXD- with respect to SELxB- will always be at least 1.4 microseconds. The output of this flip-flop controls the disk drive motor. Thus, the system can control all four motors using only one signal on the cable (MTRXD-).

DRESB- (Pin #10)

This signal is a buffered version of the system reset signal. Three things can make it go active (low):

- System power-up (DRESB- will go low for approximately one second);

- System CPU executes a RESET instruction (DRESB- will go low for approximately 17 microseconds);

- Hard reset from keyboard (lasts as long as keyboard reset is held down).

External disk drives should respond to DRESB- by shutting off their motor flip-flops and write protecting themselves.

A level of 3.75v or below on the 5v+ requires external disks to write-protect and reset the motor on line.

Device I.D.

This interface supports a method of establishing the type of disk(s) attached. The I.D. sequence is as follows.

1. Drive MTRXD- low.

2. Drive SELxB- low

3. Drive SELxB- high.

4. Drive MTRXD- high.

5. Drive SELxB- low

6. Drive SELxB- high.

7. Drive SELxB- low

8. Read and save state of RDY.

9. Drive SELxB- high.

Repeat steps 6 to 9, 15 times more.

Convert the 16 values of RDY- into a 16-bit word. The most significant bit is the first value and so on. This 16-bit quantity is the device I.D..

The following I.D.s are defined:

0000 0000 0000 0000	Reserved
1111 1111 1111 1111	Amiga standard 3.25
1010 1010 1010 1010	Reserved
0101 0101 0101 0101	48 TPI double-density, double-sided
1000 0000 0000 0000	Reserved
0111 1111 1111 1111	Reserved
0000 1111 xxxx xxxx	Available for users
1111 0000 xxxx xxxx	Extension reserved
xxxx 0000 0000 0000	Reserved
xxxx 1111 1111 1111	Reserved
0011 0011 0011 0011	Reserved
1100 1100 1100 1100	Reserved

Appendix J

Hardware Example Include File

This appendix contains an include file that maps the hardware register names, given in Appendix A and Appendix B, to names that can be resolved by the standard include files. Use of these names in code sections of this manual places the emphasis on what the code is doing, rather than getting bogged down in include file names.

All code examples in this manual reference the names given in this file.

```
                              IFND      HARDWARE_HW_EXAMPLES_I
        HARDWARE_HW_EXAMPLES_I  SET      1
        **
        **        Filename: hardware/hw_examples.i
        **        $Release: 1.3 $
        **
        **
        **        (C) Copyright 1985,1986,1987,1988,1989 Commodore-Amiga, Inc.
        **             All Rights Reserved
        **
        **************************************************************************

                IFND      HARDWARE_CUSTOM_I
                INCLUDE "hardware/custom.i"
                ENDC


        **************************************************************************
        *
        *  This include file is designed to be used in conjunction with the hardware
        *  manual examples.  This file defines the register names based on the
        *  hardware/custom.i definition file.  There is no C-Language version of this
        *  file.
        *
        **************************************************************************
        *
        * This instruction for the copper will cause it to
        * wait forever since the wait command described in it
        * will never happen.
        *
        COPPER_HALT       equ       $FFFFFFFE
        *
        **************************************************************************
        *
        * This is the offset in the 680x0 address space to the custom chip registers
        * It is the same as  _custom  when linking with AMIGA.lib
        *
        CUSTOM            equ       $DFF000
        *
        * Various control registers
        *
        DMACONR           equ       dmaconr         ; Just capitalization...
        VPOSR             equ       vposr           ;    "         "
        VHPOSR            equ       vhposr          ;    "         "
        JOY0DAT           equ       joy0dat         ;    "         "
        JOY1DAT           equ       joy1dat         ;    "         "
        CLXDAT            equ       clxdat          ;    "         "
        ADKCONR           equ       adkconr         ;    "         "
        POT0DAT           equ       pot0dat         ;    "         "
        POT1DAT           equ       pot1dat         ;    "         "
        POTINP            equ       potinp          ;    "         "
        SERDATR           equ       serdatr         ;    "         "
        INTENAR           equ       intenar         ;    "         "
        INTREQR           equ       intreqr         ;    "         "
        REFPTR            equ       refptr          ;    "         "
        VPOSW             equ       vposw           ;    "         "
        VHPOSW            equ       vhposw          ;    "         "
        SERDAT            equ       serdat          ;    "         "
        SERPER            equ       serper          ;    "         "
        POTGO             equ       potgo           ;    "         "
        JOYTEST           equ       joytest         ;    "         "
        STREQU            equ       strequ          ;    "         "
        STRVBL            equ       strvbl          ;    "         "
```

```
STRHOR          equ     strhor          ;  "          "
STRLONG         equ     strlong         ;  "          "
DIWSTRT         equ     diwstrt         ;  "          "
DIWSTOP         equ     diwstop         ;  "          "
DDFSTRT         equ     ddfstrt         ;  "          "
DDFSTOP         equ     ddfstop         ;  "          "
DMACON          equ     dmacon          ;  "          "
INTENA          equ     intena          ;  "          "
INTREQ          equ     intreq          ;  "          "
*
* Disk control registers
*
DSKBYTR         equ     dskbytr         ; Just capitalization...
DSKPT           equ     dskpt           ;  "          "
DSKPTH          equ     dskpt
DSKPTL          equ     dskpt+$02
DSKLEN          equ     dsklen          ;  "          "
DSKDAT          equ     dskdat          ;  "          "
DSKSYNC         equ     dsksync         ;  "          "
*
* Blitter registers
*
BLTCON0         equ     bltcon0         ; Just capitalization...
BLTCON1         equ     bltcon1         ;  "          "
BLTAFWM         equ     bltafwm         ;  "          "
BLTALWM         equ     bltalwm         ;  "          "
BLTCPT          equ     bltcpt          ;  "          "
BLTCPTH         equ     bltcpt
BLTCPTL         equ     bltcpt+$02
BLTBPT          equ     bltbpt          ;  "          "
BLTBPTH         equ     bltbpt
BLTBPTL         equ     bltbpt+$02
BLTAPT          equ     bltapt          ;  "          "
BLTAPTH         equ     bltapt
BLTAPTL         equ     bltapt+$02
BLTDPT          equ     bltdpt          ;  "          "
BLTDPTH         equ     bltdpt
BLTDPTL         equ     bltdpt+$02
BLTSIZE         equ     bltsize         ;  "          "
BLTCMOD         equ     bltcmod         ;  "          "
BLTBMOD         equ     bltbmod         ;  "          "
BLTAMOD         equ     bltamod         ;  "          "
BLTDMOD         equ     bltdmod         ;  "          "
BLTCDAT         equ     bltcdat         ;  "          "
BLTBDAT         equ     bltbdat         ;  "          "
BLTADAT         equ     bltadat         ;  "          "
BLTDDAT         equ     bltddat         ;  "          "
*
* Copper control registers
*
COPCON          equ     copcon          ; Just capitalization...
COPINS          equ     copins          ;  "          "
COPJMP1         equ     copjmp1         ;  "          "
COPJMP2         equ     copjmp2         ;  "          "
COP1LC          equ     cop1lc          ;  "          "
COP1LCH         equ     cop1lc
COP1LCL         equ     cop1lc+$02
COP2LC          equ     cop2lc          ;  "          "
COP2LCH         equ     cop2lc
COP2LCL         equ     cop2lc+$02
*
* Audio channels registers
```

```
*
ADKCON          equ     adkcon              ; Just capitalization...

AUD0LC          equ     aud0
AUD0LCH         equ     aud0
AUD0LCL         equ     aud0+$02
AUD0LEN         equ     aud0+$04
AUD0PER         equ     aud0+$06
AUD0VOL         equ     aud0+$08
AUD0DAT         equ     aud0+$0A

AUD1LC          equ     aud1
AUD1LCH         equ     aud1
AUD1LCL         equ     aud1+$02
AUD1LEN         equ     aud1+$04
AUD1PER         equ     aud1+$06
AUD1VOL         equ     aud1+$08
AUD1DAT         equ     aud1+$0A

AUD2LC          equ     aud2
AUD2LCH         equ     aud2
AUD2LCL         equ     aud2+$02
AUD2LEN         equ     aud2+$04
AUD2PER         equ     aud2+$06
AUD2VOL         equ     aud2+$08
AUD2DAT         equ     aud2+$0A

AUD3LC          equ     aud3
AUD3LCH         equ     aud3
AUD3LCL         equ     aud3+$02
AUD3LEN         equ     aud3+$04
AUD3PER         equ     aud3+$06
AUD3VOL         equ     aud3+$08
AUD3DAT         equ     aud3+$0A
*
*   The bitplane registers
*
BPL1PT          equ     bplpt+$00
BPL1PTH         equ     bplpt+$00
BPL1PTL         equ     bplpt+$02
BPL2PT          equ     bplpt+$04
BPL2PTH         equ     bplpt+$04
BPL2PTL         equ     bplpt+$06
BPL3PT          equ     bplpt+$08
BPL3PTH         equ     bplpt+$08
BPL3PTL         equ     bplpt+$0A
BPL4PT          equ     bplpt+$0C
BPL4PTH         equ     bplpt+$0C
BPL4PTL         equ     bplpt+$0E
BPL5PT          equ     bplpt+$10
BPL5PTH         equ     bplpt+$10
BPL5PTL         equ     bplpt+$12
BPL6PT          equ     bplpt+$14
BPL6PTH         equ     bplpt+$14
BPL6PTL         equ     bplpt+$16

BPLCON0         equ     bplcon0             ; Just capitalization...
BPLCON1         equ     bplcon1             ;     "           "
BPLCON2         equ     bplcon2             ;     "           "
BPL1MOD         equ     bpl1mod             ;     "           "
BPL2MOD         equ     bpl2mod             ;     "           "
```

```
DPL1DATA        equ     bpldat+$00
DPL2DATA        equ     bpldat+$02
DPL3DATA        equ     bpldat+$04
DPL4DATA        equ     bpldat+$06
DPL5DATA        equ     bpldat+$08
DPL6DATA        equ     bpldat+$0A
*
* Sprite control registers
*
SPR0PT          equ     sprpt+$00
SPR0PTH         equ     SPR0PT+$00
SPR0PTL         equ     SPR0PT+$02
SPR1PT          equ     sprpt+$04
SPR1PTH         equ     SPR1PT+$00
SPR1PTL         equ     SPR1PT+$02
SPR2PT          equ     sprpt+$08
SPR2PTH         equ     SPR2PT+$00
SPR2PTL         equ     SPR2PT+$02
SPR3PT          equ     sprpt+$0C
SPR3PTH         equ     SPR3PT+$00
SPR3PTL         equ     SPR3PT+$02
SPR4PT          equ     sprpt+$10
SPR4PTH         equ     SPR4PT+$00
SPR4PTL         equ     SPR4PT+$02
SPR5PT          equ     sprpt+$14
SPR5PTH         equ     SPR5PT+$00
SPR5PTL         equ     SPR5PT+$02
SPR6PT          equ     sprpt+$18
SPR6PTH         equ     SPR6PT+$00
SPR6PTL         equ     SPR6PT+$02
SPR7PT          equ     sprpt+$1C
SPR7PTH         equ     SPR7PT+$00
SPR7PTL         equ     SPR7PT+$02
;
; Note:  SPRxDATB is defined as being +$06 from SPRxPOS.
; sd_datab should be defined as $06, however, in the 1.3 assembler
; include file hardware/custom.i it is incorrectly defined as $08.
;
SPR0POS         equ     spr+$00
SPR0CTL         equ     SPR0POS+sd_ctl
SPR0DATA        equ     SPR0POS+sd_dataa
SPR0DATB        equ     SPR0POS+$06     ; should use sd_datab ...

SPR1POS         equ     spr+$08
SPR1CTL         equ     SPR1POS+sd_ctl
SPR1DATA        equ     SPR1POS+sd_dataa
SPR1DATB        equ     SPR1POS+$06     ; should use sd_datab ...

SPR2POS         equ     spr+$10
SPR2CTL         equ     SPR2POS+sd_ctl
SPR2DATA        equ     SPR2POS+sd_dataa
SPR2DATB        equ     SPR2POS+$06     ; should use sd_datab ...

SPR3POS         equ     spr+$18
SPR3CTL         equ     SPR3POS+sd_ctl
SPR3DATA        equ     SPR3POS+sd_dataa
SPR3DATB        equ     SPR3POS+$06     ; should use sd_datab ...

SPR4POS         equ     spr+$20
SPR4CTL         equ     SPR4POS+sd_ctl
SPR4DATA        equ     SPR4POS+sd_dataa
SPR4DATB        equ     SPR4POS+$06     ; should use sd_datab ...
```

```
SPR5POS          equ      spr+$28
SPR5CTL          equ      SPR5POS+sd_ctl
SPR5DATA         equ      SPR5POS+sd_dataa
SPR5DATB         equ      SPR5POS+$06      ; should use sd_datab ...

SPR6POS          equ      spr+$30
SPR6CTL          equ      SPR6POS+sd_ctl
SPR6DATA         equ      SPR6POS+sd_dataa
SPR6DATB         equ      SPR6POS+$06      ; should use sd_datab ...

SPR7POS          equ      spr+$38
SPR7CTL          equ      SPR7POS+sd_ctl
SPR7DATA         equ      SPR7POS+sd_dataa
SPR7DATB         equ      SPR7POS+$06      ; should use sd_datab ...
*
* Color registers...
*
COLOR00          equ      color+$00
COLOR01          equ      color+$02
COLOR02          equ      color+$04
COLOR03          equ      color+$06
COLOR04          equ      color+$08
COLOR05          equ      color+$0A
COLOR06          equ      color+$0C
COLOR07          equ      color+$0E
COLOR08          equ      color+$10
COLOR09          equ      color+$12
COLOR10          equ      color+$14
COLOR11          equ      color+$16
COLOR12          equ      color+$18
COLOR13          equ      color+$1A
COLOR14          equ      color+$1C
COLOR15          equ      color+$1E
COLOR16          equ      color+$20
COLOR17          equ      color+$22
COLOR18          equ      color+$24
COLOR19          equ      color+$26
COLOR20          equ      color+$28
COLOR21          equ      color+$2A
COLOR22          equ      color+$2C
COLOR23          equ      color+$2E
COLOR24          equ      color+$30
COLOR25          equ      color+$32
COLOR26          equ      color+$34
COLOR27          equ      color+$36
COLOR28          equ      color+$38
COLOR29          equ      color+$3A
COLOR30          equ      color+$3C
COLOR31          equ      color+$3E


*******************************************************************************
**
**
                          ENDC    ; HARDWARE_HW_EXAMPLES_I
```

Glossary

Agnus	One of the three main Amiga custom chips. Contains the blitter, copper, and DMA circuitry.
Aliasing distortion	A side effect of sound sampling, where two additional frequencies are produced, distorting the sound output.
Alt keys	Two keys on the keyboard to the left and right of the Amiga keys.
Amiga keys	Two keys on the keyboard to the left and right of the space bar.
AmigaDOS	The Amiga operating system.
Amplitude	The voltage or current output expressed as volume from a sound speaker.
Amplitude modulation	A means of increasing audio effects by using one audio channel to alter the amplitude of another.
Attach mode	In sprites, a mode in which a sprite uses two DMA channels for additional colors. In sound production, combining two audio channels for frequency/amplitude modulation or for stereo sound.
Automatic mode	In sprite display, the normal mode in which the sprite DMA channel, once it starts up, automatically retrieves and displays all of the data for a sprite. In audio, the normal mode in which the system retrieves sound data automatically through DMA.
Barrel shifter	Blitter circuit that allows movement of images on pixel boundaries.
Baud rate	Rate of data transmission through a serial port.
Beam counters	Registers that keep track of the position of the video beam.
Bit-map	The complete definition of a display in memory, consisting of one or more bit-planes and information about how to organize the rectangular display.

Bit-plane	A contiguous series of display memory words, treated as if it were a rectangular shape.
Bit-plane animation	A means of animating the display by moving around blocks of playfield data with the blitter.
Blanking interval	Time period when the video beam is outside the display area.
Blitter	DMA channel used for data copying and line drawing.
Chip Memory	Memory accessible to the Amiga custom chips. On the current generation of machines, this section of memory starting at address 0. *See* Fast Memory.
Clear	Giving a bit the value of 0.
CLI	*See* command line interface.
Clipping	When a portion of a sprite is outside the display window and thus is not visible.
Collision	A means of detecting when sprites, playfields, or playfield objects attempt to overlap in the same pixel position or attempt to cross some pre-defined boundary.
Color descriptor words	Pairs of words that define each line of a sprite.
Color indirection	The method used by Amiga for coloring individual pixels in which the binary number formed from all the bits that define a given pixel refers to one of the 32 color registers.
Color palette	*See* Color table.
Color register	One of 32 hardware registers containing colors that you can define.
Color table	The set of 32 color registers.
Command line interface	The command line interface to system commands and utilities.
Composite video	A video signal, transmitted over a single coaxial cable, which includes both picture and sync information.
Controller	Hardware device, such as mouse or light pen, used to move the pointer or furnish some other input to the system.

Coordinates	A pair of numbers shown in the form (x,y), where x is an offset from the left side of the display or display window and y is an offset from the top.
Copper	Display-synchronized coprocessor that resides on one of the Amiga custom chips and directs the graphics display.
Coprocessor	Processor that adds its instruction set to that of the main processor.
Cursor keys	Keys for moving something on the screen.
Data fetch	The number of words fetched for each line of the display.
Delay	In playfield horizontal scrolling, specifies how many pixels the picture will shift for each display field. Delay controls the speed of scrolling.
Denise	One of the three main Amiga custom chips. Contains the circuitry for the color pallete, sprites, and video output.
Depth	Number of bit-planes in a display.
Digital-to-analog converter	A device that converts a binary quantity to an analog level.
Direct memory access	An arrangement whereby intelligent devices can read or write memory directly, without having to interrupt the processor.
Display field	One complete scanning of the video beam from top to bottom of the video display screen.
Display mode	One of the basic types of display; for example, high or low resolution, interlaced or non-interlaced, single or dual playfield.
Display time	The amount of time to produce one display field, approximately 1/60th of a second.
Display window	The portion of the bit-map selected for display. Also, the actual size of the on-screen display.
DMA	*See* direct memory access.
Dual-playfield mode	A display mode that allows you to manage two separate display memories, giving you two separately controllable displays at the same time.

Equal-tempered scale	A musical scale where each note is the 12th root of 2 above the note below it.
Exec	Low-level primitives that support the AmigaDOS operating system.
Fast Memory	Memory not accessible by the custom chips. Care must be taken to present only chip memory address to the custom chips. *See* Chip Memory.
Font	A set of letters, numbers, and symbols sharing the same size and design.
Frequency	The number of times per second a waveform repeats.
Frequency modulation	A means of changing sound quality by using one audio channel to affect the period of the waveform produced by another channel. Frequency modulation increases or decreases the pitch of the sound.
Genlock	An optional feature that allows you to bring in a graphics display from an external video source.
High resolution	A horizontal display mode in which 640 pixels are displayed across a horizontal line in a normal-sized display.
Hold-and-modify	A display mode that gives you extended color selection—up to 4,096 colors on the screen at one time.
Interlaced mode	A vertical display mode where 400 lines are displayed from top to bottom of the video display in a normal-size display.
Joystick	A controller device that freely rotates and swings from left to right, pivoting from the bottom of the shaft; used to position something on the screen.
Light pen	A controller device consisting of a stylus and tablet used for drawing something on the screen.
Low resolution	A horizontal display mode in which 320 pixels are displayed across a horizontal line in a normal-sized display.
Manual mode	Non-DMA output. In sprite display, a mode in which each line of a sprite is written in a separate operation. In audio output, a mode in which audio data words are written one at a time to the output.

MIDI	A standardized musical instrument interface used by many musical instruments.
Microsecond (us)	One millionth of second (1/1,000,000).
Millisecond (ms)	One thousandth of second (1/1,000).
Minterm	One of eight possible logical combinations of data bits from three different data sources.
Modulo	A number defining which data in memory belongs on each horizontal line of the display. Refers to the number of bytes in memory between the last word on one horizontal line and the beginning of the first word on the next line.
Mouse	A controller device that can be rolled around to move something on the screen; also has buttons to give other forms of input.
Multitasking	A system in which many tasks can be operating at the same time, with no task forced to be aware of any other task.
Nanosecond (ns)	One billionth of a second (1/1,000,000,000).
Non-interlaced mode	A display mode in which 200 lines are displayed from top to bottom of the video display in a normal-sized display.
NTSC	National Television Standards Committee specification for composite video. The base Amiga crystal frequency for NTSC is 28.63636 Mhz.
Overscan	Area scanned by the video beam but not visible on the video display screen.
Paddle controller	A game controller that uses a potentiometer (variable resistor) to position objects on the screen.
PAL	A European television standard similar to (but incompatible with) NTSC. Stands for "Phase Alternate Line." The base Amiga crystal frequency for PAL is 28.37516 Mhz.
Parallel port	A connector on the back of the Amiga that is used to attach parallel printers and other parallel add-ons.
Paula	One of the three main Amiga custom chips. Contains audio, disk, and interrupt circuitry.

Pitch	The quality of a sound expressed as its highness or lowness.
Pixel	One of the small elements that makes up the video display. The smallest addressable element in the video display.
Playfield	One of the basic elements in Amiga graphics; the background for all the other display elements.
Playfield object	Subsection of a playfield that is used in playfield animation.
Playfield animation	*See* bit-plane animation.
Pointer register	Register that is continuously incremented to point to a series of memory locations.
Polarity	True or false state of a bit.
Potentiometer	An electrical analog device used to adjust some variable value.
Primitives	Amiga graphics, text, and animation library functions.
Quantization noise	Audio noise introduced by round-off errors when you are trying to reproduce a signal by approximation.
RAM	Random access (volatile) memory.
Raster	The area in memory that completely defines a bit-map display.
Read-only	Describes a register or memory area that can be read but not written.
Resolution	On a video display, the number of pixels that can be displayed in the horizontal and vertical directions.
ROM	*See* read-only memory.
Sample	One of the segments of the time axis of a waveform.
Sampling rate	The number of samples played per second.
Sampling period	The value that determines how many clock cycles it takes to play one data sample.
Scrolling	Moving a playfield smoothly in a vertical or horizontal direction.
Serial port	A connector on the back of the Amiga used to attach modems and other serial add-ons.

Set	Giving a bit the value of 1.
Shared memory	The RAM used in the Amiga for both display memory and executing programs.
Sprite	Easily movable graphics object that is produced by one of the eight sprite DMA channels and is independent of the playfield display.
Strobe address	An address you put out to the bus in order to cause some other action to take place; the actual data written or read is ignored.
Task	Operating system module or application program. Each task appears to have full control over its own virtual 68000 machine.
Timbre	Tone quality of a sound.
Trackball	A controller device that you spin with your hand to move something on the screen; may have buttons for other forms of input.
Transparent	A special color register definition that allows a background color to show through. Used in dual-playfield mode.
UART	The circuit that controls the serial link to peripheral devices, short for Universal Asynchronous Receiver/Transmitter.
Video priority	Defines which objects (playfields and sprites) are shown in the foreground and which objects are shown in the background. Higher-priority objects appear in front of lower-priority objects.
Video display	Everything that appears on the screen of a video monitor or television.
Write-only	Describes a register that can be written to but cannot be read.

INDEX